SOLDIERING ON ST KILDA

Aerial photograph of St Kilda taken from the cockpit of the Airspeed Consul with a 'box brownie' in August 1959. The dark island in the foreground is Dùn, on the far left background is Soay and the rest in between is Hirta, with the three peaks (left to right) of Mullach Mór, Conachair and Oiseval.

SOLDIERING ON ST KILDA

ONE MAN'S REFLECTIONS
ON HIS SERVICE IN ST KILDA, 1959-61,
AND THE PREVIOUS NAVAL AND
MILITARY HISTORY OF THIS
REMOTE BUT BEAUTIFUL ISLAND

By James Mackay

TOKEN PUBLISHING LTD
HONITON, DEVON
2002

First published in Great Britain, May 2002
by
Token Publishing Ltd., Orchard House, Duchy Road, Heathpark, Honiton, Devon EX14 1YD
Telephone 01404 46972 Fax 01404 44788
email; info@tokenpublishing.com Website: http//www.tokenpublishing.com

British Library Cataloguing in Publication data:
A catalogue for this book is available from the British Library

ISBN 1 870 192 48 6

Printed in Great Britain by Polestar Scientifica, Exeter
Designed by Inspire Creative, London

CONTENTS

To Mary

INTRODUCTION

FROM certain vantage points on the west coast of the Outer Hebrides the St Kilda group of islands (Hirta, Boreray, Soay, Dùn, Levenish and their rock stacks) can be discerned on the distant horizon, often silhouetted against the setting sun. These islands, 110 miles west of the Scottish mainland and 45 miles west of the nearest point in the Outer Hebrides, had been inhabited for 4,000 years, until the morning of 28 August 1930 when the dwindling, ageing population of 36 souls was evacuated at its own request. Thereafter, Hirta was a desert island, with no permanent human population until April 1957 when it was re-settled by servicemen and thereafter became an outpost of the Rocket Range in South Uist some fifty miles to the east. *Nach robh thu ann Hiort* – 'I wish you were on Hirta' – is what Gaelic mothers used to say (and probably still do) to naughty children as a threat. In a letter written to my sister from St Kilda on 18 March 1959 I quoted this expression but added that two years' occupation by the Forces had taken the sting out of the wild savagery and awful bleakness of the island. Then I added, 'I am looking forward to my monthly visits to it and possibly to staying for a week or two some time.'

That turned out to be an understatement. I was to spend much of the summer of 1959 on Hirta as second-in-command of the St Kilda Detachment of the Royal Artillery Guided Weapons Range (Hebrides), popularly known as the Rocket Range. On a few days each summer guided missiles were launched from South Uist and tracked by a handful of technicians manning the two radar stations on Hirta. The War Office, in its infinite wisdom, therefore required 30 men to be stationed on that island 365 days a year. Probably the task of tracking the occasional missile could have been performed just as efficiently, but at a fraction of the cost, by a Royal Navy destroyer on station during the firing season. It was a prime example of Parkinson's Law but for me it turned out to be the experience of a lifetime.

For a twenty-two year-old lieutenant of the Royal Army Educational Corps holding down a responsible position in a Gunner unit, it was extraordinary and unprecedented – and I dare say it remained a unique situation. But in the winter of 1959 I actually took over command of the detachment when the regular OC again went on leave. The Officer Commanding the detachment was entitled to twelve weeks' annual leave, but the War Office, as usual, had overlooked the provision of a deputy. As the only lieutenant at the Rocket Range (and regarded, no doubt, as a dogsbody) I very soon found myself in that unusual situation. I actually spent about half my time in 1960 and 1961 on St Kilda as Relief OC prior to demob in August of the latter year. I was the only lieutenant to command St Kilda and the only officer not of the Royal Artillery to do so. In fact, I think I can safely say that I was the only 'schoolie' to hold an independent field command anywhere in the world, at any time – a fact which, unfortunately, did not endear me to the Chief Education Officer at Scottish Command Headquarters in Edinburgh.

At Benbecula I was Mess Secretary, Messing Officer for the entire unit and HQ Troop Commander (in charge of clerks, cooks, boilermen, sanitary dutymen and other odds 'n' sods). I was Conducting Officer for visiting generals, politicians and other VIPs as well as being 'Army spokesman' whenever the

The sheep fanks in An Lag bho 'n Tuath, with Mullach Sgar beyond

media wished an interview or a soundbite. I dealt with the Honorary Chaplains to the Forces, the Presbyterian minister and the parish priest, and even played the organ in the parish church on Sundays. I began my literary career by editing the *Gannet Gazette* on St Kilda and furnishing the Public Relations Officer at Scottish Command with suitable 'local boy' stories which he then fed to the appropriate regional newspapers, and shortly before I left the Army I produced my first book, *A Guide to the Uists*, for the benefit of troops coming from Germany and America to fire their missiles. It was always a challenge, but I would not have missed my time in the Hebrides for anything.

St Kilda has an indefinably magical quality that touches most, if not all, people who go there. Even people who only spend a few brief hours ashore from a cruise liner ever afterwards regard it as an unforgettable experience. I held a three-year Short Service Commission and of the two and a half years I was stationed with the Range I spent an aggregate of 290 days on St Kilda. I might add that, when I could be bothered to take leave, I usually spent it in other parts of the Hebrides and thus got to know Lewis, Harris and Barra as well.

For me, personally, St Kilda has a very special sentimental attachment for it was here that I met my first wife Mary in the summer of 1959. In 1997 our son Alastair went there on a National Trust for Scotland work party. On his return he said that he had something to give me. It proved to be a photocopy of the very first page of the Army Visitors' Book, commenced on 12 August 1958 by Major H.F. Riach, RA when he went there to begin the complex task of taking the island over from the RAF. The next entries were Captain David Boddington, RAMC and Lieutenant-Colonel George Cooper, RA, on 28 August when the Army actually took over. Captain B.K. Warner, RA signed the book the following February and I made my mark on 19 March 1959.

I last saw St Kilda on 30 July 1961 when I returned to Benbecula to go on demob leave. Exactly forty years later, to the very day, I returned on the M/S *Black Prince*, a cruise liner chartered by the National Trust for Scotland. The prospect of revisiting the haunt of my youth was dampened by the outbreak of foot and mouth disease which led to the cancellation of the six NTS work parties scheduled for the summer of 2001, but as the epidemic receded the work parties were permitted after all, and passengers on the cruise were likewise allowed to land provided we had not been in an infected area within the previous 28 days. Hopes of making a landing were again dashed, however, when I discovered that this large liner had not made a landing at St Kilda for several years, but merely sailed around the islands.

With a heavy swell running, I had abandoned all hope of going ashore. Imagine my elation when we anchored in Village Bay and the captain announced that we would go ashore after all. Disembarkation took place according to deck and cabin number, and I had to endure a nail-biting hour, waiting for my number to come up. It was the most agonising hour of my life. There was only one thing worse than not getting ashore and that was if a lucky few made it and the rest of us did not. Knowing how very capricious the weather on St Kilda can be, even in the height of summer, I anxiously watched the flags for the slightest hint of a change in the wind direction. Mercifully the wind remained from the northwest and the ship's tenders continued to ply back and forth until the landings were completed. Had the wind veered round to the southeast, a hurried evacuation would have been ordered and further disembarkation aborted. I was overwhelmed with emotion when I set foot on the uneven slabs of the slipway again; I had to restrain the urge to emulate the Pope and kiss the ground.

Seeing the old place again, forty years on, brought back a flood of bittersweet memories. On my return home I dusted off a parcel of yellowing foolscap sheets typed on a manual typewriter. 'Why don't you write a book about the Army on St Kilda? There's a good story there that cries out to be told!' Bill McStay, the PRO at Scottish Command, had urged me. He even furnished a somewhat unusual title for the book.

I heeded his words and during my last months in the Hebrides I produced about 30,000 words, but the upheaval of settling in London, marriage and adjusting to civilian life prevented me from finishing it. The parcel had lain dormant and unread for four decades. It was an apprentice piece, written when I was very young, and frankly I approached it with some misgivings. Despite its shortcomings, however, I was amazed at the details which I had long forgotten. With the aid of the diaries I kept during my later tours of duty on St Kilda, together with letters home which my parents lovingly preserved, I have been able to re-create the period of 1959-61.

Despite the phenomenal amount of literature that exists about St Kilda, remarkably little attention has ever been paid to the neo-St Kildans of the RAF and the Army. This glaring deficiency was admirably filled by Brigadier R.A. Spackman who compiled *Soldiers on St Kilda* in 1982. In his capacity as Range Controller and Commandant, Tony Spackman paid several visits to St Kilda in the late 1970s and planned his book to mark the 25th anniversary of the military occupation of the island, but back in 1959-61, when he came up to Benbecula with the summer increment as an Instructor in Gunnery from Larkhill, he never had the opportunity to see St Kilda as I did, at the very beginning of the Army period, when so many vestiges of the old pre-Evacuation island life were still evident, when the military presence was still relatively embryonic and the facilities quite rudimentary. It is to be hoped that someone will some day bring Tony's narrative up to date. The military evacuated St Kilda in 1999 and left behind a plaque to commemorate their time there; but the history of those forty years of the British Army's most unusual garrison deserves to be told in full.

It was my good fortune to make the acquaintance of many of the surviving St Kildans and to interview them. Sadly this was in an era before the advent of the pocket tape-recorder so I do not have their actual voices, speaking very correct English in their soft Gaelic tones, but I made extensive notes and much of this material has never been published until now.

This is not in any sense an official history of the St Kilda detachment but merely one person's impressions of it over a relatively limited period. Nevertheless, I hope that it will at least partly assuage the curiosity of the countless visitors to the island who see the discordant buildings of the former Army base (which may, in time, become just as much of an archaeological relic as the cottages of the islanders) and wonder what it must have been like to live and work there. What was it like in wintertime, for example? Most visitors only see St Kilda in midsummer when the island and its weather are on their best behaviour, but it was a very different place during the long winter months which, for all practical purposes, extended from the end of August till mid-May.

Remember also that the period of which I write was at the height of the Cold War and shortly before National Service was abolished. National Servicemen received basic pay of four shillings and sixpence a day. My pay, as a Regular lieutenant, was under £9 a week, although I received two guineas (£2.10) a day while serving as Relief OC on St Kilda. On the other hand, the cost of a stamp on a letter home was threepence in old money (little more than 1p in our modern debased currency), and a soldier on St Kilda could get by quite happily on less than ten bob a week.

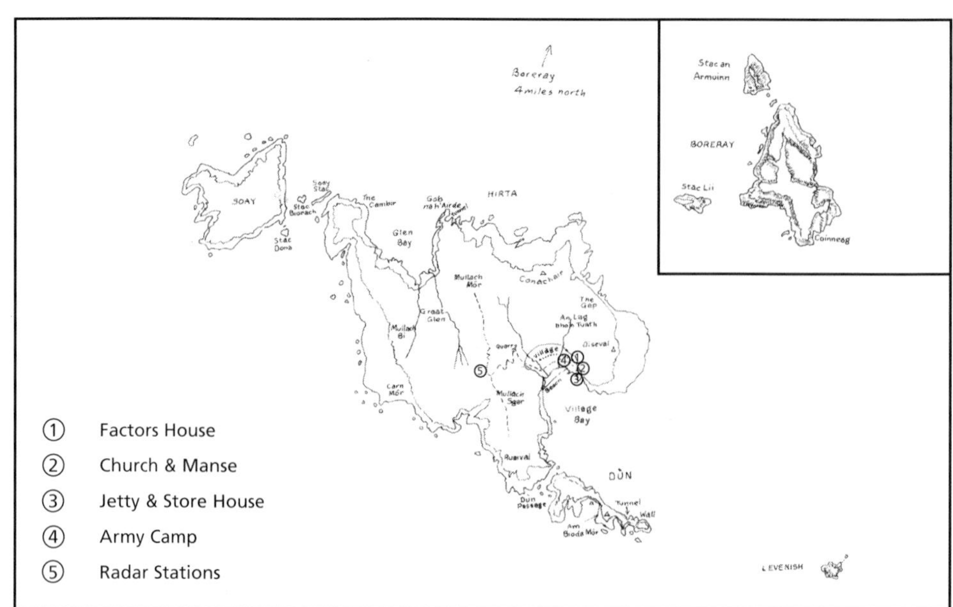

Sketch map of St Kilda

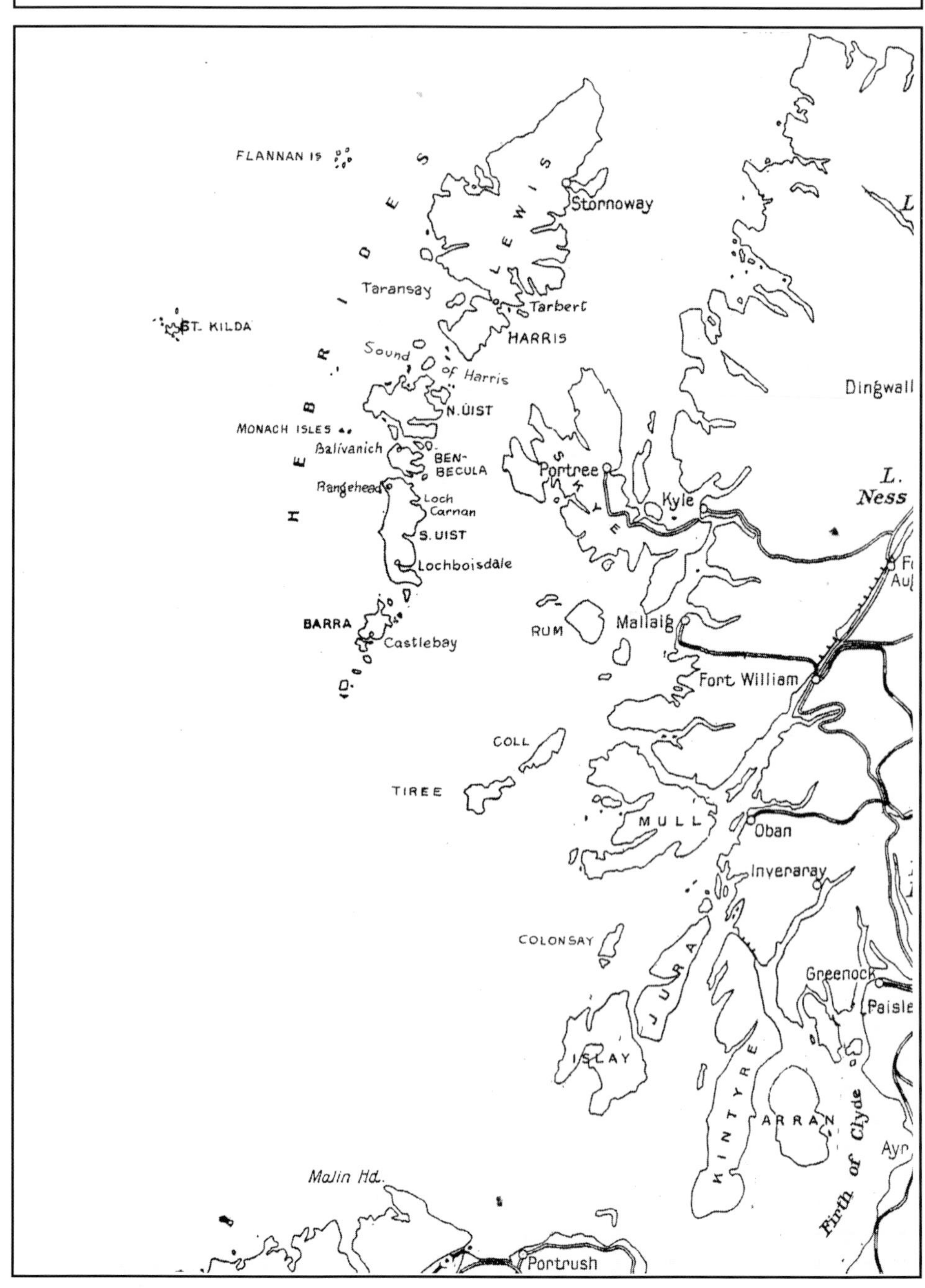

Map showing St Kilda in relation to the Hebrides, mainland and the coastline of Northern Ireland

1. THE ROAD TO THE ISLES

From:- Major A.D. McGregor, MC, TD, RA.
RA GW Range (Hebrides)
Dundonald Camp
TROON, Ayrshire
Tel: Troon 855 Ext 29
Ref: A/840.

10 March 1959

Dear Jim,

Unless you hear from me otherwise the ST KILDA party will leave from Queen Street Station, Glasgow, on Sunday 15 March at 2310 hrs.

I would advise you to return fairly early on Sunday to prepare for the journey.

Transport will be provided to take yourself and party from Dundonald to Irvine. At St Enoch's Station you will be met by WD transport and conveyed with your baggage to Queen Street Station, there you will be joined by the relieving medical officer for St Kilda, Lt. W.A. STEWART, RAMC, and perhaps also Lt Col N. BARNES & Mr COX from REME SCOTCO.

You arrive Oban 0530 hrs sailing from there at 0630 hrs and arriving Lochboisdale 1930 hrs that evening.

Arrangements exist for the payment of all meals for all ranks. You will require to fill in an AF P1922 and have it signed by the purser. The rates allowed are on the slip attached to the AF P1922. Hand the slips into our office on your return from ST. KILDA. Also enclosed is £1 which you will pay to the head steward as a gratuity.

Accommodation has been reserved at Lochboisdale Hotel for yourself and STEWART.

Maurice FRANCIS will arrange transport for you on Tuesday 17 and will either meet you at Lochboisdale or advise you by phone of the time of departure from Lochboisdale for Loch Carnan.

Subject to weather you should leave Loch Carnan on Tuesday 17 March. There will be two boxes of compo rations and a cook will join you at Loch Carnan to provide meals on the round trip.

Major FRANCIS has a hamper with Cutlery and Crockery for you.

Cpl JONES will brief you regarding Pay for the ST KILDANS.

I would advise you to provide yourself with Avomine or Dramamine against sea-sickness.

Any further points which come to mind I will pass to you by telephone.

Yours sincerely,

Mac

HERE at last were my orders to move to the Hebrides with the relieving personnel for the little garrison on the even more remote island of St Kilda, a tiny speck in the North Atlantic, about 50 miles west of North Uist and 110 miles from the nearest point on the Scottish mainland. After three weeks of inaction and prolonged leave in Glasgow, interspersed with two or three very hectic days at Dundonald Camp while we waited for the trawler which was to take us from South Uist to St Kilda to complete her overhaul, we were on the move.

Soon I would be seeing this island of which I had read so much lately and ,imbued with the romanticism of writers like Seton Gordon and Compton Mackenzie, I was keenly looking forward to my first visit to the Western Isles. My knowledge of this part of the country, like most Scots dwelling in the Lowlands, was extremely vague and superficial. Scotland's 'Rainbow West', the 'Dream Isles of the West', the 'Isles of Mist' or *Tir nan Og*, the 'Land of the Eternally Young' – these and similar cliches by which these islands are known to writers, journalists and the more enterprising Glasgow tourists embodied my impression of the Outer Hebrides as a land apart. It might have been on the dark side of the Moon for all I knew of it; but, like many other Scots, I cherished an ambition to visit the Hebrides and had an especial curiosity about St Kilda.

St Kilda, the Ultima Thule of the Victorian and Edwardian tourists who braved the uncertain weather and the cramped discomfort of the old cargo vessels *Dunara Castle* and *Hebrides* to spend a few hours in its Village Bay and marvel at the cliffs and gape at its inhabitants, had been abandoned to the seals and sea-birds thirty years earlier, but had hit the headlines again when the RAF re-occupied it in 1957. Now it was manned by Army personnel who maintained the two missile-tracking stations as part of the newly formed Royal Artillery Guided Weapons Range.

View of St. Kilda from the departing trawler Mull *(RASC flag at the stern)*

Four months previously, I was sent from the Army School of Education, where I had been undergoing preliminary officer training, to Dundonald Camp near Troon on the Clyde Coast. When I attended a War Office Selection Board at Stanmore the previous July I had been somewhat taken aback to be quizzed almost exclusively about my knowledge of Greek, the classical variety of which I had studied at school for six years, followed by a year at University. When asked if I knew anything about demotic Greek I made the cardinal mistake of admitting that I had actually qualified as a Boy Scout interpreter in the modern language. Near neighbours were the Tombazis family, and the father of my chum was the Greek Consul in Glasgow; I was the only boy in my class to study Greek but I welcomed the opportunity to learn something of the contemporary language. This was clearly regarded as initiative, a commodity which the modern Army apparently regarded very highly. I was actually rather elated when the full colonel General Staff interviewing me muttered something about Cyprus and hinted at duties as a counter insurgency and field security officer.

Honours graduates who took a teacher training course were by that time exempt from National Service. Had I wished to become a schoolmaster I would have gone straight from University to Jordanhill teacher training college and thence into a secondary school. Like everyone else at that time I seriously considered this soft option, especially as those with good honours degrees were being selected for an elite two-term course which would have meant actual employment after Easter instead of the following September. But the ending of a love affair changed my mind, especially when I realised that the young lady would be in this very select group. In days gone by, young men mended a broken heart by running away to join the French Foreign Legion. My decision was much more prosaic – I merely cancelled my deferment.

Having decided to take the Queen's shilling I did not wait to be drafted but made enquiries regarding the best method of fitting a round peg into a round hole. In May 1958 I had travelled across country to Edinburgh where I had an interview in the Castle. Brigadier Adam Teacher, a scion of the well-known whisky family, interviewed me and told me that I was just the chap the Army were looking for. The Army had never granted direct entry commissions (apart from such specialists as doctors and dentists), but it was proposed to launch a trial project in the autumn with a squad of top-grade university graduates. In due course, I found myself in a squad of thirty four, allegedly the cream of the autumn intake. The snag was that we were inducted into the Royal Army Educational Corps, a right bunch of misfits who had no intention of entering the teaching profession. Several were high flyers who were destined for the senior Civil Service but had to do National Service first. One of my comrades, in fact, recently retired a Chairman of the Board of Inland Revenue. Another, a brilliant jazz pianist, later became organist and choirmaster at Salisbury Cathedral, while a third is currently the Chairman of Grampian Holdings. Others were destined to become professors and barristers, so I imagine that they became rather reluctant 'schoolies'. But while they struggled with schemes of work or tutored the Brigade Squad (the young hooray henries and chinless wonders who were destined to become ensigns in the Household Cavalry once they had acquired the basic educational requirements to squeeze into Sandhurst) I had an increasingly scary time on various secondments, to the Infantry School of Small Arms to gain proficiency with the 9mm Browning and the Sterling sub-machinegun, to the Royal Warwickshire Regiment on anti-IRA duties in Ballykinler, Northern Ireland, and finally to 50 Medium, a regiment which had but lately returned from a stint in Cyprus where the Greeks and Turks were knocking the stuffing out of each other, when they were not both having a go at the British Army. Cyprus was looking less and less attractive as the days and weeks passed.

There I was, attached to 50 Medium Regiment, RA, where I spent a fairly uneventful, aimless month, supervising the scraping and repainting of 5.5 inch guns in preparation for the annual Administrative Inspection. All this was pretty dull, relieved only by two facts: on the one hand, I could go home to Glasgow every weekend and, on the other, I met Major McGregor. In one corner of Dundonald Camp, tucked away on its own and far from the gaze of inspecting staff officers, was an independent formation rejoicing in the impressive title of the Joint Services Guided Weapons Establishment (Hebrides) (Army Element). Admittedly, this was not as impressive as Two One (Gibraltar 1779-1783) Battery, to which I was attached, but nevertheless a name to intrigue the casual passer-by.

At that time, this embryo unit consisted of no more than a handful of clerks, commanded by Major Alexander D. McGregor. Only his wife Peggy, Medical Officer of Health for Aberdeen, called him Sandy; to everyone who served with him he was Major Mac. It was his task to prepare JSGWE for its ultimate move to the Outer Hebrides, to form the administrative staff of the Rocket Range in South Uist.

I had arrived at Dundonald Camp on a Sunday morning in December 1958. Being a Sunday morning, there was a deserted air about the Officers' Mess, everyone from the regiment – with the possible exception of the Orderly Officer – having departed for the weekend. The sole occupant of the ante room when I walked in was a small, dapper, middle-aged man, with twinkling eyes and sandy hair turning white. He was clad in a cinnamon coloured tweed jacket and matching plus-fours and looked like a country gentleman, which is exactly what he was, with his own landed estate in Aberdeenshire. He apologised that there was no one there to meet me, but he did his best to make me feel at home.

'Educational Corps?' he asked, noting the collar badges on my service dress tunic.

'Yes sir,' I replied.

'Ah. We're expecting an education officer for RAGWR next March.'

'RAGWR?' I was puzzled.

'The Royal Artillery Guided Weapons Range,' he explained. 'Hebrides,' he added after a pause. 'Yes, we are moving north in the early spring, to the Rocket Range on South Uist – you must have read about it in the papers – and we have an education officer down on our establishment.'

'That's interesting, sir. I thought the Rocket Range had packed up – strangled at birth, so to speak.'

'No, not quite,' he replied, 'but the RAF dropped out of the scheme, so it will be much smaller than was originally planned. There's nothing much up there just now, of course – except St Kilda, that is. We've got about thirty men out there at the moment.'

'St Kilda?' I asked. 'But isn't that the island where the RAF went out last year and built part of the Rocket Range? Surely it isn't still occupied – and at this time of year too?'

Yes, indeed. The RAF were running the show there until two or three months ago when we took over. They built quite a nice little camp for us – we've got all mod cons there now – electricity, hot and cold running water and such like. Yes, it's very comfortable out there. As a matter of fact, I'm off to St Kilda tonight myself. I make the trip every month by the *Mull* – she's an old wartime Admiralty trawler which the RASC run now. In between dumping ammunition in the Firth of Clyde she does a monthly run from Cairnryan near Stranraer to St Kilda. I go up to South Uist as a rule, and pick up the boat at Loch Carnan – that's our own port on South Uist. From there it's an eight-hour voyage to St Kilda, through the Sound of Harris, or thirteen hours if the weather's bad and the skipper decides to go the long way round by Barra Head.'

'It all sounds very interesting,' I commented, 'and you must see quite a bit of the Highlands and Islands in your job.'

'Believe me,' he said, warming to his subject, 'you certainly do. Even the trip out from Oban to South Uist is great fun – providing,' he added hastily, 'that you get some decent weather for it. You can go ashore at Tobermory and have a walk round the harbour, and when you get to Barra in the afternoon you have quite a long wait at Castlebay while the *Claymore* unloads her cargo. Last month I managed to hire a little rowing boat and had a close look at Kishimul Castle, stuck on a rock in the middle of the bay. At Lochboisdale I stay in the Hotel while I'm waiting for the *Mull*. I have my own cabin aboard her too,' he continued enthusiastically, 'right up alongside the bridge. Another thing – I take a tin of Nescafe with me. There's a kettle always on the boil in the galley and I go in there and brew up whenever I feel like a good hot drink. Aye, there's no doubt about it, many people less fortunate than myself pay a lot of money for a Hebridean cruise while I enjoy it for nothing – and I'm paid for it too!'

In the course of the next few weeks I ran into Major McGregor on several occasions and from these subsequent encounters I learned a lot more about this strange, unconventional unit which was slowly being formed in the Hebrides. It soon became apparent to me that Mac was 'selling' the Uists and St Kilda to me, and I admit that from the very beginning I was keen to go there as the education officer. On one occasion he asked me if I knew anything about sailing or cruising. Apparently the Nuffield Trust had awarded a large sum of money to the Range for the purchase of recreational equipment and Mac had decided to spend it on a boat. It had always been one of his ambitions, hitherto unfulfilled, to 'mess about in small boats'. Now his opportunity had come – and what better way was there to explore the sea lochs and countless little islands of the Hebrides. I had to confess that my knowledge of boats was limited to a fortnight's cruising on the Thames the previous summer, but evidently this marked me down as eminently suitable for the Range. The only obstacle to this pleasing prospect, however, was Cyprus...

My month at Dundonald Camp ended with a week's Christmas leave, but shortly before I left Troon two things occurred which made my posting to the Rocket Range even more uncertain. The first was the annual convention of all RAEC personnel in Scottish Command, which took place in Edinburgh in early December that year. As I was on regimental duties at Troon I was not present at this convention, but the RAEC sergeant instructor attached to 50 Medium attended, and told me on his return the following week that an officer had already been earmarked for the Hebrides Range. I was bitterly disappointed, and the fact that the said officer, a Lieutenant Davis, married with a family, was moving heaven and earth to get this undesirable posting altered was little consolation.

The other incident occurred one day when my Troop Commander, Captain Paul Holland, and I were driving through the town and gave a lift back to the camp to a strange officer whom we had not met before. He was a Gunner captain – a very senior one, judging by his row of war ribbons – and on his shoulders he wore the Lion and Crown flash of War Office-controlled units.

'You must be one of those Guided Weapons chaps,' surmised Paul. 'Just back from St Kilda?'

'Yes,' replied the stranger dourly, 'thank God! And I hope I never see that bloody dump again!'

After the rosy picture of the Ideal Army Unit painted so vividly by Major Mac, I was taken aback by the rank heresy of this captain.

'What's up with it?' I enquired. 'Don't you like it out there?'

'It's a terrible place, and anyway, I would rather not discuss it, thank you,' he replied with some asperity. Thus snubbed I remained silent, but wondering all the while why Mac and this officer should differ so radically in their opinions about St Kilda. I began to have my doubts about the Hebrides as the ideal posting for me – or anyone else – after all. Perhaps it was just as well that Scottish Command had found a 'volunteer' instead of me.

A week later the regiment went off on Christmas leave and I went home for a few days before returning to Beaconsfield. I did not see Major McGregor again, as he was on another of his frequent trips to St Kilda when I left Troon. In any case I had given up all hope of being posted to his unit and, after seeing the intense look of disgust on that captain's face at the mention of St Kilda, I was not so sure that I minded not going. Instead, I buckled down to some concentrated work on unlearning the declensions and conjugations of classical Greek and practising a Cypriot accent.

The day after I got a massive cocktail of jabs to protect me from the dreaded lurgi and Makarios' Revenge, the government announced a cease-fire in Cyprus. Peace talks progressed at breakneck speed and the Emergency was officially over. No longer bound for Episkopi or Dhekelia, I was what was known in Army jargon as RTU ('returned to unit'). On 18 February 1959 our Commanding Officer, Major Jim Sleator, announced our postings. There were gasps when no fewer than nine postings to the Brigade of Guards were read out, but the one which raised a laugh was mine.

'Mackay,' began the major. 'Ah yes – you were down for an overseas posting I believe?'

'Yes sir,' I replied cautiously, wondering what was coming next.

'Well, you've got it,' he announced triumphantly. 'You're going to the Rocket Range in the Outer Hebrides!'

The way he emphasised the 'Outer' betrayed his sense of self-satisfaction – we did not exactly love each other – and I suppose that this posting to the back of beyond must have given him some sardonic amusement. Nevertheless, it was just what I wanted; and, surprisingly, as I thought at the time, there were some chaps who actually envied my posting, though it was some time afterwards before I fully appreciated how lucky I had been.

Back at Dundonald Camp again in March, life seemed to be going on in much the same desultory fashion as when I left three months earlier. Only in the corner of the camp where my new unit was located was there much sign of activity. The old, flaking sign-board proclaiming the home of the Joint Services Guided Weapons Establishment had disappeared and a new sign, in gleaming blue, scarlet and gold, indicated that the unit had now become the Royal Artillery Guided Weapons Range (Hebrides). Still, the nearest we were to the Hebrides was the island of Arran whose magnificent peaks dominated the view to seaward – and many purists will argue that Arran can scarcely be included among the Hebrides, even the Inner Hebrides.

But inside the spider-hut which constituted the office and nerve centre of the unit I was immediately transported hundreds of miles in spirit, for covering the walls were maps, in all scales, of the Uists and Benbecula, and a six-inch-to-the mile map of the goal itself, St Kilda. I was highly intrigued by this map and spent a great deal of time examining it, noting the very tight contour lines that indicated the towering cliffs.

'We're sending you up there next week', said Mac when we met. 'You will take the advance party to South Uist and then go out on the *Mull* soon afterwards. Now come and meet the Commandant, Colonel Cooper. He and I will be going out to South Uist two or three days later, and will see you when you return from St Kilda.'

Lieutenant Colonel E. George Cooper, on first sight, was the very epitome of the Army colonel one has seen described in so many novels: small in stature but very heavily built, with a massive bull neck, florid face, balding, but distinguished by a bushy black moustache and matching eyebrows which heightened his fierce mien. When he spoke, he barked, and when he laughed, it was always a hearty guffaw. His first question was to ask me what games I played. He himself had been a fine Rugger player and had played for Berkshire before the War, and the Army after. He definitely conformed to the stereotypical picture of a colonel which existed in the minds of most civilians after seeing Colonel Blimp. In many ways this was true of Colonel Cooper, and to many of the General Staff at Scottish Command Headquarters and the War Office he later came to be known as the Baron of Benbecula. But those who served under him never had a better commanding officer. He earned the respect and loyalty of his men and welded the diverse elements of his new command into an efficient, and above all else, a very happy unit.

Colonel George was a born fighter and thus admirably suited to the challenge of organising the Range. During those two years in which he commanded RAGWR he had often to fight against apathy and ignorance of our needs at War Office level, and there was none more bellicose or truculent in championing the causes of his men than Colonel George. He was a maverick, with an unconventional but highly pragmatic approach to soldiering that, to a very large extent, explains my own extremely unusual military career. He was adept at bending rules and cutting corners and never afraid to take on the War Office. The bark 'Miss MacInnes – bring book!' resounding all over the Orderly Room meant that the colonel was on the war-path again, and Mary Ann MacInnes, his long-suffering secretary, would scurry into his office to take down the latest broadside against the brass-hats. He was considerate and fair to his men at all times, and to this was due his immense personal popularity. In August 1960, when it was decided to limit the tour of duty in the Hebrides to two years, no fewer than 65 per cent of the unit volunteered for a second tour.

In some ways Colonel George and Major Mac seemed ill-assorted. Whereas Mac was a country gentleman who had held a commission in a prewar yeomanry regiment (hence his Territorial Decoration), the colonel's last ribbon was the much narrower green edged with yellow of the Territorial Efficiency Medal which revealed that he had come up through the ranks. He had, in fact, been a chartered accountant in Civvy Street, and a non-commissioned officer in a Territorial Gunner unit. What both men had in common, however, was a very active war. The colonel had fought in Burma with the 14th Army while Mac had been captured, escaped across the Pyrenees, and later earned his Military Cross in one of these interminable river crossings as the British slowly advanced through Italy. For a small and rather unassuming, kindly man, Mac had a most impressive array of ribbons, three rows of them which included the General Service Medal with clasp for the ill-starred Suez campaign.

The only other officer at Troon was Captain John Sims, the equipment officer, on loan to us from 50 Medium. He dealt with the 'Q' matters which affected us on the mainland, while his boss, Major Maurice Francis, the unit's quartermaster, held the fort at Benbecula where he and a small band of veterans of the old Joint Service days prepared the camp in readiness for the big move of RAGWR at the end of the month.

Apart from Maurice, the only other officer at Benbecula in the preliminary phase was Captain Alan Earl, Royal Signals, another war veteran who had been commissioned from the ranks. Our little band of permanent staff was subsequently completed by the arrival of Lieutenant Harold 'Nobby' Hall, a relatively elderly REME officer. All four of these officers proudly wore the 'mark of the beast' as the ribbon of the Long Service and Good Conduct Medal was familiarly known. It was a singular fact that none of the Range staff had obtained their commissions as a result of training at Woolwich or Sandhurst, and this also may have accounted for the unconventional atmosphere as well as our constant loggerheads with Scotco and the War Office. By contrast, however, the appointment of Officer Commanding St Kilda was a twelve month posting for a Gunner captain, invariably a regular officer who had trained at the Royal Military College before commissioning.

My first task apparently was to take the advance party, consisting of a REME sergeant and ten men, by rail and steamer to South Uist, and having got there I was to await the *Mull* and then continue on to St Kilda with a number of relieving personnel. In the meantime there was nothing for me to do, and the simplest thing was to have some more leave. After two days at Dundonald Camp I went off home again to Glasgow and awaited further instructions from Major McGregor.

I returned to Dundonald on Sunday morning, 15 March 1959, packed my trunk, assembled my belongings, had a medical and dental check-up, and early in the evening set out by road with the advance party. On the platform at Queen Street Station I met another young lieutenant in uniform, disconsolately talking with a girl who turned out to be his wife. Willie Stewart looked younger than his years and terribly fed-up at the prospect of leaving his bride of only a few weeks to brave the uncertainty of a fortnight on St Kilda while the island's doctor had some well-earned leave. While the young couple took their fond farewell, reminiscent of Vronsky leaving Anna Karenina for the Serbian front, I checked that the men were settled in.

Oiseval from the sea, showing the network of sheep tracks on the sheer cliffs

'Captain Mackay?'

I turned to face a sergeant whose untidy, beretless appearance did not immediately endear him to me, even if he had elevated me in rank. Before I could say a word, however, another voice, familiar in spite of its angry tone, cut in from behind me.

'Sergeant Court, you bloody idle man! Where's your hat?'

Major McGregor, returning from a weekend's leave in Aberdeen, had just stepped off the train and immediately recognised his old bête-noir. With this bawling out in public, Sergeant Court retreated shamefacedly and Mac, still simmering, said,

'That, as you know now, was our Sergeant Court. A good soldier – ex-boy, y'know – but a helluva man. Been out on Kilda too long. Needs a spell under the RSM to bring him back to normality. Well, Jim,' he softened, 'you're off now, are you? Best of luck – and don't lose any of these buggers on the way.'

Settled in our first-class compartment, Willie and I introduced ourselves as the train pulled out of the station. It was a pity that it was so dark, he complained, as he would have liked to have seen the mountains. This struck me as a trifle strange, but in the course of the conversation I discovered that Willie – born, bred and educated in Glasgow – had scarcely been outside the city boundary in his entire twenty-five years. His one excursion into the outside world had been on call-up for National Service when he had spent two or three weeks at the RAMC training centre at Crookham in Berkshire. Thereafter he had been posted back to his native city and was currently employed at Cowglen Military Hospital on the south side (long gone and now to a large extent the site of the National Savings Bank), a stone's throw from his home.

'Well,' I thought, 'I wonder how you are going to like St Kilda. I expect it will be quite a change for you…'

During a half-hour wait on a cold, draughty platform at Stirling where we changed to the midnight train bound for Oban, we were mysteriously joined by a party of twenty-three of the brightest specimens of the Royal Pioneer Corps. The sudden appearance of the Pioneers worried me. I had not been briefed about them, and yet – where else could they be going on the Oban train if not to the Hebrides? I had heard such awful stories about the Chunkies (as they were derisively known) during my limited military career so far, and it was the dread horror of all young education officers to be posted to a unit where they had to introduce them to the three Rs. At that moment, however, I was not so interested in their education as in their discipline and general behaviour. I had visions of them whooping it up in Oban in the wee small hours or pulling MacBrayne's steamer apart on the way out to the Uists. My fears proved to be totally unfounded and the Pioneers, both then and later on when I knew them so much better, were good as gold. Moreover, while the average height of these Pioneers seemed to be about five foot two, both the sergeant and the corporal in charge of them were strapping six-footers, so it was unlikely that I would have any trouble with them after all.

There can be few more depressing sights than Oban Pier at six o'clock on a bleak, blustery March morning, and as I shepherded my little party from the railway station, stumbling in the darkness across the railway lines and blundering into large, smelly crates of fish and huge coils of tarry rope, my enchantment with the Hebrides began to evaporate. By this time the Pioneers were huddled close together in their greatcoats, on the pavement outside the station, but making no move to follow us down to the waiting steamer. I turned back and approached the sergeant who gave me a very smart salute. I later discovered that Pioneer NCOs were invariably seconded from the Brigade of Guards, hence their height and iron discipline.

'Excuse me for asking, sergeant, but are you not going to board the ship?'

He looked aghast. 'Oh no, sir. We're waiting for a truck to take us to the Hebrides.'

I chuckled at this. 'But the Hebrides are a group of islands, so you'll have to catch the steamer.'

He shook his head vigorously. 'No sir, they're a group of mountains somewhere over there,' and he waved a hand vaguely in the direction of the hills.

'Please show me your travel documents,' I said quietly.

He produced a collective travel warrant. My heart sank when I saw *'Guided Weapons Range, Hebrides'* typed across the top. His heart sank too, when I patiently explained to him that my men were also bound for the Hebrides. He reluctantly agreed to follow me, but had quite a job persuading his Pioneers. For an agonising moment I thought I would have a mutiny on my hands, but eventually the men were persuaded to go up the gangplank.

The ship was not a prepossessing sight. The usual ship on this route, the *Claymore*, was on the Mallaig-Stornoway run and in her place was the old *Lochearn*, about half her size and a tenth as comfortable. We had breakfast in relays and then explored the ship to find somewhere suitable to lie down and catch up on the sleep which we had lost the previous night. Willie and I finally got stretched out on the narrow upholstered bench which ran round the wall of the diminutive first-class saloon. It was here that we ran into Colonel Barnes and Mr Cox, the only other occupants, who were likewise attempting, none too successfully, to get some sleep. Any thoughts we may have had in this direction vanished as soon as the ship weighed anchor; the vibrations, creakings and assorted groans from the bowels of the vessel in response to her engines made sleep utterly impossible. We compromised by sitting in our mackintoshes, hunched up in a corner apiece, and dozily contemplating one or other of the uninspiring oil paintings riveted to the bulkheads.

As we berthed at Tobermory the sun came up and stirred us out of our cramped lethargy. Half an hour ashore gave us the opportunity for a brisk walk along the sea-front, to buy postcards and barley-sugar, the latter as a precaution against the open sea ahead. The voyage through the Sound of Mull was calm and very beautiful, and even Willie, I think, forgot his wife for a moment to remark on the wonderful scenery of Morven on the one side and the rugged grandeur of Mull on the other. As we breasted Rudha nan Gall at the northern tip of the island we got our first glimpse of the far-off Cuillins of Skye, rising like fairy castles into the clouds, and to the south we beheld the little islands off the coast of Mull, with the peculiar shape of the aptly named Dutchman's Cap beyond.

Ahead lay the low islands of Tiree and Coll. At the latter, the steamer hove to off-shore while a bright red painted cutter chugged out from the rocky bay of Arinagour to meet her. Several people destined for the island jumped out from an opening in the ship's side on to the undecked cutter, while five calves were lowered one by one in a box contrivance over the side of the cargo deck, protesting in loud bovine fashion as they were swung willy-nilly into the pitching and yawing little boat and narrowly missing the heads of its passengers.

By contrast, loading and unloading at Scarinish Pier in Tiree was a much more leisurely and dignified business. I was amazed at the variety of cargo which came off here – concrete blocks and timber planking, a monster of a Post Office van and even a coffin bedecked with wreaths – a *Tiridheach* returning from the cities of the south to his native island for the last time.

We had just finished lunch as the ship came out through the narrow strait between Tiree and Coll, and at once felt the uneasy surge of the long Atlantic swell that is never absent, even on the calmest of days. Ahead of us was nothing but open sea; over the stern Mull and the hills of the mainland were fast receding. It was strange to think that we were still in the United Kingdom, out here on the open seas with nothing but the merest vestige of land smudging the horizon behind us. One of the soldiers who had just lost his lunch to the fishes remarked wryly, 'And they call this a home posting…' It seemed as if we were destined for some foreign country, and I suppose in many ways we were. To the Highlanders of the mainland and Inner Hebrides the Western Isles were *Innse Gall* – 'the Foreigners' Islands' – an allusion to the fact that many centuries previously they had formed part of the Norse dominions. Even now, with their Gaelic language and age-old traditions yet unchanged despite increasing infiltration and influence from the mainland, these remote, rocky, treeless islands for which we were bound had an aura of the unknown.

As I pondered on these lines, we had our first sight of the Outer Hebrides. Before us, along the distant horizon, were a number of grey-blue humps stretching in a nondescript line into the haze of the north, to re-emerge as the westernmost limb of Skye. Gradually these humps rose and became more clearly defined, until we could discern the main island of Barra, with its twin peaks Tangaval and Heaval, and southward the string of lesser islands with musical names like Mingulay and Vatersay, Lingay, Sandray and Berneray.

Slackening speed, the ship swung into the channel between Barra and Vatersay and I beheld for the first time the beautiful setting of Castlebay, gleaming in the long rays of the evening sun. The row of cottages straggled round the bay, with the tower of the Church of Our Lady, *Reul na Mara* (Star of the Sea) above the centre of the village, and of course Kishimul Castle, Barra's most famous landmark, gracing the bay itself – these immediately reminded me of the film *Rockets Galore* which I had seen in London only a month earlier. What sort of hostile reception would we get?

There was a lively air of hustle and bustle at Castlebay as the passengers debouched on to the pier. The entire canine population of Barra appeared to be gathered there to greet us, with continual yapping and barking. At the western end of the pier half a dozen French crabbers from Camaret-sur-Mer were tied up in tight formation, brightly painted and ornately decorated, whose swarthy Breton crews in clogs and voluminously baggy trousers gave the scene an exotic flavour. The strains of a melodeon wafted across from the wheelhouse of one boat and, with the soft blue sky and turquoise sea contrasting with the rich green and brown of the land, I might have imagined myself in some fishing village on the coast of Brittany. But here also was a kilted figure, a Cameron Highlander going home on leave, and the incessant lilt of Gaelic which left me in no doubt that we were in fact in the Outer Hebrides. To someone who had been raised in Skye during the war, the Barra Gaelic sounded strange. Two centuries earlier a man could have travelled from West Kerry in Ireland to Sutherland in Scotland and been able to understand and converse with all the people he encountered in between, but such has been the relentless progress of the English language and the fragmentation of Gaelic that the Irish no longer understood the Scots, or vice versa. Later I learned that the dialect and intonation of the language in Barra was relatively close to that of the Gaeltacht of southwestern Ireland.

We walked up the hill from the pier, past the post office, the bank and the shops, most of which seemed to be owned by MacNeills, and at the Church turned to admire the view. Across the bay lay Vatersay, with its green machair and long sandy beaches just as Compton Mackenzie had described Little Todday in *Whisky Galore*. We paused in one of the shops to buy the inevitable postcards. The shopkeeper who served me said mournfully that he wished the Rocket Range had come to Barra, where unemployment was high and the people would have welcomed the project – 'Not like these *Uibhisteachs* up north,' who, he hinted, were protesting loudly at the Ministry of Defence imposing on them.

Stac Lii, the largest gannetry in the world

At the railway bookstall in Oban that morning I had come across a little book entitled *The Postmark on a Letter* by R.K. Forster. Since early childhood I had been an avid stamp-collector, and although I had packed away my albums at home for the duration of my military service I still took the opportunity to add items that crossed my path. At Beaconsfield we had a contingent of Gurkhas from whose officers I scrounged a number of envelopes bearing Indian stamps with Nepalese postmarks. As Nepal had not yet joined the Universal Postal Union, her own stamps had only local validity, but mail going abroad went through the Indian system. I had the good sense to keep these curiosities intact, for I appreciated that Indian stamps were quite common, but those with Nepalese postmarks were not. This subconsciously laid the foundations of a lifelong interest in postal history; but what really triggered it off was this little book, priced five shillings in hardback. I read it from cover to cover on the voyage and by the time we reached Barra I had resolved to form a collection of the postmarks from all the offices in the Outer Hebrides.

Thus I marched into the sub post office and asked if I might have impressions of the various handstamps in use. Had the postmaster rebuffed me or stated that this was forbidden by regulations my incipient interest would have been killed at birth, but Mr MacNeill was most obliging and favoured me with clear impressions of the counter stamps, the double-circle used for cancelling letters and cards and even the large rectangular mark applied to parcels. He was curious, though, and asked me about this strange hobby. I told him I was just starting, and showed him the little book which had stimulated my interest. Later I would discover that there were no fewer than ninety-nine post offices in the Outer Hebrides, from Port of Ness at the north end of Lewis, to Vatersay south of Barra, and over the next two years I managed to visit every one of them. The number was nicely rounded up by St Kilda – but more of that in due course.

The last lap of our voyage took us along the eastern seaboard of Barra, a wild, rocky coast, here and there relieved by patches of green and little clusters of brightly whitewashed cottages. Past the islets of Gighay and Hellisay we skirted Eriskay, where Bonnie Prince Charlie first set foot on British soil and which, at a much later date, Marjorie Kennedy-Fraser immortalised with its *Love Lilt* and tales of its singing seals. As darkness fell the ship approached South Uist and minutes later we were turning into Loch Boisdale, with the lights of the little township of the same name beaming a welcome.

This was the end of the road for Willie and me, there being no officers' mess as yet at Benbecula, twenty-eight miles away to the north, where the thirty-five soldiers who had accompanied us this far would be billeted in the old wartime RAF camp. We were to stay in the Hotel for the next few days until the Mull was ready to take us out to St Kilda. A mere day's journeying had transported us from the civilised chaos of Glasgow to the unhurried timelessness of South Uist. In the Lochboisdale Hotel we dumped our gear, ate an excellent supper, marvelled at the salmon and sea-trout mounted in the Anglers' Room, and relaxed. We had arrived in the Hebrides.

2. PUFFINS AND PIRATES

WILLIE and I rose late, to a solid breakfast of bacon, eggs and coffee, the only concession to the Hebrides being the oat cakes which were optional instead of toast. Colonel Barnes, now in uniform, and Mr Cox, in sensible tweeds, sat at a nearby table. The only other occupants of the dining room were a couple with a little girl, and a tall, willowy young woman on her own. I was intrigued by the couple who conversed in the clipped tones of Mayfair and from their elegant appearance might have stepped straight out of the Society pages of *Country Life* or *The Field*. Murdina, our waitress, told us afterwards that the gentleman was Colonel Cameron, Younger of Lochiel, and his wife 'a Macdonald of the Isles, no less' – this in awed tones. Later I learned that the colonel had won his Military Cross while leading the Allied troops who had the distinction of liberating the tiny mountain republic of San Marino from Nazi occupation.

The unaccompanied girl was 'the lady from the Department', and on enquiring further which or what department that was, Murdina answered,

'Why, the Department of Agriculture of course. She comes over from Inverness every so often and stravaigues about, inspecting folks' cattle and sheep.'

Murdina had very pretty eyes, large and dark, and one of those soft Hebridean voices to which it is a joy to listen. I subsequently discovered that she was a Gaelic singer, prominent in the ceilidhs of the Uists.

'So you're off to St Kilda, are you? And will you be seeing any of those queer four-horned sheep they have out there?'

'Four-horned sheep?' I returned incredulously.

'Aye. I've heard there are rams which grow two sets of horns –'

'That sounds like one of the soldiers has been pulling your leg,' I cut in sceptically.

'Oh no,' she protested. 'It was my grandfather who told me he saw a St Kilda ram's head mounted on a board in a hotel in Stornoway once, and it had four horns sticking out of its skull, as sure as I am standing here telling you of it now.'

I had read briefly about the island and its quaint Soay sheep, the last remnant of the aboriginal sheep of northern Europe, but had they possessed four horns I was sure that Major McGregor would have told me all about them, as one of the prime attractions of St Kilda. Murdina, however, was adamant, so I decided that I would have to solve this mystery for myself when I got out there.

The next two days were spent peacefully, exploring Lochboisdale and its surrounding district, climbing the craggy, boggy eminence of Ben Kenneth which overlooked the loch, and writing long letters in the evenings, describing all the wonders of the island. Colonel Barnes energetically hiked along the road past the next township of Daliburgh and crossed the velvet machair to the broad white beaches bordering the Atlantic itself. I believe that, with no junior officers present to inhibit him, he even took off his socks and shoes, rolled up his battledress trouser legs, and paddled about blissfully in the surf. *Tir nan Òg* – the Land of the Ever Young – the poets called it, and I am sure that it had this effect on him.

Soay Sheep on guard (Alastair Mackay)

On one occasion, passing some whitewashed cottages in the village itself, we heard the strange clack-clack of machinery, and on peeping through the low doorway we found a dozen men and boys seated at tweed looms, treadling away at a furious rate as though their very lives depended on it. It looked so picturesque.

'One electric motor,' observed the colonel, 'would do all that work – in half the time and at far less cost. Besides,' he went on, 'I notice that these machines were made in Keighley.'

He pointed to the manufacturer's mark stamped on the frame, with the pride of the Yorkshireman recognising his county's enterprise in this outlandish place.

On the morning of the third day we looked out of the dining room window across the loch to see a strange vessel steaming cautiously into the anchorage. She was much smaller than the *Lochearn* and set much deeper in the water; from her lines she was in the trawler class, but her drab grey-blue paint overall proclaimed her to be no ordinary trawler. As she hove to, we could make out the unusual flag which fluttered raggedly from her stern – the navy blue ensign with crossed swords, banner of the motley fleet operated by the Royal Army Service Corps. This regiment, known affectionately by the rest of the Army as the Jamstealers or the Galloping Greengrocers, was later renamed the Royal Corps of Transport. Whereas the tank landing craft (LCTs) which provided communication between St Kilda and the outside world in summertime were crewed by officers and men of the RASC, this old tub was manned by a civilian crew.

This was the good ship *Mull*, long looked for and come at last. She was an 'Isles' Class trawler built for coastal patrol work during the Second World War. She was steam powered with a single screw, displaced 700 tons and was a mere 164 feet long. A brass plate informed us that she was constructed by Cook, Welton & Gemmell of Beverley – a point which gave Colonel Barnes further inordinate pride in his native county. Built towards the end of the War, she was transferred to the Royal Army Service Corps in 1946. In the early years of her varied career she was based successively at Bangor, Singapore and Cairnryan, and in 1954 she was engaged in the melancholy task of ferrying back from remote islands off the coast of northern Europe some of Britain's war dead for re-interment in the United Kingdom. She began the most important phase of her career in September 1958 when she commenced on the Hebrides Winter Maintenance programme. She left the Hebrides, not exactly covered in glory, in January 1973 and was eventually sold to Ocean Services Limited who disposed of her to a Greek company operating a coastal service in the Aegean Sea. And there, I have no doubt, she is still afloat, almost sixty years after she first entered the water.

Hurriedly we finished our breakfast, packed our grips and paid our bills. 'Remember the four-horned sheep,' cried Murdina as we ran down from the Hotel to the pier.

A number of soldiers, well wrapped up in duffel coats and PVC mackintoshes, lined the rail as we stepped gingerly up the gangplank. A smallish man, wearing a dingy navy-blue battledress blouse and white-topped peaked cap, stepped out of the wheelhouse on the bridge above us and welcomed us aboard. 'My name's Ross,' he said, 'I'm the First Mate, and this is Mr Elson the skipper.' Captain Elson had three gold stripes on his epaulettes to Donny Ross's two, but apart from that his main distinguishing features were the faded British Empire Medal ribbon above his breast pocket and the fact that he sported neither collar nor tie. He ran a sloppy ship and Colonel Cooper, making a play on the skipper's surname which was rather similar to a famous brand of chemical toilet, had dubbed him 'Sanitary Dan'.

'How do?' he said briefly. 'That's the lot of you, is it? Good. We'll be off then. I want to turn Barra Head by noon if we can.'

And with that he was back in the wheelhouse again, ringing down to the engine room. Ross ushered us aft, while we struggled with our baggage round stanchions and pipes and all the other bits of gear which clutter up the decks of a ship of this size.

'Down there,' he pointed into the very bowels of the ship, from which arose a foetid stench of diesel oil and human sweat, 'is the wardroom. You can dump your kit in there.'

One by one we descended the iron steps into the officers' quarters. God knows what the seamen's berths were like. On our left, two curtains concealed the sleeping berths of the Chief and Second Engineers. Snores emanated from the former. On the opposite side of the narrow passageway an open door revealed the wardroom itself, a small cubby-hole of a place where there was barely room enough to edge round the table riveted to the deck. An upholstered bench, not unlike the one in the saloon of the *Lochearn*, ran round the table on three sides, but whereas MacBrayne's steamers had red upholstery this one could not be described for the grime thickly ingrained in it. Likewise the table-cloth, which at one time had probably been white, was now a nauseating shade of grey, mottled with assorted gravy and soup stains. A youth of about sixteen, wearing a seaman's jersey with RASC FLEET picked out in red across the chest, and sporting sideburns and several days of fuzz on his cheeks, lay stretched out along one side of the bench, fast asleep. As we entered, however, he stirred and sat up, eyeing us dozily for several seconds before sidling out hastily without a word being exchanged. The fug in the wardroom was well-nigh overpowering and when we left the shelter of Loch Boisdale and encountered the open Minch, we thought it more prudent to get up on deck again, where the salty spray and biting wind were at least wholesome.

I shall never cease to marvel at the amazing ability of the British soldier to make himself comfortable in the most uncompromising surroundings. The boys who accompanied us on this trip were no exception. At first I could not find them anywhere – until I looked at the hatches which covered the top of the engine room. There, scarcely a foot or two from the sea water that swilled rhythmically back and forward in the scuppers as the ship pitched into the full Atlantic swell, and only slightly sheltered from the sou-wester which whipped keenly round the open companionways, lay the men, huddled together, head to toe in their duffel coats for mutual warmth, flat out on top of the hatches – the warmest part of the entire ship.

In the galley Chris Foster, our Army cook sent out specially for the round trip, busied himself preparing a meal of hot soup and an indeterminate stew out of compo tins. At that time I believe he made the St Kilda trip every month to provide meals for those hardy enough to eat them, and even in the roughest gale never failed to come up with the stew. I heard how, on the previous trip, Colonel Cooper himself had gone out to St Kilda in a force nine gale. Even the bridge had been awash on that occasion and the colonel had taken refuge in the wireless room, when suddenly the ship's radio officer lurched for the door, stumbled over his portly visitor, and had been sick all down the colonel's battledress. At that precise moment Foster had entered the cabin with a bowl of steaming broth, and asked the colonel if he wished to have some. Whereupon Colonel Cooper, with his customary sangfroid replied, 'No thank you, Foster; I've just had somebody else's.' This story the Second Engineer related to us with a hearty chuckle, at which poor Willie seemed to get some sort of convulsion and made a hasty dash for the rail.

We stood round the stern rail or sat on the tarpaulin covering the after hold, scooping tinned meat and veg out of our mess tins and quaffing pints of stewed syrupy tea as the *Mull* rounded Barra Head. A thin drizzle obscured the details of the island of Berneray as we passed close inshore, though serving to heighten the effect of the stupendous cliffs, half as high again as Beachy Head and infinitely more impressive. Perched on the very top was the light-house, the highest above sea level in Scotland. As we came round the cliffs we really felt the full force of the open Atlantic. Visibility was reduced to a few hundred yards by the spindrift skimmed off the top of the waves by the rising westerly wind. I shuddered and went below to join Willie who was by now reclining on the bench in the wardroom, exhausted by his futile efforts to retain his breakfast. In the heat of the open coal fire burning cosily in the grate and lulled by the steady motion of the ship as she bit deeply into the oncoming waves, I dozed off.

'You'll have to move out till we've had our tea.'

I was rudely awakened by the sing-song accents of the Second Mate, a small wizened Aberdonian who, plate of fish and chips in hand, was trying to get past me to his place at the table. As I sat up and took stock of the situation the remainder of the ship's officers filed in and rummaged noisily through a drawer for their cutlery. Willie had already risen and was leaning unsteadily against the side of the companionway, looking up at the grey sky and debating whether it would be beneficial for him to go out on deck again.

The time was now after five o'clock. 'We should be due at St Kilda in another hour or so,' I thought. I went up on deck and stumbled forward to the companionway leading to the bridge. Here I found Colonel Barnes and his civilian adviser studying the Decca radar for signs of the island. As yet it was not visible owing to the thick mist, but some telltale splotches of light on the radar screen betrayed its presence less than ten miles ahead. Another hour and we would be safe in Village Bay. I spent the rest of the time in the wheelhouse watching in fascination Old Paddy, a septuagenarian who had gone to sea in the days of sail, expertly handling the wheel. Of all the motley crew recruited by the RASC from the ranks of the Merchant Navy to man the *Mull*, Old Paddy was the most colourful. Over six feet tall, grizzled and wrinkled by sixty years afloat, he was a real 'salt' in the best seagoing tradition. He kept us amused during the voyage with his fund of superstitions and sea-lore, spoken in a soft musical brogue.

'D'ye see them seagulls following the ship there?' he would say. 'Well, them's the ghosts of ould mariners come back to ha'nt the ship they sailed in.'

'Come off it, Paddy, this old tub was only laid down twenty years ago. I saw the date on the ship's bell. Don't tell me anyone would come back to haunt the *Mull*. It wouldn't be worth their trouble.'

'Aye, ye may joke about it – but I know for a fact it's true,' he answered reproachfully. 'And don't you be calling her an ould tub either. She's a bloody fine ship, I tell yez.'

'Will you come back and haunt her when you're dead, then?'

'Ach away with yez,' he countered in disgust. 'Sure an' I'd be havin more to do with my time than ha'nt the likes of youse bums.' This was addressed specifically to Donny Ross who was chaffing the old boy, a favourite pastime of his.

'Hey, look!' cried Cox. 'What's that out there?'

He pointed into the mist ahead. We strained our eyes and our imagination to try to make out what he had seen. Sure enough, about a mile ahead, a dull grey shape was gradually coming into definition. It resembled a thumb sticking up – with sheer sides and a gently rounded top. Could this be St Kilda at last? Eagerly we scanned it with binoculars; but as we drew closer it became apparent that this was only a mere stack of rock, Levenish by name, which rose less than two hundred feet out of the ocean. The mist and poor visibility generally had given the illusion of greater size to this rock; nevertheless it looked formidable enough as the surf broke on its almost sheer flanks and shot right up the side and over the top.

A hurried glance at the chart revealed that Levenish was less than two miles from Hirta, the main and only inhabited island of the group, and suddenly we came upon it. The sky seemed to darken above us, and then the mist cleared slightly to reveal those terrible cliffs soaring over a thousand feet into the clouds. The effect was frightening since it was quite unexpected. The *Mull* seemed so tiny and helpless ploughing through the heavy seas at the base of this fantastic mass of sheer towering rock.

As we steamed round the wrinkled bastion of Oiseval which guards the northern side of Village Bay, we looked up spellbound at the buttresses and spires which gave the cliff the awe-inspiring effect of some great medieval Gothic cathedral. A few solitary fulmars wheeled and soared in the eddies and currents of air high above us, their rigid wings silhouetted against the leaden sky. But the bay itself held even greater surprises in store for us. The sky had cleared to the west and the long rays of the setting sun threw the jagged ridges of Dùn, the island enclosing the southern side of the bay, into brilliant relief. A colossal archway, higher than Fingal's Cave in Staffa, which almost split Dùn in two, let a shaft of sunlight sweep through on to the relatively calm waters of the anchorage.

Before us lay the great Village bowl of St Kilda, dominated on all sides by hills which rose a thousand feet and more in less than half a mile of horizontal distance. Huge screes and gullies tore at the face of Conachair, the giant in the centre, below which spread the meadows of the erstwhile inhabitants. Across these fields, in a tightly formed crescent about a quarter of a mile back from the storm beach, ran the line of the old Village Street, whose roofless houses were an eloquent but pathetic reminder of a vanished race. In violent contrast to the deserted village was the hum of activity nearer the shore. From our anchorage we could hear the throb of the electric generators, and the glare of sodium lights clashed harshly with the soft evening sun. Above the old jetty, still seemingly as serviceable as the day it was built in 1901, a crowd of neo-Kildans scurried about and prepared to launch one of their small boats.

A flag suddenly broke from the mast-head in front of the Nissen huts which constituted the Army camp. I had to look twice with my binoculars, before I could convince myself that I was not having hallucinations; for there, fluttering proudly in the breeze, was the Jolly Roger, age-old badge of piracy on the high seas! Our apprehension was in no way diminished by the arrival alongside of the island's boat, a fourteen-foot dory, which appeared to be manned by as colourful and wild a crew as ever plied a bumboat in some far-eastern port. Two of the four-man crew sported magnificent moustaches, veritable handlebars which stretched from ear to ear, all of them were badly in need of a haircut, and not one of them wore a vestige of uniform clothing. The coxswain, with his unruly mop of tight red curls cascading over the scarlet kerchief knotted about his neck, needed only a huge pair of gold earrings and a knife between his teeth to finish the picture of the Complete Pirate. The dashing air of bravado with which he brought the dory alongside would have reflected creditably on any swashbuckling buccaneer leading a boarding party. I half expected Donny Ross to yell out, 'All hands on deck to repel boarders!' but instead he broke the spell with 'Throw us a line, Ginger.'

A shaky rope-ladder was uncoiled and dangled over the side for us to make our descent into the tiny boat bobbing far below. The four of us with our baggage and the waterproof sacks of mail put the dory dangerously low in the water; but, nothing daunted, Ginger cast off again and revving his outboard engine sped off towards the shore. We passengers sat near the stern to avoid the columns of spray which belted across the bows with resounding smacks as we met each wave. Willie at my elbow was almost sick with fright; certainly it was not a very pleasant experience. I looked from one to another of the crew who perched unconcernedly in the bows. The tall man in the white T-shirt and blue jeans was Corporal Denham, the island's electrician. His bushy moustache was only surpassed by that of his companion, Bombardier Johnny Harris, whose golden locks and red chubby face gave him a somewhat cherubic appearance – if you could imagine a cherub with the broadest of West Country accents. The third man wore a tartan shirt and when he smiled he revealed a huge gap where several front teeth had been knocked out. Still, on this island without women, appearances did not count for much. The fourth was Corporal Donald 'Ginger' Stewart, the only Scot among the crew – and a Highlander from Argyll at that.

The view from the bridge of a landing craft as it approaches the island

The Village from the summit of Conachair, showing a landing craft beached

About a hundred yards short of the jetty, Donny Stewart cut the motor and brought the dory round in a sweeping turn, aiming for a yellow buoy. The lads in the bows hung over the side and scooped up a heavy rope attached to the buoy. With this they proceeded to haul the boat along through the dense mass of seaweed and between the gigantic rocks which obstructed the entrance to the jetty. The water swirled back and forth round the base of the jetty and we would have been hard put to it to scramble ashore, but a massive raft, improvised out of diesel drums, telegraph poles and steel girders, lashed to bollards on the jetty, took the brunt of the swell and prevented the dory from being dashed to pieces against the rocks. We had to leap from the boat on to the raft, and from there to the slippery weed-covered steps of the jetty. We were ashore, after thirteen hours at sea, and the detachment commander was greeting us heartily.

Major Hamilton 'Tony' Riach was almost as unconventional as his men in dress. Hatless, his white hair plastered across his brow by the spray, he was clad in a thin silk khaki shirt, with sleeves rolled up past the elbows, and a pair of baggy corduroys tucked into gumboots. At his side stood a captain who was more sensibly and regimentally clad in battledress blouse, beret, denim trousers and the ubiquitous gumboots and seaman's thick white woollen stockings which seemed to be the only article of clothing uniform to the whole detachment. Captain Brian 'Will' Warner had arrived a few weeks earlier to understudy Tony Riach and take over command of the island.

Colonel Barnes shivered in the keen evening air, and after perfunctory introductions were over he asked the major,

'Isn't it a bit early for shirt sleeve order?' To which Tony Riach replied airily, 'Oh, I don't know. We've been like this since last August…'

I would later discover that winters on St Kilda were exceptionally mild and generally frost-free, owing to the influence of the Gulf Stream which washed the shores of the island; and having gone so long in shirt sleeves the soldiers there had become acclimatised to quite intemperate weather on those occasions in February and March when the north winds brought icy rains and the odd snow shower down from the Arctic.

At the top of the jetty we were met by a third officer, a captain whose face and arms were a mass of unseasonable freckles and whose long curly red hair peeped out untidily below his beret.

'I'm David Boddington, the doctor out here,' he said. 'Pleased to meet you.'

Round his neck he wore a pair of long, heavy binoculars, and even as we spoke while walking up from the jetty, his attention was seldom concentrated wholly on the conversation, for occasionally he would lift his binoculars to his face and peer intently across the meadows and exclaim with some precision, 'Ah! Seven redwings, and a wren too, if I'm not mistaken.' He was a Bird Watcher. I use capitals advisedly for, apart from my son Alastair, I have never come across someone in whom the obsessive compulsive behaviour of the twitcher was so keenly developed. Later on I learned that, less than a year previously, David had been stationed at Cowglen Military Hospital in Glasgow, and quite by accident heard that the Army were taking over St Kilda and would require a doctor. I gathered that, far from volunteering for the post, David had actually badgered the Deputy Director of Medical Services and his staff in Edinburgh into sending him out there. St Kilda, last refuge of the Great Auk and first known breeding place in the British Isles of the Fulmar, was and still is an ornithologist's paradise. Like most other fellow-enthusiasts, David would have cheerfully given his right arm for the opportunity to visit this interesting but terribly remote and inaccessible island. Everyone else on the medical staff in Scottish Command being married or engaged, there was no rush of volunteers and in due course David saw his dream come true. He had arrived on St Kilda on 28 August 1958 when the RAF left the island; ever since, without a break, he had devoted his time to the study of St Kilda's wildlife which, as well as a large variety of birds, included seals, sheep and field-mice, all distinctive to the place.

Having foregone Christmas leave in order to study the breeding habits of the island's colony of Atlantic grey seals, he had now reluctantly yielded to the entreaty of Colonel Cooper and agreed to come off for two weeks vacation, on condition that he could get back in time for the commencement of the lambing season. A Fellow of the Royal College of Obstetricians and Gynaecologists might seem a little redundant on an island bereft of women, but David was just the man to have around if any of the St Kilda ewes got into difficulties while giving birth.

His locum gazed around bleakly and then back at David, whom I think he must have regarded as slightly round the bend. To Willie Stewart birds were either 'seagulls' or 'crows', and he drew no finer distinction, or in fact saw any need for such. On one point they were agreed, however, and that was the sooner the ship returned to St Kilda in two weeks' time the happier they would both be for their own separate reasons.

David ushered us into the Mess, which was housed in part of a Romney hut (a much larger version of the Nissen hut), not far from the jetty. We dumped our baggage in the tiny porch and entered the main room which was large but rather austerely furnished. On one side was a dining table set for seven, with heavy Suffolk chairs around it. On the other side a suite of rather tired looking easy chairs and a settee were grouped round a card table on which sat a battery radio-set. At the far end of the room, in the corner diagonally opposite the one from which we had entered, was another door which led on to a hallway. This door was open and through it we could see soldiers bustling to and fro, carrying plates laden with food. The officers' ante room and the men's cookhouse were cheek by jowl in this democratic camp. Tony strolled in behind us with Colonel Barnes.

'I expect you are pretty hungry, sir,' he said, taking up a dinner plate from a pile on the table. 'It's self-service here,' and he waved towards the door.

We fell into line behind him and trotted out into the hallway and up the short flight of steps into the men's dining hall.

Most of the tiny garrison had already eaten their supper, but the men who had followed us ashore were now queuing up at the hotplate for an appetising meal of compo steak and kidney pudding. Colonel Barnes said nothing. 'When in Rome…' he probably thought as he stood in line with his plate. Tony joked and bantered with the man in front of him in the queue, one of the old hands now returned for another tour of duty on the island. Juggling plates of hot soup, steak and kidney, and prunes and custard, we stepped gingerly down into our dining room and set to ravenously.

Later David took me across to the Medical Centre to show me his own special domain. Just as Neil Ferguson, the postmaster up to the Evacuation, had held several offices simultaneously, David was not only the Medical Officer of St Kilda, but also the Rations Officer, Meteorological Officer, Barber and Postmaster. His Medical Inspection Room boasted equipment that would have put Cowglen to shame, with its dental surgery, barber's shop and fully-fledged operating theatre. The Post Office consisted of a red-painted triangular corner of the hospital, where the men brought their letters. David collected the letters, dispensed stamps, made out Army Form FF 49 in triplicate whenever a letter had to be registered, then put the mail into a polythene bag. This, in turn, went into an oilskin bag and this was sealed in a regulation Post Office mailbag. It was then that he told me that the mail went to Stranraer where, miraculous to relate, it was stamped with the old St Kilda postmark which somebody had apparently resurrected when the RAF re-occupied the island. He showed me some of the fan mail which he received from all over the world, stamp collectors writing for specimens of the postmark. Many of them offered stamps of their own country in exchange, and as a result David had acquired a sizeable collection. His abiding passion, however, was the bird life and he told me about his plans for ringing the birds. '46,000 pairs of fulmar and 60,000 pairs of gannets out of a total world population of 80,000,' he informed me, his eyes shining at the prospect. His duties as honorary Nature Conservancy warden did not sit lightly upon him.

Afterwards David took us up to the Factor's House, a substantial two-storey building at the top of the meadow behind the main camp. This house, as its name suggests, had been at one time the residence of the factor, or agent of the proprietor of St Kilda, who occupied it twice a year during his brief visit to the island to collect the rents and supervise his master's business. After St Kilda was evacuated in 1930 the new owner, the Earl of Dumfries (later fifth Marquess of Bute) had maintained it after a fashion and used it as rough and ready accommodation for his ornithological guests. Thus it was still in fairly good shape when the RAF re-occupied the island, and after they had renovated it and installed electricity it became their officers' sleeping quarters.

The architect who had designed it, back in the 1830s, had not bothered with such refinements as an internal staircase connecting the upper and lower levels. Instead, he had cleverly made use of the steep slope on which the house was built, so that the front door led into the ground floor rooms while a pathway led round the side of the building to the back door which opened on to the upper storey.

Cox and I elected to share the spare bedroom on the ground floor. Across the passage way slept the new Commanding Officer, Will Warner, but between those two rooms was a small cubby-hole, which in days gone by had been a tiny pantry. In this Tony had erected a camp bed for the colonel who sacrificed comfort to gain the privacy of a room to himself. Upstairs, Tony was to share a bedroom with Willie, while David had the other room which only had a single bed.

We sorted ourselves out and had a wash. A singular feature of St Kilda was that only the officers lacked 'en suite' facilities. The sergeants who lodged in the old Manse had an internal bathroom, while the other ranks accommodation block incorporated ablutions; but the officers had to endure the inconvenience of creeping out into the dark night when they needed to take a leak. The wash house, a brick and concrete edifice resembling a wartime pillbox, was sited on the opposite side of the pathway facing the house. In spite of its almost vulgarly utilitarian external design it was surprisingly well-equipped inside. It boasted a bathroom, shower and toilet, a brace of wash-hand basins and, most wonderful of all in this god-forsaken spot so far from civilisation, a Hoovermatic spin-drier and washing machine.

'We have to do our own laundry,' David explained, 'Even sheets... The nearest laundry is in Oban, and that's damn' near two hundred miles and several light years away.'

'Can I use my electric razor here?' I asked.

'Sure. And you can have a bath too, if you want one, We've got constant boiling water – a hundred and fifty gallons of it – at any time of day or night. It's marvellous, isn't it?'

I was amazed at the comfort of the place. Even in the Outer Hebrides, sixty miles to the east and closer to civilisation, most people had no modern sanitation and very few, as yet, had electricity; while away out here on this tiny speck of rock in the ocean a handful of men enjoyed all the benefits which our modern society could think of. I reflected aloud on this.

'That's nothing,' said David. 'You haven't seen our canteen yet. Come on down when you're ready.'

We joined the others and walked down across the close cropped grass of the Minister's Meadow to the beckoning lights of the camp. The canteen was not a large room – about the size of the taproom in a small country pub – but its unique character was derived from its décor. Dominating the centre of the wall above the bar was a huge placard on which was painted a puffin.

'It's the commonest bird on St Kilda in summertime,' explained David. 'Over two million pairs of them nest here. So we call our canteen the Puffin Club, and those of us who serve on St Kilda long enough qualify for a Puffin tie. Sarn't Tutt,' he called to the barman, 'Show Lieutenant Mackay one of our ties.'

Sergeant Tutt rummaged below the counter and came up with a box from which he produced a maroon silk tie whose motif consisted of a number of puffins.

'There you are,' said David. 'Perhaps you will get one some day, if you stay here for at least a month.'

I do not know when the much coveted Puffin tie of the St Kilda detachment was taken over by the St Kilda Club, which reduced the residential qualification to a single night on the island. More recently anyone can wear it who signifies his support of the Puffin Club merely by buying it. The Puffin Club later became the Puffin Bar, complete with a rather fine mural of Andy Capp, almost supine, with a foaming tankard in one hand and eventually it became the Puff Inn, the remotest (and cheapest) pub in the British Isles. Today it has grown out of all recognition in both size and the splendour of its fittings. In July 2001, when the base ceased to be a military establishment under the Ministry of Defence, the Puff Inn had to apply to the licensing authority in Stornoway in order to continue. I understand that no objections were raised by the neighbours, the gannets, fulmars and puffins, and the licence was duly granted – although I have no idea how the Stornoway police can check that proper hours are adhered to.

'What do you think of our pin-ups, sir?' smiled Tutt, nodding over his shoulder toward the gallery of scantily clad young ladies whose photographs adorned the wall above the shelves of canned pineapple juice and sticks of shaving cream. 'Pretty good, eh?'

I studied them for a moment. 'Where do you get them from?' I was intrigued to note that these glossy pictures of rising starlets like Diana Dors and Joan Collins had not been cut out of magazines.

'Oh, we have a dodge here for getting pin-ups,' Tutt replied. 'Q Wilson who looks after our film shows does them for us. Whenever we get a film with a nice bit of tit – like Diana Dors here, for instance, revealing her talents in *The Long Haul* – Q Wilson turns the film over, frame by frame, in the projector until he gets the most revealing shot. You'd be amazed just how much these film stars show. Of course, it's normally quicker than the human eye can follow, but taking it one frame at a time, you often see quite a lot. When he gets the frame he wants, he blows it up on the enlarger and takes a print off it. Full plate, it looks not bad up there behind the bar...'

The Factor's House: Tex Geddes leaving the officers' toilet block

And sure enough, the gorgeous pouting Miss Dors was revealing an astonishing amount of her ample bosom. Of course, one can see much, much more on television any night of the week nowadays; but back in the Prim and Proper Fifties, before the Swinging Sixties, the only films that showed women with bare breasts were travelogues and documentaries about obscure and very primitive tribes.

'Did you bring any cash out for us?' Tony Riach was at my elbow.

'Oh, sorry sir, I forgot. Yes, here you are; twenty-five pounds in nice crisp new ten-shilling notes. I have to take the same sum back to Benbecula in old notes.' I produced the wad of notes which Corporal Peter Jones, the pay NCO back at Troon, had given me some days earlier.

'There you are,' replied Tony, handing me an envelope. 'Fair exchange is no robbery, they say. Go on – you'd better check it.'

I opened the envelope and drew out the

Generator sheds, REME workshops, ORs' accommodation block, Conachair in the background

filthiest, raggedest, limpest banknotes I have ever handled. They were disgusting, they positively stank and many were virtually reduced to an unrecognisable pulp. Some had dark splodges of diesel oil almost totally obliterating them. Conversely others were stiff, impregnated with Guinness beer. Some were none too skilfully repaired with sticky tape, and I even found a few which had names or initials scrawled in ball-point pens on their tattered backs. Tony explained this extraordinary situation.

'We don't carry a large stock of money on the island,' he said. 'There's really no need, since we have only thirty boys here at most for months on end. Every week, at pay parade, the chaps only draw enough money from their pay credits to keep them going in pocket money during the week. Over the ensuing seven days all this money gradually drifts into the canteen. Then comes the next pay parade when I draw sufficient cash from the canteen account to pay the men. Thus the same money keeps circulating every week. The cash taken in by the canteen for goods sold, and the amount of money to which each soldier is entitled are treated purely as book transactions through the Pay office at Troon, thus minimising the actual sum of money to be handled out here. Consequently the same notes keep changing hands constantly and after a bit of the rough usage they get out here they become a trifle soiled, as you can see for yourself. Sometimes the chaps mark the notes, to see how long it takes for these particular notes to come round to them again. It's quite a game.'

This seemed an appropriate moment to ask Tony a question I had been dying to put to him since we landed. 'Tell me, what's the significance of the pirate flag you were flying when we arrived?'

'A symbol of one of my many battles with Higher Authority, my dear boy,' he replied. 'We often get ships of other nations in here – Spanish and Danish trawlers, French lobster boats and so on – and I petitioned the War Office that we should be made a Flag Station – like Gibraltar or Malta – and be entitled to fly the Union Jack when any of these foreigners called in. It would have meant a free issue of flags for us; but, of course, these bods in Whitehall can't see beyond the ends of their noses. Said it would be too expensive, and also require special legislation to make St Kilda a Flag Station. So we didn't get our flag. Then I threatened to fly my own flag instead; and since they haven't replied to that one, I've gone ahead and made a Jolly Roger. Damned effective it is too, don't you agree?'

A spirited game of darts was going on in another corner of the crowded little canteen. Behind the bar, Sergeant Tutt replaced the well-worn disc of *'My Fair Lady'* with selections from *'Carousel'*. The babble of voices clamoured from all directions. I sauntered out of the canteen, into the Rec Room, where four men were playing table-tennis while a number of others, sprawling in easy chairs, looked on. At one end of the room was a large cinema screen, while at the far end small glass windows indicated the projection booth. Above the little windows a sheet of foolscap headed *'Puffin Bioscope'* announced that George Formby was keeping fit… *'All seats reservable'*.

Beyond the Rec Room was the dining hall and the exit. I joined Willie and Mr Cox who were on the point of retiring to the Factor's House. Outside, the sky had cleared, revealing the starry heavens framed by the black outline of the lofty hills around the bay. As we groped our way across the Minister's Meadow, something bolted ahead of us, giving us a fright. Our torch beam caught the outline of a wild goat-like creature for a second or two before it bounded over a low stone wall and disappeared.

'One of the sheep,' said Cox.

'You didn't notice its horns?' I asked.

'I don't think it had any,' he replied.

'I must ask Captain Boddington in the morning about the four-horned variety.'

We stumbled over the litter of fallen stones which lay strewn in front of the entrance to the Village Street at the top of the meadow. On the uneven granophyre paving ahead of us small dark shapes flitted and scurried back and forward into the shadows.

'Look!' cried Willie. 'Rats!'

'These aren't rats, Willie. These are mice – the famous St Kilda field-mice. But what whoppers they are. I'll show you one in the morning.' David Boddington had appeared out of the shadows, carrying a small aluminium box in his hand. 'I'm going to set a catch-alive trap for one tonight.' And with that he disappeared across the meadow again.

'God, what a place this is,' sighed Willie. 'Wild sheep and mice like rats. Ugh. The sooner I get off this island and return to Civilisation the better!'

Cox and I undressed silently and got into bed, fatigued by our long and eventful day. For long enough, however, I could not sleep on account of the unaccustomed drone of the generators whose steady throb reverberated across the bay from one steep hillside to the next. 'What a place it is, indeed,' I mused. 'So much to see and in such a short time, too.'

3. THE DESERTED VILLAGE

BREAKFAST next morning was at half past six. We made our way, still half asleep, down across the meadow in the darkness and ate a hurried meal which compared all too poorly with our previous breakfast. Shortly after seven, as the first grey fingers of daylight began to creep over the horizon beyond Levenish, we clambered aboard a one-ton truck and began our sight-seeing tour of the island. One of St Kilda's most striking, and most recent, features was its road. Although it is barely a mile and a half in length it is nevertheless quite a feat of engineering, rising as it does in a series of hairpin bends and one-in-three gradients, from the tarmac square outside the OC's office at sea level to the Marconi radar station at the top of Mullach Mór twelve hundred feet above the bay. All during the long hot summer of 1957 three hundred men of 5004 Squadron of the RAF Construction Branch toiled seven days a week to construct it and earn for their commanding officer the OBE.

The original plan had been to build the road well back from the sea, running along the base of Conachair where materials, in the form of the quaint stone cleits and the tumbled screes of dolerite and granophyre were ready to hand. The Air Ministry even considered demolishing the Village and use the rubble from it in building the road. Fortunately, the National Trust for Scotland (who owned the island) and the Nature Conservancy Council (who leased it) forced the Air Ministry to revise its plans and construct the road along the foreshore instead. It was subsequently discovered that, had the original plan been implemented, not only the present Village, with its houses of 1838 and 1860, would have been destroyed, but the site of the medieval village would have been destroyed and incalculable damage done to several other structures of immense archaeological interest. Just thirty years later, in 1987, St Kilda became Scotland's very first UNESCO World Heritage Site, but it might so easily have been obliterated had the 'men from the Ministry' had their way.

Building the road along the top of the escarpment overlooking the rock-strewn storm beach entailed the spanning of the Amhuinn Mór, a diminutive stream running through a gully, which one of the national dailies described, in an account of the tasks ahead of the RAF Hard Rock Task Force, as *'a sixty foot gorge'*. A standard Bailey Bridge was thrown across the burn, past which the road turned sharply upwards towards the quarry where the RAF had obtained most of their building materials. After a short, sharp drive we were already several hundred feet above the sea. From the quarry we had a fine view of the old village spread below us. I was amazed at the abundance of stone walling in the village glen. Three large walls, perhaps ten feet thick, ran down from the line of cottages towards the bay, while running round the entire area was the head dyke, an enormous wall separating the village and its meadows from the rougher pasture and heather beyond. The boundaries of each croft were clearly delineated by lesser dry stone dykes running parallel to the three main walls and at right angles to the street. Behind the houses were several enclosures, sheep-folds and kailyards, the smaller circular structures in which cabbages had at one time been cultivated, sheltered from the wind and the ravages of the sheep.

General view of cleits on the slopes above Village Bay

Everywhere, as fascinating and as puzzling as the stone heads of Easter Island, were the cleits, strange stone beehive structures with bushy grass-topped roofs. Here the islanders had stored dried sea-birds, their staple diet, peat, hay, fishing and fowling gear and even spare clothing. Some were quite large and a few of them may even have been the primitive 'black houses' of the period prior to the erection of the 1830 houses. Others were much smaller, about five or six feet high and just as broad, with the walls gradually sloping inwards so that the roof could be formed with slabs of granophyre laid across the top and covered with a protective layer of soil and turf. David told us that he had counted 118 cleits within the head dyke, and there were about five hundred more dotted all over the entire island outside it, some on the very summits of the hills. In fact there are almost 1100 cleits on Hirta, and perhaps a further 150 distributed on the other islands.

'I have numbered each of the cleits within the Wall,' said David, 'so that when I spot an unusual bird I can record in my field notebook its exact location by reference to the nearest cleit.'

'Well, that's one use for them,' I joked, 'but I doubt if they would serve any useful purpose nowadays.'

'Ah, that's where you're wrong,' David maintained. 'We use some of them at this very moment. One of them is a paint store, another is the explosives store, and two of them are used as potato clamps. The National Trust and the Nature Conservancy also use some of them for storing their gear. They look very primitive but they are amazingly efficient. The solid roof keeps out the rain, while the gaps between the stones forming the walls let the wind through to keep everything nicely aired.'

'Still – over six hundred of these things – seems a bit wasteful to me, if the total population of the island never exceeded two hundred. Why do you suppose they built so many of them?'

'I couldn't really say. Of course they had different uses. Some are located halfway down the cliffs and obviously were stores for fowling rods and nets; others away up on the top of Conachair and Oiseval were used for storing peat – in fact some of these still have stacks of peat in them that must have been cut at least twenty-nine years ago. But right enough, there do seem to be far more of them than were really necessary. Perhaps boys had to build a cleit to prove their manhood, or perhaps cleit building was a form of punishment, or recreation even. I don't know, and I don't suppose any of these bright archaeological chaps know either.'

Left: The large cleit popularly regarded as Lady Grange's House. Note the head dyke in the background

Right: Tobar Gille Chille (the well of the servant of the cell or chapel), one of the oldest structures on Hirta

We drove on again, jolting dangerously as the truck lurched round incredible corners and tipped us unceremoniously down towards the tailboard as it took the steep gradients. Eventually we came to a road junction, and turning to the left we proceeded down a gentle incline to the Decca radar station. We jumped out and stretched our legs, gazing around to take in the wonderful scenery. We seemed to be directly above the island of Dùn, but whereas from the camp we had a broadside view of this spectacular island, we were now looking at it hull down, and from this angle its ridges and pinnacles seemed even more frightening than before. Behind the squat concrete building which housed the radar the cliff fell away in a steep grassy incline towards the sea a thousand feet below.

'Don't go too near the edge, sir,' warned Tony.

'I don't think I will, replied Colonel Barnes. 'But why did you say that?'

'Last year one of the Decca technicians thought he would take a photograph of the radar from that angle, and backed down the grassy slope a bit to get it all in. It seems he backed a bit too far – and the next thing he knew was that he had slipped and fallen into the sea.'

'Good lord! Did he survive that?' The colonel peered cautiously over the edge.

'Apparently he had been a naval frogman during the War, and kept his head when he went into the drink,' Tony continued. 'The sea is fantastically deep at this part, but it was still a helluva dive. Anyhow, he managed to swim ashore along the coast a bit – but he lost his camera.'

'I should think that that little escapade must have put him off photography for the rest of his life,' Colonel Barnes commented dryly.

While the colonel and his civilian technical adviser inspected the interior of the building, David, Willie and I strolled outside. Now, in broad daylight, we were able to get a good look at the Soay sheep, a flock of which was grazing nearby. They were quite unlike any sheep I had ever seen before. They had short tattered fleeces which varied in colour from a light caramel to a deep chocolate. Their legs were long and they bounded with the agility of the chamois over the crags, or picked their way nimbly along the narrow paths round the cliff below. Some of the ewes were horned, others were hornless; the tups presented a magnificent sight with their curving black horns, black beards and shaggy black manes. Tony fancifully likened them to miniature buffalo.

'Odd looking brutes, aren't they?' remarked David.

'I couldn't agree more,' I added. 'But tell me, is it true that some of the rams have four horns?'

'I've heard that story myself,' said David, 'but I very much doubt it – unless, of course, there are some like that on Soay. Until the islanders evacuated St Kilda, you could only find this breed of sheep on Soay, which was their natural habitat. Then the Marquess of Bute, who bought St Kilda from the MacLeod of MacLeod in the early Thirties, had some Soay sheep – about forty I believe – brought over from Soay to Hirta. Now there are over a thousand of them here on this island, and that doesn't take account of the original flock on Soay itself. The latter haven't been visited since 1932. Soay is an extremely difficult island to land on because of its sheer cliffs on all sides, and it may well be that a four-horned variety of tup is to be found there. The St Kildans themselves raised Blackface or Cheviot sheep here, but all of them were rounded up at the time they left in August 1930. I have a hunch that some sheep evaded the round-up, so there is probably a strain of Blackface in the flock to this day.'

Soay sheep

'You seem to have done quite a bit of work on the sheep.'

'Yes. I find them fascinating. Their behaviour patterns are especially interesting.'

'Oh. In what way?'

'Well, one of the things about them is the sexual behaviour of the tups. They don't start to get interested in the ewes till they are two years old. Until then they go through some kind of homosexual phase. They form into bands – I call them Tup Clubs – and roam around together in a little coterie of their own. They congregate in the cleits at night; at other times you will see them playfully butting each other.'

'Ah well, there's safety in numbers I suppose. But who'd have thought of sex rearing its beautiful head in this dump?' queried Cox who had joined us.

On the subject of four-horned rams, the jury is still out; but some years later I visited the Isle of Man and discovered that four horns was a common characteristic of the Loaghtyn sheep. Like the Soay sheep, they are believed to have been introduced to Man by the Vikings more than a thousand years ago.

We drove back up the road, along the ridge of Mullach Sgar, past the road junction and up the side of Mullach Mór to the Marconi station. From this point we could look northwards at Boreray and its attendant rock stacks, Stac Lii and Stac an Armuinn, home of the world's greatest gannetry. To the west, the flank of Mullach Mór fell away steeply to the Great Glen of Hirta. Unlike the Village Glen, this valley bore no visible sign of recent human habitation and few sheep grazed on the sour marsh grass which grew there. A stream, Allt a' Ghlinne ('river of the glen') trickled down to the coast where it fell in cascades over a hundred-foot cliff. On the far side of the glen, the ridges of Mullach Bi rose up like the Dùn, of which it was in fact a continuation. Beyond them was the tall promontory of the Cambir which jutted out to form the north-westerly point of Hirta. Behind it, separated from Hirta by a channel no more than 400 yards, lay the inaccessible island of Soay, twelve hundred feet high, whose sides fell in near vertical screes to end in sheer cliffs of two hundred feet. Nowhere was there a beach or convenient rocky ledge where one might scramble ashore. All round the foot of the cliff the mighty ocean pounded relentlessly, and a closer examination through field-glasses revealed colossal rocks and boulders which would make an approach by any kind of vessel quite impossible. And yet the St Kildans had managed to land on Soay from time to time, and their lack of skill in boat-handling was well known. So, clearly, a landing was not totally out of the question.

My attention was drawn to patches of white which gleamed on the sides of the Glen and were scattered down the banks of the stream. 'The wreckage of a Sunderland flying-boat, from the War...' David explained laconically. You could imagine the great aircraft lumbering along, probably in a thick fog, unaware that the island was even there... then suddenly, the crash into the hillside, and that was that. I shivered. A year in my University air squadron had taught me to fly on instruments when enveloped in cloud or fog, but unless you were flying at an altitude sufficient to avoid the highest mountains, flying blind was always a dangerous business.

'St Kilda is hardly the place to lark around in an aeroplane,' David observed.

If anything, the drive downhill was even more scary than the drive uphill, for the road seemed to corkscrew at a very steep angle. I tried to keep my eyes off the vertiginous road and gazed down on the bay and the crescent of the deserted village. Obligingly the truck stopped to let me jump out while the rest of the party went on. Willie and David still had to do the hand over of the Medical Centre, and Colonel Barnes wished to visit the island's workshops and generator sheds. A hundred yards from the road was the stream, Amhuinn Mór on the far bank of which was the end of the Street and the last of the cottages. From what I had read of St Kilda I had gathered that the Street was a comparatively modern development. Early in the nineteenth century a wealthy baronet, Sir Thomas Dyke Acland, had sailed in his own yacht – appropriately named Lady of St Kilda in compliment to his wife – and had been so appalled at the squalor in which the St Kildans lived that he had left £20 with the minister, to be awarded to the first man who took the initiative and rebuilt his house. The primitive communism of St Kilda had many admirable qualities, but it stifled any attempts at individual activity and for several years no one made a move to win the prize. In the end, the minister shrewdly realised that improvement would only come from the pulpit, and in the 1830s he used the money to prime the pump of a wholesale rebuilding of the village.

The Village Street, east end; the road and RAF quarry can be seen in the upper left-hand corner of the picture.

The new village was laid out in a crescent of sixteen cottages, representing the cutting edge of Hebridean black house technology. The houses did not face the bay, but stood at right angles, their thick, rounded gables taking the brunt of the south-easterly gales. The houses were constructed of double dry stone walls, the cavities being filled with soil. Driftwood from the Caribbean provided the roof trusses and rafters while the roofs were thatched in the traditional manner. The cottages had two apartments, the lower end being occupied by the cattle and the upper end forming the living and sleeping quarters of the family. The cottages were set sufficiently far apart from each other for the proprietor of St Kilda, three decades later, to erect a further sixteen houses along the Street, alternating with the 1838 cottages. This time, however, the houses were the standard, mid-Victorian, single-storey dwelling of agricultural labourers in many parts of the Highlands and Islands, comprising a kitchen, boxroom and bedroom separated by internal wooden partitions, with outer walls of dressed stone, a proper wooden door and two large glazed windows, all fronting directly on to the bay. At either end of the zinc-sheeted roof stood an earthenware chimney pot. These fine, modern houses came complete with various articles of furniture donated by an increasingly charitable public. Some of the earlier black houses were retained as additional accommodation, but mostly they were relegated to the role of outhouses and cowsheds. Not surprisingly, the St Kildans missed the cosy fug of the older cottages and complained long and loud about the draughts and leaking roofs. The zinc-sheeted roofs were speedily replaced by tarred roofs of a more substantial construction, but even they had to be strapped down tightly with stout hawsers to prevent Atlantic gales from tearing them off.

Almost twenty-nine years had elapsed since the last St Kildan had turned the key in the lock of his front door and carted his few personal belongings down to the jetty where the *Dunara Castle* waited to take them all away to a new life on the mainland. In successive summers after the Evacuation of August 1930, a few loyal islanders had returned to their

The houses at the west end of the Village Street as they were in 1959, roofless and in ruins

The island's tiny circular burial ground. The marble 'book' (centre) was erected after the Evacuation by Alexander Gillies Ferguson in memory of his parents. Most islanders were content with a simple uninscribed stone slab.

old homes, mainly to act as caretakers for the Marquess of Bute and serve as guides to the tourists for whom the now deserted isle was an even greater attraction than ever. At the same time, however, the ravages of winter storms and the looting and vandalism of visiting trawlers had hastened the dilapidation of the cottages. They appear to have been systematically stripped of doors and window-frames and probably a great deal of the roofing materials as well. Ironically, the older cottages had stood the test of time rather better than the 1860 houses, although they, too, were now totally roofless. Ten years before my first visit to St Kilda, the last roof in the village had collapsed. The corrugated iron shack which served as the post office was still standing when Morton Boyd took his expedition to the island in 1952, but even that had vanished before the arrival of the RAF in 1957.

Altogether there were about forty houses of different periods in the Street; most of them were actually on the Street itself, but one or two of the smaller, older dwellings pre-1830 were set back behind the others, especially around the middle of the village where a side street led off to a large circular enclosure, the island's ancient burial ground. Built on the same pattern as a sheep fank, although designed to keep the sheep out rather than in, it was surrounded by a high dry stone wall, greater height being imparted by the fact that it was on a slight eminence below which the ground fell away sharply. A narrow entrance at the eastern end led into the little cemetery, the last resting place of generations of St Kildans. Each grave was simply marked by two standing stones, the larger one at the head and the smaller at the foot. These rough stones bore no marks of any kind, but the graveyard contained three proper tombstones. One had been erected by the Revd Neil Mackenzie who buried several of his children here; another marked the interment of Margaret Mackay, sister of, and housekeeper to, the Revd John Mackay who ministered to the St Kildans from 1859 till 1889, while a third, in the form of a marble open book, had been erected after the Evacuation by Alexander Gillies Ferguson in memory of his parents.

It took me more than two hours to make even a cursory inspection of the buildings along the Street. Stooping through the low wide doorways of the 1830 cottages, where people and cattle had entered together, I paused to look around at the disorder and decay of fallen masonry and thatch now rank with weeds. Here and there would be the rotting staves of a barrel or wash-tub; in others, the rusting iron rings which tethered the cow in the lower room of the house could still be seen jutting out of the rough wall. In one 'hallan-end' lay the whitened bones of a sheep which had crawled in there to die.

It was in the remains of the more modern houses that I savoured the pathos which must have surrounded the departure of the St Kildans. They had walked out carrying little more than hand baggage, either because they were unable to take their heavier possessions on account of the limited cargo space on the steamer, or because they half-hoped that some kind Fate would allow them to return to their homes if the mainland should not turn out to be the Golden Land they imagined it to be. In fact, they were no sooner off the island than many of them begged to be repatriated; but the Labour government had spent at least £1,000 on their removal and was not minded to incur a similar cost in putting them back there. Although some of them returned for short visits during the summers of 1931-9, till shortly before the outbreak of the Second World War, most of them had never come back. Consequently their bulky chattels, treasured family heirlooms such as huge brass-knobbed bedsteads and oaken chests of drawers, remained to moulder away slowly with the passage of the years. Now, little remained of the furniture except the occasional bed with weeds sprouting up through the mattress and blankets. What did remain, however, was a profusion of smaller articles, hardware, rusted biscuit tins, broken crockery and the like. I took numerous black and white photographs of this detritus of a vanished race. Some time later, the work parties organised by the National Trust for Scotland made a concerted effort to clear all this rubbish out of the derelict houses as a preliminary to the task of preventing further deterioration of the ruins. Huge pits were dug in the lower meadow into which this junk was deposited and buried. In more recent years these pits have been the subject of archaeological digs and I was amused to note that the old bedstead which I had photographed in March 1959 was one of the prominent exhibits in the splendid exhibition entitled 'St Kilda Explored' which was staged in Glasgow's Kelvingrove Museum in 1996.

In his *Last Voyage to St Kilda*, published in 1931, Alasdair Alpin MacGregor mentioned how he had inadvertently left behind his razor strop hanging on the window sill of the postmaster's house, and prophesied that in years to come archaeologists would find it and thereby deduce that the St Kildans were a clean-shaven race. The commonest articles I found were rusted enamelled chamber pots, one house having no fewer than three of them abandoned in the bedroom. Just what the archaeologist or sociologist was to deduce from this, on the lines suggested by MacGregor, I do not know. The St Kildans may have used them as cooking utensils; one nineteenth century writer actually stated that he had seen the islanders employing chamber pots for this purpose, although this may have been a gross distortion of the facts. It is far more likely that they were used for defecation and urination within the privacy of the houses, the contents being then tipped out on to the middens which stood across the narrow Street, opposite each house.

There was certainly no shortage of the more conventional kitchen hardware and I found frying pans and enamel saucepans in great abundance. There were also several broken porcelain teapots, as well as the iron three-legged pots in which the islanders had boiled puffins, made fulmar broth, cooked their porridge and dyed sheep's wool prior to spinning it – all with a cheerful lack of fastidiousness. These and many other articles of everyday life which could have been duplicated elsewhere in the Highlands and Islands even in the 1950s lay strewn about. There was, in fact, as much of antiquarian interest lying in these ruined cottages as you would find on any municipal rubbish dump in England – precious little. And yet there was something poignant in the sight of these common objects which had once graced the lives of these poor people and brought a breath of the civilisation, if not the luxury, of the outside world to their tiny, remote island.

The fact that a few of the houses at the eastern end of the Street had been cleared of all rubbish indicated that the NTS volunteers of the previous summer had already been hard at work. The biggest surprise of all was to find in one of these otherwise empty houses a complete bath-tub, with hot and cold water taps – this on an island which had not possessed running water before the Evacuation! But there it was, its blue and white enamel finish still reasonably intact; even the taps retained the gleam of chromium. I asked David about it afterwards and the story he had to tell reflected on the stupidity of some Staff officers who never deviate from the rules and regulations.

A St Kilda 'mailboat' c1897. The letters and coppers for postage were placed in a Van Houten coffee tin sealed with ship's canvas and attached to an inflated sheep's bladder as a float with a piece of wood on which was carved ST KILDA MAIL – PLEASE OPEN.

Finlay McQueen launching a St Kilda 'mailboat', 1896 [photo Richard Kearton].

Apparently when the RAF occupied St Kilda they found in the manse (where successive ministers and missionaries had once resided) this bath, connected up to an Aga heater. This appurtenance of upper-class hygiene had been installed in the mid-1930s by the Marquess of Bute to provide some 'mod cons' during his summer visits, when the manse had fleetingly rejoiced in the rather grand name of House of Oiseval. The RAF had renovated and refurbished the manse as the sergeants' mess and the old bath was then taken out. Rather than let it rust away in idleness, however, they decided to fit it into the Medical Centre, there being no bath provided in the plans for that building. All was well for a time, and the RAF congratulated themselves on a masterpiece of improvisation, until some senior Medical Staff Officer had come out to inspect the island's medical facilities. He declared that the bath was not on the requisite G 1098/1198 Scale of Equipment, Hospitals, Troops for the use of, and ordered that it be got rid of... David thereupon had the bath removed once more and put it into one of the roofless houses where he had his zoological 'laboratory'. A further eighteen months were to elapse before the Powers That Be decided that it might not be a bad idea to install a bath in the Medical Centre after all. In the meantime, the detachment had to get by with only two baths in the OR's Ablutions, to serve the needs of an average of twenty-five men for nine months of the year and often twice that number in summertime.

I had scarcely examined the last house in the Street when a hooter sounded across the bay; the *Mull* had steam up and was due to sail. I hurried along the uneven paving to the Factor's House and gathered up my kit. Down on the jetty the party leaving the island was in the process of embarking; some were already scrambling aboard the cutter while others were sitting on kit-bags and suitcases on the jetty, eagerly waiting their turn. All were dressed unfamiliarly in khaki; even Major Riach had covered his thin silk shirt with his battledress tunic. I was puzzled by the last medal ribbon on his chest; I had not encountered it before and assumed that it was some foreign decoration and asked him what it was.

'That, my boy, is the ribbon of the Territorial Medal for the Honourable Artillery Company. The red and blue stripes were King Edward the Seventh's racing colours, actually.' And with that, Tony swung his valise out on to the cutter and jumped in after it.

David, Colonel Barnes, Cox and I brought up the rear. Hurried farewells were exchanged with Willie Stewart and Will Warner, now left in sole command of the detachment. There were waves, assorted rude gestures, derisive cheers and shouted comments from the soldiers we left behind us. One man was heard to remark, in a rich Scouse accent, as the *Mull* gave a final blast on her hooter, 'Ta ta, fucking *Altmark*!' (a reference to the notorious Nazi prison ship). Even as we clambered up the rope ladder and tumbled on to the deck, the anchor was being weighed with a rattling of chains and the wheezing of the winch. Already Chris Foster was busy in the galley preparing lunch and David was doling out sea-sickness tablets.

My first trip to St Kilda was at an end. There was so much which I had not managed to see. As the *Mull* began to move out of the bay, I scanned the shore with my binoculars and caught the unmistakable shape of a gun.

'Surely you don't have artillery out here?' I asked David.

'Oh, you mean the old gun?'

'Mm. That's odd. It appears to be pointing towards the camp and not out to sea.'

'It's an old naval gun left over from the First World War. It seems there was a naval detachment stationed here at the time, but I'm afraid I can't tell you anything more about it than that.'

A naval gun from the First World War, indeed! Whatever would I find next?

The voyage back to South Uist was calm and uneventful. This time we sailed via the Sound of Harris and cut our voyage down from thirteen to eight hours, much to David's relief. Like Willie, he was not too good a sailor, and disdaining the wholesome mess of compo stew at mealtimes, contented himself with an occasional nibble at a hard tack biscuit. St Kilda and Boreray remained in view almost to the very entrance of the Sound, two lonely heaps of rock sticking defiantly out of the Atlantic, on the edge of the sunken plateau known as the Continental Shelf, beyond which the ocean bed dropped to hundreds of fathoms. As we passed Shillay and Pabbay, the twin smudges on the horizon vanished in the evening haze and our attention turned instead to contemplation of the intricacies involved in navigating the *Mull* between the reefs and skerries which beset the channel.

The author leaning against the wall of House No 2, the former residence of Finlay McQueen, most redoubtable of the old St Kildan fowlers

4. SAILORS ON ST KILDA

PROBABLY the first servicemen to visit Kilda were the redcoats who went there on a bootless errand in the summer of 1746, thinking that Bonnie Prince Charlie might be taking refuge there. Campbell of Mamore was in command of this flotilla which consisted of HM ships *Furnace* and *Terror* and several troop-carrying wherries which left Tobermory on 10 June. Off Eigg they were joined by HMS *Trial* and when they rounded the Butt of Lewis two 42-gun men-o-war, the *Loo* and the *Eltham* under Commodore Thomas Smith, considerably swelled the ranks. With more than 120 regular soldiers and a comparable number of Argyll levies on board, the expedition reached St Kilda on 19 June. The troops went ashore that afternoon, doubtless relieved to be on reasonably dry land again. They spread out and combed the island, eventually winkling the terrified islanders out of their caves and crevices whither they had fled at the approach of the ships. 'They knew nothing about a Prince, or a Pretender, or His Majesty King George for that matter. They had heard that the MacLeod of MacLeod had been at war with a great woman somewhere, and that he had got the better of her.' This sounds like a garbled account of the incarceration of Lady Grange which would, of course, have been very fresh in the minds of the St Kildans.

Meanwhile the Prince was accompanying the redoubtable Flora Macdonald, disguised as her Irish maid Betty Burke, as they criss-crossed South Uist. By the time the soldiers returned to the Outer Hebrides, the Prince had taken a boat from Benbecula 'over the sea to Skye' and thence escaped back to France. At any rate the troops of the 'Butcher' Cumberland established the precedent for the courtesy calls of the Royal Navy whose frigates occasionally visited St Kilda at long intervals during the nineteenth century. The St Kildans owed a lot to the Royal Navy. Ships like the *Jackal* (1876) and the *Flirt* (1877) brought them supplies and provisions in the winter months when they might otherwise never have seen a stranger from September till May. It was a naval officer, Captain (later Admiral) Otter of HMS *Porcupine*, who first surveyed the island and led the agitation for the provision of a jetty in Village Bay from 1860 onwards. In 1861 Alexander Grigor was conveyed by the same frigate to take the Census on St Kilda, and ten years later he journeyed aboard HMS *Jackal* for the same purpose. Otter was again at St Kilda in 1863, this time in command of HMS *Seagull*.

Arising out of several visits of the frigates *Flirt* and *Jackal* in 1876-7 the Home Office submitted a proposal to the Admiralty that HMS *Jackal* should visit the island twice a year and transmit provisions and mail, but after prevaricating for almost a year their Lordships decided that as St Kilda was 'the property of a private individual and within the jurisdiction of the Parochial Board of Harris' they did not consider that 'the services of H.M. Ships should be called into requisition to supply the needs of a civil population'. Nevertheless it was invariably the Royal Navy that came to the rescue when St Kilda faced famine or epidemic, and in the end it was HMS *Harebell* which supervised the Evacuation in 1930.

After sensational reports in the popular press in May 1912 that the St Kildans had been found by the trawler *Strathmore* to be on the verge of total starvation due to the failure of their crops the previous autumn, Winston Churchill, then First Lord of the Admiralty, despatched the armoured cruiser *Achilles*, then based at Lamlash, Arran with the Second Cruiser Squadron, to the island with emergency supplies of food. The orders reached the ship on a Saturday morning as the crew were preparing for Captain's Rounds and getting ready to take part in the Fleet Regatta the following Monday; but within the hour she had steam up and set off at full speed for St Kilda which was reached just after six o'clock the following morning. The bay was like a mill pond and St Kilda wore an air of serene tranquillity. Boats were lowered and crammed with foodstuffs and stores – even a generous supply of tobacco for the men – and the flotilla of tenders and cutters set out for the shore. Admiral Sir Angus Cunninghame-Graham (who visited St Kilda in 1959) had been a midshipman on board the cruiser and he it was who commanded the cutter which led the little expedition. The ship's captain took the precaution of also dispatching a rating armed with a rifle, in case the mob, driven mad by lack of food, would attempt to rush the boats. When the leading cutter reached the jetty, however, not a soul was in sight. The entire population was actually in the church attending early morning worship. Cunninghame-Graham and his men waited until the sounds of Gaelic singing died away and the congregation streamed out of the church.

What an anti-climax. Far from being mobbed by ravenous St Kildans, the Navy men were stared at in silence. Even when Cunninghame-Graham explained the nature of his mission, the 'starving' islanders would have nothing to do with the boats, refusing to unload them on the Sabbath. The perplexed sailors had to unload the stores themselves and stack the crates on the end of the jetty with tarpaulins over them, not so much as protection against the elements but to conceal the provisions which might otherwise have given offence to the Sabbatarian sensitivity of the inhabitants. During the course of the day, the captain sent ashore a hamper of buttered bread which had just been baked on board ship. This the St Kildans would accept, but still they refused to touch the stores until the stroke of midnight.

Through the night, however, the St Kildans worked with a will and soon had all the provisions stowed away in their Store House. That afternoon the captain invited the entire population to come aboard and inspect his ship. The St Kildans had never been on a British warship before and spent several hours examining the engine-room and the gun turrets in minute detail. They were entertained to hornpipes by the sailors who also emptied the ship's canteen of sweets and biscuits for the children and cigarettes for the men. At daylight on the Tuesday the cruiser got under way and returned to Lamlash, too late for the Regatta but with the feeling of having accomplished a great humanitarian mission.

Another sailor on that relief expedition was F.J. Goddard who later recalled the chagrin and bitter resentment of his shipmates when they found that their goodwill expedition had been ignored by the *Daily Mirror* which gave prominence to its own relief mission. When the trawler broke the news on its return to Aberdeen, the *Mirror* promptly chartered the Clyde tug *Victor*, enlisted the generosity of Sir Thomas Lipton and Sir Joseph Lyons and despatched sufficient groceries to keep St Kilda high on the hog for an entire year. Even the London Hospital was press-ganged into sending Dr Taylor and a vast array of medical supplies. The tug reached the island the day after HMS *Achilles* but the subsequent report hardly mentions the Navy at all and gives all the credit to the *Victor*. Inevitably, the story was 'developed' by other newspapers over the ensuing days and the Navy was completely overlooked.

Whether the St Kildans were actually starving or not remains to be seen, but the matter, stirred up by the tabloid press, was not allowed to rest there. Questions were asked in Parliament about the remoteness of St Kilda and the *Daily Mirror*, never a paper to throw up the chance of a good crusade on behalf of the underprivileged, took up the cudgels and advocated that the great miracle of the age, wireless telegraphy, was the answer to St Kilda's isolation. Under the auspices of this worthy newspaper, a fund was started which was to enable the island to have a radio station. H. Gordon Selfridge, proprietor of the famous department store in Oxford Street, responded immediately by donating £100 to the fund. The *Mirror* announced that arrangements for the purchase of wireless telegraphy plant were in hand and that it was hoped to complete the installation within the next few weeks. Permission to erect the station was readily given by the MacLeod of MacLeod and an application to the Postmaster General for a licence was made. On 12 June 1912 John H. Webb, on behalf of the *Daily Mirror*, applied for the licence. It was proposed to communicate via the Flannan Lighthouse which had wireless, but the intransigent Commissioners of Northern Lighthouses flatly refused. Webb then asked for a licence to communicate via Lochboisdale and as the Scottish Office had no objection the Post Office issued the licence in January 1913. Although the *Daily Mirror* had hoped to have the station installed by July 1912, a whole year elapsed before it became fact.

A contract was awarded to the Marconi Wireless Telegraph Company to install a 1.5 kilowatt petrol motor generator and a standard 10-inch coil transmitter with a range of 75 miles. But before this work could be put in hand, disaster struck St Kilda for the second time in twelve months.

On 12 June 1913 the *Dunara Castle* paid her first visit of the summer season and brought not only the mail but an unwelcome visitor – influenza. The St Kildans had always been prone to attacks of the common cold after a ship had called, but this proved to be a serious epidemic which prostrated the entire community the following week. On 15 June the Hull trawler *Mercury* visited St Kilda and found twenty children seriously ill, all the women helpless and the islanders on the verge of starvation. They appealed to the skipper, William Rilatt, to send a telegram from Harris to the *Daily Mirror* as they were sure that that worthy newspaper would soon stir up the authorities.

The *Daily Mirror* responded nobly and contacted the Admiralty, but when that department appeared to be dilatory, the newspaper whisked a reporter ad a photographer off to Glasgow, chartered the tug *Flying Serpent*, the fastest on the Clyde, and began arrangements for another relief expedition. The Admiralty, however, despatched another cruiser, HMS *Active*, from Lamlash on 21 June and thus saved the *Daily Mirror* considerable expense, but gave the paper some nicely timed publicity for its wireless station which was shipped to St Kilda on 7 July. Mindful of the criticism the previous year, the *Mirror* bent over backwards this time to give the Senior Service due credit. When the cruiser reached the island it was found that it was not just the St Kildans who were suffering. The cows had not been milked for days and one of the first tasks of the bluejackets was to relieve the poor beasts.

The Royal Navy to the rescue during the flu epidemic of 1913; a Marine milking a cow while a sailor looks on

The job of erecting the radio station and its two great aerial masts went to the London building contractors, Messrs Kilby & Gayford whose foreman, F.H. Dexter, superintended the erection. The contractors' men arrived on 10 July and the station was completed within twelve days. Dudley Ward Miller of the British Telegraph Instruments Company tested the transmitter and instructed the missionary Malcolm MacArthur in operating it. The first messages were sent early on the morning of 29 June to King George V, the *Daily Mirror* and J.M. Hogge, the Liberal MP for East Edinburgh who had taken a keen interest in the St Kildans' welfare.

The tricky business of erecting one of the 75-foot radio masts alongside the Factor's House, July 1913

A metal plate was fixed to the base of one of the two 75-foot aerial masts that stood to the west of the Factor's House, inscribed 'This wireless station was installed by the *Daily Mirror* for the use of the inhabitants of St Kilda in time of acute distress – July 1913'. No trace of this plate or its mast now remains, but the concrete base of the mast can still be seen. The name of M. Crook and the initials of the missionary and eight others (including F. Dexter and Dudley Miller) were scratched in segments of the wet concrete and exist to this day. At the foot of the circle was scratched the date 20 July 1913 above the little plaque (which was removed at some later date, probably part of the looting which took place in the 1930s). The centre of the concrete base was subsequently filled in by men of the Hardrock Task Force and set with a four-line inscription in lead: 5004AC SQN RAF 1957-58. The station's call-sign was TDM (initials of the *Daily Mirror*) in honour of the newspaper which gifted the radio to the St Kildans.

The Marconi wireless station ceased operations in March 1914 when the General Post Office (which owned the plant) tried to sell it to the lessee, the *Daily Mirror*, for £350. The newspaper considered this too much, and as St Kilda was no longer newsworthy, began surreptitiously dismantling the station. As a compromise, the GPO agreed to buy the plant if a guarantor for £200 a year could be found. As no guarantor came forward, however, the station was closed down in August and the St Kildans seemed doomed to return to their isolation.

Several of the St Kildans I interviewed in 1959-60 vividly recalled the day in August 1914 that the newly appointed missionary, Alexander MacKinnon, rang the bell that summoned them to church, and broke the news to them from the pulpit that Britain was now at war with Germany. The early months of the War passed St Kilda by, but by the beginning of 1915 even this lonely Hebridean backwater was involved in the conflict. The outbreak of the First World War gave the wireless station a reprieve. On 5 November 1914 the Admiralty asked the Marconi Company to re-open it. The Post Office agreed in principle, but did nothing further.

On 12 January 1915 the Admiralty sent Armed Trawler *Amsterdam* to St Kilda with a detachment comprising Captain Frank Athow, Royal Marine Light Infantry (Retired), Acting Chief Petty officer Sydney Morris (formerly of Ipswich Coastguard), a petty officer, twelve ratings and a Royal Marine batman. Captain Athow was appointed Intelligence Officer and Censor at St Kilda. Athow and his party went ashore on 15 January, but bad weather prevented the landing of all their gear, and some of their equipment was damaged by exposure to the elements. Temporary accommodation was arranged in the islanders' houses and the Factor's House while their huts were being erected on the level ground at the rear of the church and schoolhouse.

When the sub post office was opened in 1900 it was located in the Factor's House, in one of the downstairs rooms next to the front door, but when the *Daily Mirror* radio station was installed in 1913 the post office moved to a corrugated iron shack adjoining the postmaster's house (5 Main Street). The wireless equipment then occupied the attic rooms while its petrol-driven generator was located

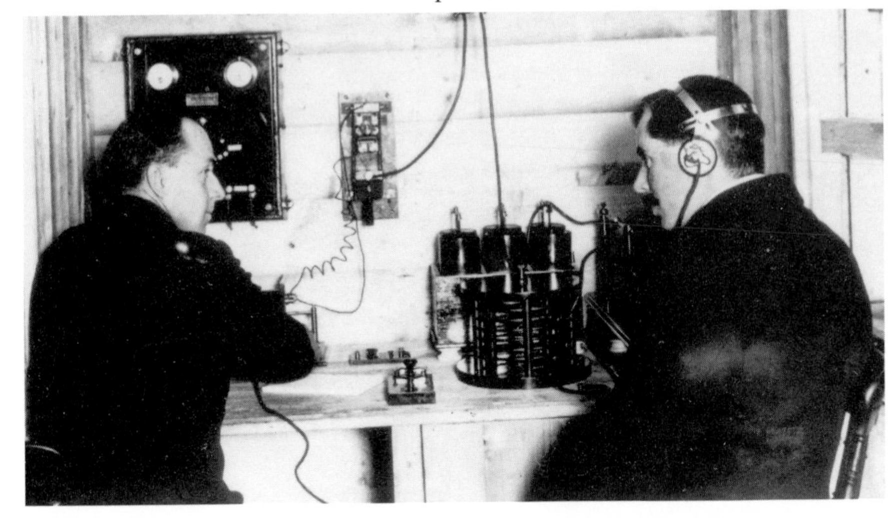

Dudley Ward Miller (left) giving instruction in radio transmission to the missionary, Mr MacArthur, July 1913

The rather unprepossessing prefabricated huts which formed the naval camp. Of the two figures, the man on the left is John T. Mackenzie, factor of the MacLeod estates, during one of his periodic visits to the island

downstairs. When the naval garrison arrived in 1915 the ground floor rooms of this cottage were occupied by a Mrs M.E. McLennan, a widow who had been recruited as nurse and midwife some time in 1914. For this reason the naval generator and wireless equipment had to be accommodated elsewhere. HMS *Calyx* called on 23 January and Rear-Admiral T.B. Wardle, commander-in-chief of the Tenth Cruiser Squadron, reported on Athow's progress. By that time the naval apparatus (a Marconi portable field-set) and generator had been set up in two prefabricated huts, each seven foot square, which had been shipped in from Stornoway and erected on the ground between the manse and Store House above the jetty. In addition, the naval camp consisted of two barrack huts, a store hut, cook house, food store, latrine and ablutions block. Ironically, the naval wireless was found to be hopelessly inadequate. It was only half a kilowatt, with a range of less than ten miles on Q tune. The *Daily Mirror* set, on the other hand, was 1.5KW but even this had difficulty in communicating with Lochboisdale, although at night communication was easily effected with Malin Head.

Some doubts were expressed about Athow's fitness for the post. When questioned by Admiral Wardle, he could not explain why the *Daily Mirror* apparatus had not been taken over, or why huts were to be built instead of utilising the Factor's House. Rear Admiral D.R. de Chair, who visited St Kilda in HMS *Alsatian* on 26 January, reported that Athow had been on the retired list for 15 years and had no knowledge of wireless telegraphy. Nevertheless, he later succeeded in 'cannibalising' the *Daily Mirror* apparatus with the Marconi field-set and the surplus *Daily Mirror* gear was stowed away. By 11 February wireless communication with Lochboisdale and Malin Head had been established, using the *Daily Mirror* equipment.

Captain Athow left St Kilda on 20 May by steam drifter for Oban and was succeeded by a Warrant Telegraphist as officer in charge. On 1 May it was decided that personnel should be changed every six months, supplied from ships of the Grand Fleet at Scapa Flow, *Cyclops* and *Warspite*. When HM Yacht *Iolaire* visited St Kilda on 7 June 1915 her captain found that the personnel arrangement was unsatisfactory; as a result of his report it was decided that, from the end of July 1915 onwards, personnel should come under Rear-Admiral R.Tupper, CVO at Stornoway and were seconded from the depot ship *Manco* based there. Incidentally, this led to a change in the island's postal address. Hitherto St Kilda's sub post office had come under Lochmaddy head post office, but now it was transferred to the control of Stornoway for the duration of hostilities. The garrison now consisted of a Warrant Telegraphist, a Chief Petty Officer, a Petty Officer Telegraphist, three W/T learners, four signalmen and four able seamen, their armament consisting of two Webley pistols with 600 rounds of ammunition and twelve Lee Enfield rifles with 800 rounds.

Originally, during the hours of daylight one signalman was on watch on the summit of Oiseval which offered the widest field of view. A seaman was on watch on the beach to relay signals made by the man on the hilltop to the headquarters where one of the learners would pass the message to one of the telegraphists. The signals between the hilltop and the beach were made by semaphore flags. At night a signalman kept watch on the beach while a learner was on duty in the W/T hut with the telegraphist sleeping alongside.

A general view of the Village in July 1913 showing the Factor's House (left) with the two radio masts alongside. On the right are the Church and Manse, with the little jetty in the foreground

A postcard of early 1915 showing the seven ratings of the Royal Naval Signal Staff. The names on their caps indicate that they were seconded from Warspite and Cyclops, which places this photograph in the period before responsibility for St Kilda was transferred from Scapa Flow to Stornoway

A picture postcard of World War I vintage showing Village Bay with Dùn in the background. A Royal Naval vessel is anchored in the bay. A cow grazes in the Minister's Meadow and beyond can be seen the Navy huts to the left of the Church

In an era when wireless telegraphy was still relatively embryonic, the importance of St Kilda in the constant battle against the German submarine menace cannot be overstated, and excellent use was made of its peaks in maintaining a constant surveillance of the surrounding seas. On Saturday 19 June 1915 Rear-Admiral Tupper himself, aboard HM Yacht *Hersilia*, had paid a visit to St Kilda to enquire into 'the reputed necessity for telephone communication from the look-out hills to the NE and SW of the islands. On 1 July he submitted a detailed report to the Admiralty, recommending that this should be implemented and three weeks later the Post Office granted the requisite permission.

Shortly after leaving St Kilda, on the voyage back to Stornoway, Tupper received a signal that a German submarine had actually been sighted on the west side of the island at 2pm. 'It took three hours to convey this information to the War Signal Station owing to the difficult country between'. An armed trawler was on the south-east side of Hirta at the time, while the admiral's yacht was some way to the north-east; both could have successfully engaged the enemy had they received this intelligence promptly. This incident vividly illustrated the absolute necessity for rapid communications between the hill-tops and the wireless station. A third cable linked the wireless station to 'the beach station on the island' although it is not known where precisely this vantage point was located.

Plans were laid in the event of a surprise attack. By day all hands were called to headquarters by fog horn and would immediately take up their rifles and ammunition. The telegraphist and learner on watch would remain in the W/T hut to burn the books and make any necessary signals. One of the seamen was told off to burn the books in the Officers' Hut. By night, the men slept alongside their weapons. Rear Admiral W. de Salis (retired, and now serving as a Captain, RNR) reported in June that no Morris tubes had been supplied with the rifles and that most of the men had never fired a rifle, although they had been instructed in aiming and adjusting sights. 'I authorised the officer in charge to expend 20 round per man for instructional purposes'.

De Salis found that the minister and nearly all the able-bodied men were away on Boreray for the annual sheep-shearing, so he was unable to ascertain how many local men could be recruited to assist in the defence of the island. 'As far as I could gather 10 or 12 would be the probable number, but as none have ever handled arms and the natives I saw did not appear likely to be very apt learners, I do not think that they would be of any use.' He recommended that four local men should be recruited as watchers on the south side of the island 'and if a telephone could be supplied their value would be very much increased.' He thought that they could be obtained at a wage of about 15 shillings a week. He noted that mists frequently remained on the hill tops and prevented the signalman on the summit of Oiseval from communicating with the beach, so he recommended that the defence of the island would be improved by the installation of a telephone here also. Then he added prophetically:

As the result of my inspection I am of the opinion that the best arrangements possible, with the material available, have been made, but I think it doubtful if the present garrison would prevent a submarine's crew, armed with rifles and supported by one or two guns on board the submarine, from landing.

After the men had had some rifle practice I would suggest that the six best shots should be stationed in rifle pits from which the landing place could be commanded but consider that the men should be kept together until they have been tried with a rifle.

One machine gun in charge of a reliable man would be of great value and I would suggest also that a small observation mine at the landing place, with the key in a suitably placed and protected shelter, might also very possibly prove effective.

The officer in charge has arranged for a good search of Boira Islands [Boreray] while the men are paying their annual visit this week and has offered a reward should any storage place of submarines be found. I steamed round the islands but did not see any suitable place for a submarine to use.

As a result of this report a further 1000 rounds of ammunition and Morris tubes were sent, along with a Royal Marine NCO to instruct the men in the use of the rifles. A fortnight later Rear Admiral Tupper visited the island and subsequently reported to the Commander-in-Chief, Home Fleet:

I visited St Kilda on Saturday the 19th June. On landing at 6.30am I was met by Mr Greenhill, Warrant Telegraphist, who showed me round the buildings and W/T station. Everything was found to be in good order. I then went to the top of the hill Oisirbhal where the look-out is stationed and selected a stone hut to which the telephone cable is to be laid. I then visited the other look-out place from which could be seen the proposed place for the Westward lookout and decided that a peak eight hundred yards nearer the W/T station and equally good for the look-out would be preferable for the Westward cable to be laid to.

I then met the men of St Kilda who had assembled close to the landing place and asked for volunteers to assist the Navy as lookouts. Four men were forthcoming but when I offered them 1/6 per diem for their services, i.e. 6 hours per diem, the minister, the Rev. A. MacKinnon, said it was too little as food etc had risen in price. I pointed out that they had just received a large consignment of food gratuitously and then asked if St Kilda men did not feel that they wanted to do something to help their country during the war. I told them that the telephone cables required laying from two lookout placed to the W/T station about 800 and 2300 yards respectively and asked whether they would not do that and what they required for payment for doing it. They said they would lay the cables themselves for the country without payment. I thanked them, said that was the right spirit, and that His Majesty would be very pleased to hear it and I accepted their offer. I then asked for volunteers as lookouts and after discarding one man who seemed to be the leader of the malcontents, I engaged four men at 2/- per diem for the duration of the war to keep lookout and also do whatever Mr Greenhill required. I further got the other men to agree verbally that they would trench the cable where necessary for 2/6 a day per man for a day of 10 hours. The leading man [Neil Ferguson] and the clergyman agreed to this; I told them about six would be required.

I then arranged with the clergyman in case of attack for the women and children and such of the men who could not help in the fighting, to retire to a certain locality safe from shell and rifle fire and for the remainder to be drilled in the use of revolvers and to assist the RNVR ratings as ammunition carriers etc.

I found that Mr Greenhill had no means except W/T of attracting attention of distant vessels by night or by day in case he required assistance or to communicate with patrol vessels.

Rear-Admiral Tupper conversing with islanders on the jetty, in the summer of 1915.

Tupper also recommended that the garrison be victualled from HM Depot Ship *Manco*, as provisions could be sent across from Stornoway periodically by patrol boats. He mentioned the fact that it was the usual custom to send about twenty head of cattle in mid-summer but that it was doubtful if the usual steamers would be calling at St Kilda that year: 'I may be able to effect their transfer as compensation for the laying of the Telephone cable but did not promise to do so'.

As a result, the second lookout was stationed on Mullach Geal. Both lookouts were connected by telephone to the man on the beach and he, in turn, was linked to the W/T station. Greenhill was given orders to keep a careful watch on the movements of all steamers, logging their description, course and speed. Similarly details of any submarines, giving bearing, position, course steered and speed were to be signalled to the Naval Centre at Aultbea. 'You are similarly to report Men-of-War, Patrol vessels and any vessel behaving in a suspicious manner giving if possible their nationality when not British.' Should Greenhill wish to attract the attention of a

British warship or patrol vessel he was to fire 'one Sound Rocket by day, and one Sound Rocket and one Signal Rocket by night' in addition to making a wireless call.

The eastern signal station (Oiseval) was manned by a RNVR man with a long-distance telescope and a telephone in a 'native hut' (presumably a cleit). The western signal station (Mullach Geal), at an altitude of 1146 feet, was manned by a St Kildan who also had a telescope and a telephone in a 'stone native hut' rendered waterproof by a tarpaulin. When he revisited the island on 29 July aboard HM Yacht *Iolaire*, Tupper inspected the new telephone arrangements. He assembled the islanders near the church and told them that His Majesty would be very pleased. He wanted the able-bodied men to drill daily and learn to shoot, and that a Sergeant was there and ready to teach them so that they might be able to defend the island in case of an attack. 'At this point a submarine was reported to the Northward of the island, steering NE, so I got the natives to sing the National Anthem right through, and to give three cheers for the King. I then hurried on board and put to sea, but could not find the submarine which was reported to have submerged as we were coming round in the Yacht.'

Tupper put up a request for Field Allowance for the officer and crew, considering their isolated position, infrequent mails and poor food. The men had had no leave since the outbreak of war, and he proposed to send them on leave one at a time. The grant of Field Allowance was approved on 7 November 1915, but a request for an additional sixpence a day for the cook was turned down.

FOR four years St Kilda became the hub of operations for District A of the Auxiliary Patrol Vessel Flotilla based at Stornoway. For most of the period from March 1915 till the end of the war, the Atlantic between the Butt of Lewis and St Kilda was constantly patrolled by a steam yacht and ten armed trawlers augmented from time to time by various drifters and whalers, while the area between St Kilda and Barra Head was patrolled by a yacht and nine trawlers. The services of the *Hebrides* and *Dunara Castle* to St Kilda were suspended 'for the duration' but the island had a visit from one or other of the armed trawlers every two or three days, carrying mail and provisions, so that communications were at their peak. These ships were constantly rotated, so that the total number of vessels involved was quite large. In 1915 alone the patrol records show that St Kilda was regularly visited by HM Yachts *Maid of Honour, Vanessa, Hersilia, Lorna, Yarta, Calanthe* and *Iolaire*. The armed trawlers included *Washington, Lily Melling, Calliope, Pointz Castle, Caldy, Noogana, Sasebo, Princess Alice, East Coast, Bush, Roto, Swan II, Ijuin, Margaret Duncan, Mary Bowie, Salome, Cormorant, Romilly, Yokohama, Ben Strome, Lacerta, Champion, Natal, Stanley Weyman, Gloria, Ophir III, Roxano, Earl Warwick, Pearl* and *Walwyns Castle*. The last-named, which arrived from Devonport on 20 July 1915, would play a poignant part in the military history of St Kilda almost thirty years later; for the moment, however, Admiral Tupper merely noted that her 'crew was entirely untrained. There was only one man on her who knew anything about a gun.' The steam drifters *Coulardbank* and *Celandine* were soon added to the flotilla and performed useful service in shuttling mail and provisions to and from the island. In September 1917 the *Coulardbank* even transported twenty head of cattle from St Kilda all the way to Dunvegan in the Isle of Skye, and presumably a similar arrangement applied in 1915 and 1916, as Tupper had promised.

By September 1915 the flotilla had been augmented by a number of whalers. Most of them were appropriately named: *Cow Whale, Rorqual, Humpback* and *Right Whale*, but there was one which stood out from the others. The *Meg* was a French whaler which joined the flotilla on 6 September and served on the St Kilda run until 15 November when she was transferred to Falmouth. She was skippered by Commandant Jean B. Charcot, arguably the leading French polar explorer of his day. He had commanded the *Français* in the French south-polar expedition of 1903-5 and the *Pourquoi-Pas?* on the expedition of 1908-10 (and would lose his life in 1936 when the latter ship disappeared in the Antarctic). On 17 September Admiral Tupper went for a cruise to St Kilda on the *Meg*, subsequently reporting to the Admiralty 'Dr Charcot handles her very well; target practice was carried out. The crew of Frenchmen and Englishmen have settled down together.'

Probably the most exotic of all the vessels involved in the St Kilda patrols was the 158-ton yacht *White Eagle* which belonged to Talbot Clifton of Lytham Hall, Lytham, Lancashire but which he kept at anchor at Lochmaddy, North Uist. Along with two motor launches moored alongside, Clifton had a house near Lochmaddy and two large, powerful motor cars which, with his ghillies (gamekeepers), he offered to put at the disposal of the Admiralty. He had already distinguished himself (in December 1914) by carrying vital despatches to and from Albert, King of the Belgians, but he was chagrined when his offer was turned down on account of the yacht's poor condition. Undaunted, he decided to carry on regardless in a purely unofficial capacity. Late in 1915, as the resources of the flotilla based at Stornoway were stretched to the limit, Tupper was only too glad to avail himself of Clifton's services, although he was at pains to point out that this was an unofficial arrangement and there were no funds available. The patriotic Clifton accepted the situation with good grace and was suitably bucked when Tupper equipped the little yacht with hand-grenades and 'bomb-lances'. Despite the unspecified 'poor condition' of the *White Eagle*, it has to be admitted that there were times when Clifton and his ghillies managed to get out to St Kilda and back in weather that deterred the armed patrol vessels of the flotilla.

St Kilda's baptism of fire came in late July 1915. On Sunday 25 July two German submarines, one disguised with two sails to make it look like a fishing smack, sank the trawlers *Strathmore* and *Roslin* and the French steamship *Danae* on the west side of Lewis. The following day the Norwegian steamer *Fimreite*, which had been boarded by HMS *Cedric* and found to be carrying contraband, was sunk by a German submarine, the Norwegians and the Royal Navy prize crew being subsequently picked up by the armed trawler *Pointz Castle*. Tupper immediately sent two yachts and fourteen trawlers to hunt for the submarines which were believed to be heading south.

On Tuesday 27 July the armed trawler *Pearl*, then patrolling near the southern end of District A, spotted a submarine west of Barra Head and pursued it all the way north to St Kilda. The submarine was the U 41 outward bound from Kiel and the full details of what became of her were not revealed until November 1919 when Naval Intelligence had had the time to study captured Kriegsmarine files. In light of the fact that this was one of the most advanced submarines of the period, and was armed with two 22-pounders, the action of the *Pearl* was all the more remarkable, for she had only a single 3-pounder Hotchkiss. Under the command of Sub-Lieutenant Albert Allman, RNR, the *Pearl* doggedly chased the submarine for seven hours, and hit her with gunfire six times, killing the German first lieutenant and severely disabling her. Early in the engagement the submarine fired two rounds at her pursuer before submerging, but *Pearl* was able to follow her thick oily wake and eventually overtook her. The submarine surfaced again just south of St Kilda and turned to engage her pursuer. Neil Gillies would later recall, 'They were going at it hammer and tongs for ages; we could clearly hear the exchange of gunfire all afternoon.'

Eventually the submarine escaped into a providential mist. Although it had not been sunk, it had clearly been badly damaged and, as the postwar report reveals, it barely limped back to Kiel. Admiral Tupper commended Allman 'for his plucky attempt'. As a result a reward of £150 to the crew of the *Pearl* was authorised on 14 September and Allman was awarded the Distinguished Service Cross – St Kilda's only war hero.

At 7.50pm on 27 July Lieutenant-Commander L.C. Cockerell, RNR, in command of the yacht *Vanessa*, received a signal that the indefatigable Allman in *Pearl* was in hot pursuit of a second German submarine in the same day. At that point this sub was about 38 miles SW by W of St Kilda. The yacht, accompanied by the armed trawler *Noogana*, was then at 58º 4′ N, 7º 59′ W. Cockerell immediately altered course to cut her off and wired St Kilda what speed the sub was doing. The answer was 16 knots. Cockerell again wired St Kilda to send out the armed trawlers *Caldy* and *Calliope* then stationed in Village Bay. They sailed about 20 miles NW and then turned NE by E. At 9pm Cockerell altered course, having observed a steamer stationary about six miles away. Ten minutes later he realised that the submarine was alongside the steamer. At first he assumed that the submarine was about to attack the steamer by gunfire, but five minutes later the sub left the ship and steered NW, while the steamer went off at full speed SW. Cockerell ordered action stations and set off after the sub at full speed, but the enemy gradually pulled ahead and vanished at 10.30pm. Cockerell then decided to chase the suspicious steamer, which later turned out to be the SS *Campania*, a Swedish freighter. He caught up with her at 1am, although she was going flat out at 12 knots. He put an officer, a chief petty officer, three men and an engineer on board, the last-named to go straight to the engine-room and ensure that no pumps were used except those for the main engines.

'I took her into St Kilda where I boarded her at 1am,' he reported. 'The Captain was awfully angry and evidently hostile, denies the submarine was alongside, will give no particulars so I decided to send her to Stornoway, strengthening the guard by two extra men and sending *Noogana* to escort her. There is no doubt about the submarine being alongside; my lookout man and officer of the watch can verify this. The submarine steamed away from me at least 18 knots per hour, I could not look at her at 14 knots.' It later transpired that the *Campania*, although allegedly neutral, was engaged on some kind of intelligence mission for the Germans.

Tupper, aboard the yacht *Iolaire*, visited St Kilda on 29 July to see the scene of these epic encounters for himself. The weather was excellent and he went ashore to inspect the new telephone arrangements. 'A submarine was sighted off St Kilda whilst I was approaching the Island, and again just before I left, but I was not fortunate enough to see it from the yacht although we thoroughly searched for it,' he later reported. He clambered up to the summits of Mullach Geal and Oiseval, an exercise which he noted was 'very hard work, the gradients being very steep'.

At 7am on 4 September 1915 the French steamship *Roumanie* was sunk 35 miles north-west of St Kilda but the crew were rescued by the armed trawler *Bellona III* and taken to Stornoway. On this occasion the submarine had used torpedoes but the stricken steamer was later found to be still afloat and at 3pm on 6 September she was spotted close to St Kilda. As a result the wireless station signalled Aultbea whence an Admiralty tug was despatched. Tupper himself embarked on the *Maid of Honour* at midnight and set off for St Kilda to observe the salvage operation, but was delayed by extremely thick fog which continued the following day. At 4.30pm on 7 September St Kilda loomed up out of the fog. The previous night, however, the *Pearl* had located the steamer and with her sister ship *Quercia* had gone to the rescue. The latter vessel succeeded in taking the *Roumanie* in tow, but the hawser parted as a severe gale suddenly sprang up and the doomed ship disappeared. The following day a few charred planks were all that remained of her, but the search was not abandoned till 13 September.

On 17 November Admiral Tupper cruised off the west coast of the Hebrides in the *Maid of Honour* and reached St Kilda at 10pm. A severe gale blew up from the south-west and the ship had to ride out the storm, so that it was not till the following morning that the doughty admiral was able to scramble ashore and hand over 'the mails and confidential papers'. He then inspected the naval huts and commented favourably on 'their much improved cleanliness and general appearance'. The admiral's yacht left St Kilda at 10pm after experiencing some difficulty in getting away. 'We had to leave the kedge anchor, as we could not weigh it in the surf,' he reported to the Admiralty.

At 1.40pm on 20 December a large submarine with a single periscope was sighted on the surface at the entrance to

Village Bay, making ten knots in a south-westerly direction. The visibility was atrocious and the submarine soon disappeared. She may have been deterred by the two armed trawlers in the bay at the time. Up to the end of 1915 two trawlers were permanently based at St Kilda, but as demands for the patrol vessels increased in other sectors the island was merely visited frequently from the beginning of 1916 onwards. At the same time HMS *Manco* was despatched to the Channel and her place as depot ship and headquarters at Stornoway was taken by the *Iolaire*.

The Admiralty records show the importance of St Kilda over the ensuing years. There are frequent sightings of enemy submarines and the fact that they were often estimated at anything up to 30 miles from the island indicates the eyesight of the St Kildans and the efficiency of the powerful telescopes on the summits. At the same time, the wireless station often picked up distress signals from ships in the North Atlantic which had been boarded, attacked, shelled or torpedoed and as the submarine campaign escalated these signals became more and more frequent. In January 1916 Tupper was promoted to the rank of Vice Admiral and appointed to command the Tenth Cruiser Squadron on 28 February. Pending the arrival of his successor, Rear Admiral W. De Salis, MVO, then holding the RNR rank of Captain, commanded the flotilla. Rear Admiral the Hon. R.F. Boyle, MVO took over command on 9 March 1916 and continued in this post until the end of the war. New ships in the flotilla that year included the trawlers *Dragon, Armageddon, Amplify, Oriole, Ophir II, Remo* and *Morvina* and the drifters *Daisy IV, Vale O'Moray, Bon Ami* and *Fisher Lassie*. Although none of these vessels succeeded in engaging the enemy they performed a useful service in hunting down enemy mines, most of which were destroyed by rifle fire. The trawler crews were paid £10 for every mine they destroyed.

The place of the *Iolaire* as the admiral's cruiser was taken in 1917 by the 581-ton yacht *Sayonara*. In his biography of Sir Mansfield Cumming, founder of the Secret Service (1999) Alan Judd provides some interesting details concerning this vessel, which Cumming had purchased in March 1915 for espionage purposes. The yacht had previously belonged to an American and her first commander, Lieutenant F.M. Simon, RNR, a gifted mimic, posed as one. With a crew also masquerading as Americans, the *Sayonara* cruised off the west coast of Ireland, originally on the lookout for secret German submarine bases but subsequently furnishing vital details regarding Sir Roger Casement's attempts to arm the abortive rebellion in County Kerry. In *Secret Service* (1984) Christopher Andrew records how fishermen off the Irish coast, seeing this yacht behaving suspiciously, were convinced that the *Sayonara* was a German spy ship. There would be an echo of this in my own case, in May 1960, when the Army ship *Mull* was mistaken for a Soviet spy trawler!

Additions to the fleet the same year included the trawlers *Pavlova, Kedoma, Robert Smith, Gloria, Ardent, Settsu* and *Surf*. Of their skippers little is recorded, except when they either distinguished themselves or blotted their copybooks. In the latter category must be mentioned George Clackstone, the skipper of the trawler *Canada*, who earned a reprimand in July 1916 for falsely reporting a submarine north of St Kilda. He had lately been invalided out of the Royal Naval Reserve and was thus a civilian at the time. Admiral Boyle, noting that the skipper was known among the seafaring community as 'Mad' Clackstone, reported him to the Scottish Board of Agriculture and recommended that he be suspended from duty. Many of the officers by 1917 were from the Royal Naval Volunteer Reserve and included some talented, even distinguished, amateurs. Lieutenant-Commander Craig, barrister at law, King's Counsel and Member of Parliament, was given special leave in January 1916 to answer the Party Whip at Westminster. In 1917 the skipper of the *Cow Whale* was Lieutenant Talbot Rothwell whose son and namesake (born 1916) would later achieve fame as the script-writer of the *Carry On* films.

Very little is known regarding the naval personnel who served on the island during the First World War. Among those whom I subsequently traced was Leading Seaman James Pirie from Aberdeenshire, Able Seaman John Paton from Dundee

A German submarine of the type which shelled St Kilda in May 1918, from the souvenir booklet published by The Graphic *in November that year to celebrate the surrender of the German Navy*

and Malcolm MacLean from Port Glasgow. Pirie was a keen photographer and from him I obtained a number of fascinating pictures of life on the island during the naval occupation. The St Kildans I interviewed also recalled a Petty Officer Davies and sailors named Kerr from Govan and Edwards from London.

Conscription, which was introduced in 1916, never applied to St Kilda, although there were at least a dozen men of military age living on the island at the time. On the other hand, two St Kildans volunteered for service in the armed forces, John MacQueen who enrolled in the Royal Naval Reserve and John Macdonald who enlisted in the Royal Artillery and attained the rank of bombardier. The late Neil Gillies had an amusing anecdote concerning the latter. He had actually left the island in 1913 and entered the Regular Army. Early in 1915 Bombardier Macdonald arrived home on St Kilda from his camp on Salisbury Plain, no doubt glad of the chance to escape from the tension and restrictions of service life for a few days, only to find on his arrival that a telegram had preceded him, ordering him to return to the mainland at once. Captain Athow sent word to Macdonald at his cottage, but Macdonald with characteristic Gaelic stubbornness dug in his heels and refused to budge until he had had his full quota of leave. Knowing that Macdonald was armed (having his rifle and full kit with him) Athow thought it more prudent to let the matter go for the moment, and so the steamer sailed away without him. When his leave expired, and there being no steamer there to take him off again, Macdonald donned his uniform and went down to the naval headquarters to report for duty. He may thus be considered as the first soldier – and a Gunner at that – to serve on St Kilda and unwittingly became the forerunner of the band of hopefuls who went out there forty-three years later. No action appears to have been taken against him on his return to England, and after the War he remained in the Regular Army, retiring at the beginning of the Second World War with the rank of warrant officer, first class.

Some time before the War, an incident occurred which was to have severe repercussions on the island a few years later. On 6 October 1913 the wireless station broke down, but the *Daily Mirror* sent a Marconi engineer out to repair it. He was a German named Gustaf Flick whom the St Kildans recalled as quite a likeable chap in his own quiet way, but it later transpired that he was an officer in German Naval Intelligence. According to a story related to me by Neil Gillies, Flick had remained on St Kilda to operate the wireless and only left the island when war broke out, hurriedly packing his suitcase, taking leave of his neighbours and boarding a Norwegian trawler which just happened to be in the bay. This story, or variations of it, has got into print, but there is no truth to it. According to Marconi records, Flick was only on St Kilda for a few weeks and, in any case, the *Daily Mirror* had closed down the wireless station by March 1914. Undoubtedly he supplied Berlin with detailed information about the St Kilda station. Nothing further was heard of Herr Flick until 1922; Donald Ferguson recollected how his father Neil the postmaster received a picture postcard from St Kilda, Melbourne, asking him what he thought of this place. Flick had immigrated to Australia after the War.

At 4.05pm on 29 June 1917 a German submarine sank the Norwegian timber ship *Escondido* by gunfire, but when the nineteen survivors took to the boats, the U-boat captain told them to make for an island, fifteen miles to the south, where they would be well looked after. The Norwegians were told to ask for Neil Ferguson who would see to their needs, and that while the islanders had tobacco they would have no beer to give them. When the Norwegians reached St Kilda they immediately denounced the postmaster to the missionary, saying that he must be in league with the enemy – a charge which poor Neil was too flabbergasted to answer, but the misunderstanding was soon cleared up. The Norwegians were transferred a few days later to the armed trawler *Lord Lansdowne* and taken to Stornoway where the skipper of the *Escondido* reported that the submarine had sunk another steamer about 25 miles north-north-west of St Kilda earlier that afternoon. This was confirmed by the *Lord Lansdowne* which, shortly after leaving St Kilda, found an empty lifeboat from the SS *Southland* of Liverpool.

On 9 July 1917 the look-outs reported a submarine about twelve miles south of Hirta attacking a sailing vessel. A signal was promptly radioed to the armed trawler *Walpole* which was in the vicinity and it engaged the enemy, scoring two hits. The submarine was unable to submerge but still had sufficient surface speed to outstrip the trawler. The trawler picked up the survivors of the sailing ship *Atlantic* and landed them at Hirta, whence they were transferred to the yacht *Sayonara* the following day and taken to Oban.

The following day was one of the blackest in this sector of the Atlantic when no fewer than eight ships were torpedoed within twelve hours. Prompt signalling from St Kilda, however, resulted in the crews of the *Stoic*, *Romantic*, *Cedric*, *Mabel*, *Pacific* and *Peridot* being picked up soon afterwards. On 24 July 1917, however, St Kilda picked up a distress signal from SS *Myrmidon* which miraculously turned up at Aultbea two days later, the skipper shamefacedly admitting that what he thought was a submarine about to attack his ship had turned out to be a whale!

By the beginning of 1918 the armament of the auxiliary patrol ships was being upgraded. Armed trawlers were gradually fitted with 12-pounder guns and 7.5 Howitzers, and their 3-pounders were then allocated to the drifters and whalers. It was a case of too little, too late, as the German submarines were invariably bigger, faster and more heavily armed. On the other hand, there were reports of submarines sinking cargo vessels by gunfire after stripping their crews of donkey jackets, waterproofs and jerseys – evidence of the desperate shortage of clothing in Germany which was hard hit by the Allied blockade. Submarines were often reported to be in poor shape, rusting, with flaking paintwork, but still they menaced the shipping of the Western Approaches.

At 1655 hours on 3 April 1918 the wireless station reported a submarine twelve miles east of the island, steering NNE. The trawlers *Balmoral* and *Samuel Baker* had been at Hirta earlier that day unloading stores and mail and were just about to leave when the sub was sighted. They immediately gave chase but could not get within five miles of the enemy. The *Samuel Baker* fired off a single round from her 12-pounder at the fullest extent of her range, but the submarine, doing 18 knots, escaped into the fog at 8pm. Several submarines were spotted in the vicinity of the island on 21 April and their courses plotted at regular intervals by the wireless station. At 1650 it reported that a submarine had sunk a steam trawler, about fifteen miles south-east. This turned out to be the Belgian trawler *Delta*, on passage from Iceland to Fleetwood; her crew managed to land on St Kilda in their own boats.

Three days later a German submarine approached Village Bay about 3pm and stood off to sea for twenty minutes before continuing on a southerly course. Two whalers were sent from the Sound of Harris but saw nothing. That St Kilda had a naval garrison must have been common knowledge, for reports of enemy submarines in the area were frequently transmitted to Malin Head or

Lochboisdale and these signals would easily have been intercepted by the enemy. More frequent sightings, closer to the island, were reported over the ensuing three weeks, and then the unthinkable happened.

At 0750 hours on 15 May the wireless station reported a submarine on the surface, hove to close to Boreray, about five miles north-east. Its movements were closely monitored and signalled to Stornoway. At 0905 hours it submerged ENE, but then a signal at 1020 reported that the submarine had resurfaced at 0958 at the entrance to Village Bay. This was the last signal for several hours, and it was immediately deduced that the island was under attack. The submarine slowly and deliberately edged into the bay. With pardonable exaggeration Neil Gillies later claimed that the sub came so close that you could have chucked a stone straight down the conning tower, but the official report shows that the U-boat came to a halt 'six cables' (about 1110 metres or 1212 yards) from the shore, though that was near enough for the captain, by loud hailer, to advise the inhabitants to evacuate their houses and take shelter. It was described as about 250 feet in length, armed with two 4-inch guns, 'with a step conning tower, straight bows and new paint'.

Shortly before 11am the U-boat began shelling the wireless installation from the after 4-inch gun 'on a bearing of S by SE from the wireless station'. The first shells hit the Store House, the next rounds exploded near the church, breaching its walls and shattering the windows of the manse. The third salvo overshot and destroyed Neil Mackinnon's house before the German gunners got their range and hit the Factor's House. One shell pierced the porch at the front of the house and did considerable damage to the nurse's quarters. Fortunately Kerr and Paton, operating the wireless, just managed to get out by the back door seconds before the building was struck. No doubt puzzled by the cleits, and perhaps suspecting that they concealed artillery emplacements, the U-boat captain expended most of his ammunition on them before the bombardment ended.

The St Kildans sheltered in the Dry Burn and although 72 shells were fired no one was injured. It was not long after the bombardment that the islanders, realising the commercial value of such souvenirs, were engrossed in hunting for fragments of the shells. Neil Ferguson had an entire nose-cap which he sold to a tourist for £5 at the time of the Evacuation. Firing ceased at 11.30am and the submarine then proceeded east and rounded north and west of the island when she was lost sight of in the mist. Two armed trawlers and two whalers were despatched from Harris shortly after a signal from St Kilda at 10.20am stated that an unidentified submarine was approaching.

Later a story got around that this flotilla caught up with the U-boat and sank it, but there is no mention of this in the Admiralty secret files, and it must be dismissed as wishful thinking. In fact, as soon as the attack was suspected, a whaler and two armed trawlers, the only vessels available, were immediately despatched from Stornoway. The attacker was long gone before they reached the island; but at 1925 hours the wireless station was sufficiently repaired for it to send out another urgent signal: another submarine had surfaced at 7pm and it was feared that it had intercepted the St Kilda signals and was therefore hell bent on completing the destruction of the station. Perhaps it intercepted signals from the trawlers approaching the island for the submarine skipper had a change of heart and was last seen three miles west of Hirta heading south.

Immediately after the attack two auxiliary patrol vessels were permanently stationed in Village Bay, a wise precaution as further submarines were sighted close to the island on 23, 25 and 29 May. To make matters worse, the island was hit by a severe southerly gale on 14 June which carried away the topmast of the wireless station during the night. The sailors refitted the aerial on the shattered mast but found that the signals were almost as strong as before. Two shipwrights and carpenter ratings were despatched from Stornoway on 20 June to repair the huts and erect two new huts to replace those which were damaged beyond repair. The garrison had been once more under the command of Warrant Telegraphist A.C. Greenhill who was commended by Admiral Boyle for his cool handling of the situation. On 9

July, however, he was withdrawn from St Kilda and discharged to HMS *Victory*. As the highest rating left on the island was a telegraphist RNVR, Boyle signalled the Admiralty saying that a petty officer telegraphist was urgently requested.

The 72 shells fired by the submarine did considerable damage to civilian property as well as the wireless station. The Store House was completely demolished, while the church, manse outhouse and Factor's House were also severely damaged. The first of the islanders' cottages (occupied by Neil Mackinnon) was rendered uninhabitable, the second house (occupied by Finlay McQueen) was badly damaged and the third (occupied by Calum Macdonald) was slightly damaged. It was estimated that repairs to the hardest hit cottage would require 22 yards of wall, ten rafters, 17 yards of sarking felt and tarred, two windows, a front door, three inside doors, 60 feet of partitioning, a peat-burning grate and a fanlight to make good the damage. The 1838 house alongside had also taken a direct hit but had stood up to the bombardment much better that the 1860 house.

Petitions to the Admiralty for compensation, supported by pleas from the MacLeod of Macleod and his factor, John Mackenzie of Dunvegan, fell on deaf ears, despite the fact that St Kilda would never have been shelled had it not been for the naval signal station. The matter was eventually referred to the Air Raids Compensation Committee who rejected it, on the somewhat specious grounds that the Government's insurance scheme was not applicable in this instance. It should be noted that Scarborough, which had also been shelled by an enemy submarine, was handsomely compensated for the damage it sustained, which made the treatment of the poor St Kildans, who could ill afford to endure such loss, all the harder to understand. In the end, the matter went to the Treasury who bickered with the Admiralty and the Scottish Office, but the islanders never got a penny. Neither the Store House nor '1 Main Street' were repaired before the Evacuation; ironically, both have been beautifully restored in recent years by the work parties from the National Trust for Scotland.

A postcard of early 1919 showing the wreck of the 'Wireless House by German Submarine'. The roof shows substantial damage but the aerial masts are still standing

John Mackenzie with St Kildans inspecting the destruction of the first house in the Village Street

The target of the U-boat was, in fact, the Factor's House. The naval wireless being useless, the garrison had fallen back on the *Daily Mirror* set and for that reason the attic rooms had become the W/T Room used by the naval personnel. At the time of the bombardment the three downstairs rooms were occupied by a Nurse Gillon who had succeeded Mrs McLennan in 1916. While the upper rooms containing the wireless sustained relatively little damage, the lower rooms were almost completely demolished. Nurse Gillon was allowed £20 by the British Medical Board for damage to personal effects, while a similar sum was apportioned for the replacement of medicines, a dresser, bed and furniture. The Factor's House was eventually repaired, but solely at the expense of the MacLeod of MacLeod.

On 17 May 1918 Rear-Admiral Boyle reported to the Secretary of the Admiralty on the submarine attack. 'It is possible that any apprehension that the enemy may have had up to now of there being some concealed defences are now set at ease,' he wrote, 'and that further attacks will be made to demolish the Wireless Station.' To guard against this, he requested a constant patrol for which four trawlers armed with twelve-pounders would be required urgently. The dozen armed trawlers currently attached to the naval base at Stornoway were already fully occupied in sweeping the channels and approaches to Stornoway and Loch Ewe, while the flotilla of whalers were used for escorting oilers and providing guardships for the United States mine carriers at Kyle of Lochalsh. One solution to the problem, however, would be to provide a battery of twelve-pounders or four-inch guns on shore at St Kilda. 'This question was fully gone into when the W/T station was first installed, but in view of the recent attack their Lordships might think fit to place some permanent defence.'

Preparations to fortify the landing place on Hirta with sandbags and rocks were made on 24 May 1918. Two days later it was proposed to supply a fifteen-pounder BLC gun, equipment and range-finder with two ratings as gun-layers. A gunlayer second class and a rangetaker were theoretically seconded to the garrison on 28 May. Subsequent reports in Admiralty archives note that a fifteen-pounder was useless against a submarine (8 June), a four-inch Mark III QF gun on P.I. mounting was to be supplied (13 June) and their Lordships gave approval for this (22 June). The weapon earmarked for the defence of St Kilda was well on the way to becoming an antique when it was sent to the island, for the date on the breech, which can still barely be deciphered, was 1896.

On 24 June a lighter with a derrick was sent from Poolewe and attempted to land the gun on St Kilda, but clearly the naval authorities had sadly under-estimated the difficulties in getting such a heavy piece of ordnance ashore and the landing was a total failure. Five weeks later a second attempt was made, this time using a store drifter from Mallaig which transported the gun to Stornoway where it was hoisted out on chocks in a lighter by means of a collier's derrick. The difficult and dangerous task of landing the gun, accomplished at 7am (high tide) on 6 August, was supervised by Lieutenant Albert C. Allman, DSC, RNR, the hero of the 1915 encounter with U 41; on this occasion '21 Natives and 9 of the Trawler's crews' were employed in the task.

That there was an element of urgency was borne out by the fact that there was a further attack on St Kilda on 7 August. The trawler *Lacerta* left St Kilda for Stornoway at 0530 hours and a quarter of an hour later almost ran into a submarine a mere 6000 yards offshore. The submarine fired first, but the duel lasted 35 minutes. *Lacerta* fired 21 rounds from her 12-pounder and six from her 7.5 Howitzer, at a least range of 1350 yards. *Lacerta* was hit twice, one shell making a hole two feet long about four feet below the water line on the port bow, flooding the fore peak and leaking into the next compartment abaft the collision bulkhead. *Lacerta* hit the submarine twice with her 12-pounder, while one of the Howitzer shells exploded close under the sub's stern. The contest was a stand-off, the submarine submerging while the trawler limped back into Village Bay where it was successfully beached. After temporary repairs had been effected she was ordered on 9 August to make for Scott's of Bowling on the Clyde for a complete refit which included three new plates. On 10 August the fishing trawler *Mannofield*, bound for Fleetwood from Iceland, encountered a huge submarine of a type not previously recorded. It was about 500 feet long, with three powerful guns. The trawler made a run for it, but sustained several hits and suffered three casualties.

Work on the gun emplacement, platform and powder magazine proceeded over the ensuing weeks. The weekly reports from Stornoway to the Admiralty indicate that Boyle was unduly optimistic. Clifford Kemp, Acting Gunner, arrived at Stornoway on 9 August, destined to take charge of the gun on St Kilda. The following day masons from the Admiralty Works Department reached Stornoway, also bound for St Kilda. Their foreman, Henry Lang, arrived on 17 August, but the actual move to St Kilda was hampered by bad weather. In the meantime, separate approval had to be obtained from the Admiralty for the provision of an ammunition magazine. Fears of a renewed, all-out submarine offensive resulted in the arrival at Stornoway of HMS *Vulcan* with five British submarines, in the belief that the best way to fight fire was with fire. On 25 August Boyle reported dolefully that work on the gun mounting had been hampered by extreme weather but after a superhuman effort the mounting was 'almost ready'. Buttresses and the working platform, however, remained to be completed. At the same time, the islanders had been put to work digging out the hole in the hillside where the magazine would be sited. On the last day of August the admiral reported optimistically that he hoped that the gun would be ready for action by the end of September, but continuing bad weather bedevilled this schedule.

By 14 September the excavation for the magazine had been completed and work on the concrete floor and walls was 'proceeding'. A week later it was 'still proceeding but has been much delayed by very bad weather'. By 28 September the magazine had been roofed in and work was now in hand on the interior fittings. Ammunition for the gun had now arrived at Stornoway and would go out to the island as soon as the weather improved. By 5 October the ammunition was still lying at Stornoway, but the gunlayer and sightsetter urgently requested on 30 September had not yet materialised. On 13 October 1918 Admiral Boyle was able to report to the Admiralty that the work had now been completed and that the gun was ready for action, although the lack of the promised gunlayer and sightsetter was hampering the operation. Personnel on the island had actually got the gun working on 11 October, a single shot being fired at a target towed across the bay but with what result is mercifully not recorded. The gunlayer and rangetaker arrived at Stornoway from Portsmouth on 26 October, but their despatch to St Kilda was held up by the twin epidemics of measles and influenza which were then sweeping through the Outer Hebrides.

There is, in fact, no record of the vital gun crew ever having reached St Kilda. The War ended a fortnight later.

In the spring of 1919 the naval garrison was evacuated, but the huts were still in place that September when the factor, John Mackenzie, paid his first visit to St Kilda in peacetime, to examine the damage sustained in the shelling and report back to the MacLeod of MacLeod. What became of the huts and their equipment is not recorded, but presumably they were dismantled and hauled away eventually. Neil Ferguson, the session clerk of the church, ground officer and sub postmaster added to his plurality of offices the responsibility of greasing and maintaining the Gun, for which the Admiralty paid him the princely sum of £25 per annum. His son

The naval gun installed on St Kilda in October 1918, only days before the war ended. In 1959-61 it was slewed round and pointing at the Church.

The author beside the naval gun today, the National Trust cruise liner Black Prince in the background [colour photo by Dougal Andrew]

John (whom I interviewed in 1959) recalled how 'I used to get a shot at swinging it round and up and down. Then, after a time, the Admiralty stopped the payments so my Old Man stopped greasing the Gun.' A wooden block was rammed into the chamber while the breech-block was dumped into the bay, whence it was retrieved by Royal Navy frogmen in the summer of 1962. The underground ammunition hut was locked up; it was still in good repair when the RAF landed in 1957 and, with electricity laid on, it later became the Army detachment's recreational workshop and photographic darkroom. In later years I understand that it was used as a fuel store.

As noted in the previous chapter, the gun, now heavily rusted, had been slewed round and instead of pointing menacing out to sea was actually aimed over open sights at the centre of the church. In the summer of 1961, however, in a frenzy of 'bull' for the annual Administrative Inspection, the detachment commander, Desmond Williamson, had it winched round to face the open sea, while the breach-block, salvaged from the sea-bed, was cleaned up, restored and buffed to gleam like gold. Major Sir Hugh Walker (a rather eccentric Irish baronet with whom I shared a bedroom at Benbecula for several weeks in 1959), during a brief stint as Relief OC on St Kilda, set the men to chipping and scraping off the rust of decades and painting the gun bright yellow. If the gun was never restored to its pristine glory, at least this activity marked a change from the easygoing regime of Tony Riach. When I visited the island in July 2001 the gun had been painted a curious red-brown shade, but perhaps that was merely some form of protective undercoat. I sincerely hope that it will be properly clad in regulation grey-blue eventually.

Apart from assisting in the installation of the gun, the St Kildans were employed by the Navy in manhandling stores, digging trenches and latrine pits and generally making themselves useful to the little garrison. In addition, the able-bodied men were officially enrolled as coast watchers. Throughout the War, the islanders worked in shifts to scan the waters around the island for enemy ships and submarines and for this invaluable work the St Kildans were latterly paid four shillings a day – a princely sum that probably represented more ready cash than they had ever seen from one year's end to the next before the War. After the luxury of visits from ships every other day for four years, St Kilda reverted to its prewar isolation and uncertain communications. It was 1920 before steamer sailings by the *Hebrides* and *Dunara Castle* resumed on a regular basis during the brief summer season. More significantly, the wireless communication was abandoned altogether.

Inevitably, rubbing shoulders with the navy men unsettled the islanders, especially the younger members of the community, and from 1919 onwards there was a steady haemorrhage of the more lively and energetic spirits, the very people who should have been sustaining the fragile community. At least one of the island girls, Mary Macdonald, married a sailor and inevitably he took his young bride back with him to the mainland. To be sure, Mary brought her baby son Malcolm back to St Kilda for the summer holidays. In 1961, thirty-one years after the Evacuation, Malcolm MacLean, by now a recruiting sergeant in the Army Information Office in Glasgow, made a sentimental return to the home of his maternal ancestors aboard HMS *Adamant*. Subsequently the *Aberdeen Press and Journal* ran a story about his homecoming, illustrated by photographs of little Malcolm and his mother standing in the doorway of their cottage on the Street, and Sergeant MacLean, in uniform, standing in the ruined doorway of the selfsame cottage.

5. AIRMEN ON ST KILDA

IN the first draft of my original manuscript, compiled while I was still serving with the Rocket Range, I briefly mentioned a strange story which I had picked up, but which I was unable to confirm. According to legend (and the Outer Hebrides had plenty of those) at the outbreak of the Second World War the RAF had put one or two men on St Kilda to act as coast-watchers and prevent the Germans from using the island either as a base or as a dump for submarine fuel. As there was no RAF presence in the Uists at that time, the likelihood of airmen on St Kilda seemed exceedingly remote. I remained highly sceptical of this tale until 1964 when I gave a talk to the Greenock Philatelic Society about the postal history of St Kilda. At the end of my talk I was approached by an elderly gentleman who told me that, in September or October 1939, he had been stationed at Greenock as an officer in the Royal Naval Volunteer Reserve. One of his tasks had been to act as courier, taking secret despatches by armed trawler out to St Kilda where a sub-lieutenant RNVR and two naval ratings were stationed as coast-watchers. He recalled that they all lived in the old manse – Lord Bute's House of Oiseval. Further investigation led me eventually to the widow of an officer who had been briefly engaged in this duty and from her I obtained some photographs of Hirta, taken with a box Brownie camera in the autumn of 1939.

I have never been able to ascertain just how long this system continued, but it had fallen into abeyance by early 1940. Later, when RAF Coastal Command established bases at Balivanich (Benbecula), Port Ellen (Islay), Crossapol (Tiree) and Machrihanish (Kintyre), their long-range aircraft patrolled the Western Approaches far more effectively than small detachments of coast watchers could. On at least one occasion during the War, a German submarine was caught in the bay, recharging and replenishing its water tanks, by aircraft patrolling west of Benbecula, and the fact that German submarines were surreptitiously making use of St Kilda was confirmed by one of the islanders.

Alexander Gillies Ferguson, whom I interviewed in September 1960 shortly before his death, was one of the most remarkable of the St Kildans. Leaving his native island as a young man, he had settled in Glasgow where he eventually became a prosperous merchant trading in Harris tweed as well as the products of St Kilda. He regularly travelled out to the island in his own yacht *Colonsay*, dealing with the islanders direct and thus cutting out the laird's factor. It was this enterprising gentleman who published many of the St Kilda postcards and also supplied the rubber datestamp which adorned these cards in the 1930s when the Post Office refused to re-open the sub office for the summer season. The brother of Neil Ferguson, the erstwhile postmaster, 'AG' revisited the island in the summer of 1942 and claimed that he had found the swastika flag flying from the flagpole he had erected on the jetty in the post-Evacuation period. 'The Nazis failed to find a store of petrol I had hidden under the kirk pulpit, and I won't say what I did with their flag…' During my own perambulations around the Village area I came across several cartridge cases which bore German markings, but these may have come from ammunition used by marauding trawlermen who had come ashore to kill a sheep or two.

St Kilda had sinister associations with the RAF during the War, and to this day there are fragments from the wreckage of three aircraft which crashed there. Most spectacularly visible of the wrecks when I was on St Kilda was the Beaufighter which had flown smack into the summit of Conachair, doubtless on a day of poor visibility when the island was wreathed in cloud. Most of the fuselage and the wings must have fallen into the sea hundreds of feet below; little more than the engine and the twisted propeller blades impaling the cliff-top were visible. Even the cannon shells which used to litter the hillside had all but vanished by the summer of 1959, many of them retrieved by RAF personnel for conversion into table lighters and other mementoes. The aircraft's armament, two Hispano-Suiza 0.5 cannons, were dug out of the hillside in 1960 and there was some notion of getting them repaired and mounted alongside the naval gun, but as there was no trace of them when I revisited St Kilda in 2001 I presume that they were either buried or removed to some place of safety.

The history of this aircraft and its crew was fully researched by Father John Barry of St Mark's, Edinburgh and this formed the basis of Brigadier Spackman's account in his book of 1982. The crew of two were both flight sergeants, W. Duxbury (pilot) and S.A. Thornton (navigator and wireless operator). They had trained together at RAF Catfoss and had been posted, early in 1943, to No. 304 Ferry Training Unit at Port Ellen. There they collected Beaufighter LX 798 from the Bristol manufacturers and embarked on a training course prior to posting to the Middle East. This entailed long flights over the Atlantic. Late on the evening of 3 June 1943 they took off on a flight with six other aircraft. As well as LX 798, two other aircraft on this flight lost their bearings in poor night visibility and were heard asking the direction finding stations for a fix. For about half an hour round midnight LX 798 was heard requesting a fix, but there was no response from any DF stations. About 0030 hours on 4 June LX 798 suddenly went off the air.

A sweep of the Atlantic about 230 miles west of Donegal was carried out over several days but there was no sign of the missing aircraft. Thereafter the search was widened, but without any results. Then in late August another Beaufighter from the same training unit reported sighting the tail unit of a wreck on Conachair. HMS *Propontis*, an armed trawler, was sent to investigate and on 27 August a shore party from this vessel clambered to the summit of Conachair. They found wreckage scattered over a hundred yard area, but while the tail was intact, complete with the identification serial, the fuselage was missing. It was concluded that the plane exploded on impact, shedding wings and tail, with the fuselage hurtling on and over the cliff edge. Presumably it lies somewhere on the seabed below Conachair, with the remains of its crew still in the cockpit. It seems probable that the Beaufighter descended through thick cloud to get visual bearings and had the misfortune to hit the summit of the highest hill for more than fifty miles around. Another twenty feet, and it would have cleared the summit.

In the summer of 1957 Morton Boyd succeeded in scaling the cliffs of Soay – the first time the island had been visited since 1932. There, amid the screes of the steep hillside, he found the wreckage of an aircraft. Boyd, a wartime squadron-leader, tentatively identified the aircraft as a Warwick, but due to the ravages of the high winds of fifteen winters, little was left of the plane. What the weather had left, the seabirds had made short work of, and of the luckless crew there was apparently no trace, other than a solitary bone which David Boddington later identified as the seventh rib from an adult male skeleton. When I accompanied a party of soldiers who succeeded in landing on Soay in the summer of 1960 and examined pieces of the wreckage on the south-east cliff of that inhospitable island we came to the conclusion that it was probably a German aircraft. It was not until the summers of 1978 and 1979 that three expeditions, apparently landing from helicopters, succeeded in carrying out a more detailed examination of the wreckage and identified it as a Wellington Mark VIII bomber. The remains of several bodies were excavated but no identity discs were found. The only tangible evidence regarding the ill-fated crew was a solitary cap badge of the Royal Canadian Air Force.

Subsequent patient and diligent research by John Barry shed further light on the mystery. Only 394 Mark VIII Wellingtons were ever constructed and a study of those which had gone missing over the North Atlantic eventually narrowed down the possibilities to LA 993 which disappeared on 23 February 1943. As it was last seen at 1523 hours that day in the vicinity of Boreray, four miles to the north, it seems highly probable that this was, indeed, the plane which crashed on Soay. The identity of this aircraft seemed to be confirmed by the fact that five of the crew were Englishmen but the sixth, the navigator, was a Canadian. Oddly enough, the body of one of the English crew-members, Sergeant Alston, was washed ashore on the north-east coast of Lewis on 2 March and this cast doubt on the identification of his plane as being the one that hit Soay; but it is not improbable that his body was thrown clear by the explosion on impact, and then, like so many of the St Kilda mailboats, it drifted with the wind and current. So far as I am aware, however, there is no record of any mailboat having drifted right round the Butt of Lewis to find a landfall on the east side of that island (although several have been picked up on the northwest coast of the mainland, between Durness and Melvaig).

Doubt as to the exact identity of the Wellington on Soay was cast by the strange assortment of footwear: five different RAF walking-out shoes and one Army boot, but not a single fur-lined suede flying boot which would have been worn by aircrew operating over the North Atlantic in February. This has led some investigators to consider the alternative of another Wellington, HX 448 which disappeared on 28 September 1942 on a flight from Silloth and Limavady to Rockall. On this plane no fewer than five of the crew were Canadians, and ordinary footwear would have been preferable to flying boots in September. Perhaps some day further investigation of this poignant site will settle the matter one way or the other.

The most extraordinary, and certainly the best documented, of the three wrecks on St Kilda was that of the Sunderland flying-boat ML 858, based at No 302 Ferry Training Unit, Oban. It was delivered from Stranraer on 14 May 1944 and its crew arrived a week later for final training before being posted to North Africa on convoy protection duties. The crew consisted of six New Zealanders, an Australian who had joined the RNZAF, and three Britons. The captain, Warrant officer C. Osborne, RNZAF, was an experienced Catalina pilot who had already been in action off Sierra Leone and had logged 802 flying hours as a pilot. The whole crew had already trained together at Alness on the Cromarty Firth before transferring to Oban where they embarked on a three-week conversion course before being posted to operational duties. The Sunderland was moored off the island of Kerrara opposite the town of Oban.

At 2200 hours on the night of 7 June 1944 the flying-boat took off with a full crew for a night training flight. The course lay south to Colonsay, then almost due north to Barra Head, then north-west to St Kilda before turning back to Oban. The aircraft was fully armed and the crew were prepared to engage any enemy encountered on the flight. The weather was bad, with low cloud, drizzle and poor visibility above 300 feet. The crew were required to report by radio every hour on the hour. A normal report was received at 2300 hours but no report was made at midnight, or ever again. As Sunderlands could land on the sea if they developed engine trouble and could then be towed back to base, a massive air search was ordered at dawn, involving many aircraft from the Coastal Command bases at Stornoway, Benbecula, Islay and Tiree, but the search was hampered by the continuing bad weather.

Aerial views of St Kilda

The search continued for three days but on the afternoon of 10 June three separate reports came in that wreckage had been spotted on the north-west side of Hirta. A high-speed launch was despatched immediately from Stornoway and reached St Kilda at 1850hrs. The rescue crew climbed to the ridge, found a considerable amount of wreckage strewn over the slopes of the Great Glen, and reported finding nine bodies, charred and mangled by the crash and further ravaged by the voracious black-backed gulls, so much so that identification would have been impossible if it had not been for the dog-tags each man wore. One boy was found to have over £120 in the pocket of his flying suit. Not all had perished in the wreckage, however. In a nearby cleit one airman was found, wrapped in his parachute, but dead from burns and exposure nonetheless. This gave rise to the rumour that one man had survived the crash and fed off the flesh of his dead comrades. Although this has been officially denied, it provided the novelist Hammond Innes with the plot for his novel *Atlantic Fury* (1962).

The launch party was only able to establish that there were no survivors and to identify the aircraft. It was not until 13 June that the Royal Navy could despatch HMS *Walwyns Castle*, an armed trawler-minesweeper, from Oban. It will be remembered that this ship had formed part of the flotilla of auxiliary patrol vessels that frequently visited St Kilda in the First World War. On board were the Station Commander, Wing-Commander Campbell, and the Revd Lachlan MacLeod of St Columba's Church, Stornoway. By a strange coincidence, his son Calum and I served together in the RAEC at Beaconsfield and we met again at New College, Oxford in the autumn of 1959. When Calum asked me where I was stationed I told him that I had just come back from St Kilda and it was then that he told me that his father had been there during the War. Subsequently I contacted the minister who furnished me with a very graphic account of what happened. After a most uncomfortable twelve-hour voyage from Stornoway in the teeth of a north-westerly gale, the recovery party reached Hirta and began the arduous and gruesome task of recovering what was left of the bodies.

'It was a fearful task, carrying the bodies down the steep slope to the jetty and trawler,' he wrote. 'Wing-Commander Campbell, the Station Commander of Oban was with us, and although I tried my best to convince him that the boys should be buried where we found them, or in the cemetery near the village, he would not listen, and they were buried at sea among the stacks to the north of the island; not in Stornoway notice!'

This was in response to a query from me that there was a rumour that the airmen had been interred at Stornoway. Why Campbell would not allow the minister to bury the men in the island's kirkyard is a mystery, for their remains could have been retrieved at a later date, or tended there as official war graves. Instead, they have no known resting place where their nearest and dearest might have mourned them.

In the late 1970s the National Trust for Scotland repaired and completely refurbished St Kilda's church. On Ascension Thursday 1979 Father John Barry, who had done so much to retrieve the memory of the lost airmen of St Kilda, conducted a service of dedication of a brass memorial plaque commemorating the crews of the three crashed aircraft. It hangs on the wall of the church to this day, arguably the saddest and most moving of all the many war memorials to be found around the United Kingdom. The simple plaque is headed 'IN MEMORY OF the Royal Air Force personnel who lost their lives on St Kilda'. Below, there are three panels. On the left are the names of the crew of the Beaufighter and in the centre are the names of the crew of the Sunderland, but the panel on the right remains blank, with a three line inscription at the foot: 'The crew of an unidentified aircraft, believed to be a Wellington, which crashed on Soay'.

There was grave concern that if the wreckage of the Sunderland were left as it was, other pilots might be at risk when, spotting the wreckage, they flew low over Hirta to investigate whether it was a recent wreck and whether there might be survivors. Had this happened in poor visibility, such aircraft might have been brought down by the vicious downdraughts all too familiar to those engaged in airdrops in more recent years!

On 9 July 1944 a crash crew from No. 56 Maintenance Unit at Inverness, accompanied by two Royal Navy explosives experts, arrived at St Kilda by armed trawler from Stornoway, with orders to dismantle the huge aircraft. The team took up residence in the manse and after fruitlessly searching in appalling weather for two days eventually located it and set charges to blow it up. The explosions had surprisingly little effect, so the Navy demolition team departed, leaving it to the RAF crew to hack the twenty-ton aircraft to pieces with axes and hacksaws, a task which took them a full month, working from dawn till almost midnight each day. As far as possible, the pieces were buried, no fewer than thirty-seven enormous holes being dug (eight feet long, by four feet wide and four feet deep). What could not be buried was painted red-brown to camouflage it from the air. Despite the sterling efforts of the RAF, many pieces of the aircraft can still be seen in the gullies, burns and crevices below the summit of Gleann Mór.

In the years following the Second World War, the Royal Navy came again to St Kilda. This time it was HMS *Clyde* of the Royal Naval Volunteer Reserve which used to make an annual training cruise in Hebridean waters and spend a day out at Hirta where the part-time sailors could go ashore and stretch their legs. The detour to St Kilda also served the purpose of transporting scientists and officials of the newly formed Nature Conservancy Council, who have always had a special interest in the little archipelago. In 1957, following the death of the Marquess of Bute, St Kilda was bequeathed to the National Trust for Scotland and they, in turn, leased it to the Nature Conservancy, so from that time onwards visits became more frequent. One of the naval visitors of this period was Lieutenant-Commander Mackenzie of Edinburgh whose grandfather and great-grandfather had been factors to the MacLeods of Dunvegan. In September 1960 I visited his cousin, Miss Mackenzie of Dunvegan, who showed me a photograph of the naval commander standing in the doorway of the Factor's House where his grandfather had stayed on many occasions during his twice-yearly calls to collect the rent from the St Kildans.

The year before Lord Bute died, however, the British government decided to create a great military complex in the Uists, incorporating vastly improved airport facilities at Benbecula, a Royal Air Force base near Sollas in North Uist, an Army camp at Balivanich, a naval base at the South Ford and Loch Carnan on South Uist, and a guided weapons range near Ardivachar on the north-west coast of South Uist. In connection with this joint-services complex it was proposed to re-occupy St Kilda where two radar stations would be installed, partly to keep surveillance on shipping that might stray into the danger zone, and partly to track the missiles and plot their splash-down in the Atlantic. As a precautionary measure, the government formally annexed the lonely islet of Rockall, 180 miles west of St Kilda. A bronze plaque to that effect was duly set in concrete on the summit of that rock, the operation being carried out by naval helicopter. The object of this exercise was to prevent some unfriendly power from establishing some kind of vantage point from which to spy on the Rocket Range. It seems ludicrous at this remove in time, although it accurately reflected the paranoia of the Cold War period. The plaque later disappeared in mysterious circumstances and inevitably a Soviet spy ship got the blame although the terrifying wind and weather may well have been responsible. The presence or absence of the plaque, of course, did not materially affect the annexation, which had a spin-off many years later, but for very different reasons. The discovery of oil in the North Sea and the Atlantic triggered off a dispute between Britain and the Irish Republic, the latter laying claim to Rockall because it might have been visited by St Brendan the Navigator in the seventh century. As we used to say on St Kilda: 'Beyond us there's Rockall, then f—-all – except America!'

On Sunday, 10 June 1956, HM Air Force Vessel *Bridport* sailed from the Firth of Clyde with a heterogeneous crowd of passengers, bound for St Kilda. Led by Air Commodore L.G. Levis, they included officials of the Ministry of Supply, the Scottish Office and the Nature Conservancy Council, staff officers of all three armed services, and two of the former inhabitants, the redoubtable Alexander Gillies Ferguson (then aged eighty-three) and his nephew Neil Ferguson Junior. The purpose of the visit was to carry out a reconnaissance of the island as a suitable site for a radar tracking station in conjunction with the proposed Rocket Range. Among the Nature Conservancy representatives were C.M. Harrison (later Director-General) and James Fisher, the well-known naturalist, author and broadcaster.

RAF personnel in the Great Storm of April 1957, trying to prevent their tent from taking off

According to Major John Burrill, RA from Scottish Command, the two St Kildans, as soon as they set foot on their native soil, were off like a shot, over the hills and round the cliffs, and spent most of the three days ashore not in guiding the strangers but in trapping sea birds. Indeed, some days later, when the party broke up in Glasgow, old Alex presented the Air Commodore with a dead fulmar as a token of his esteem.

In spite of indifferent weather, the reconnaissance was a great success; so much so that plans were set in motion for the re-occupation of the island the following spring. Over the ensuing winter, detailed plans were evolved for the building of a road and a military base, installing electricity, sewage system and piped water, and erecting and equipping the Decca and Marconi radar stations. By March 1957 everything was ready down to the last detail and in April the RAF Task Force 'Hardrock' set out from its base at Wellesbourne Mountford in Warwickshire. The name of the operation was derived from a line in Martin Martin's description of St Kilda (1698): 'The whole island is one hard rock'.

LCT 4002 of 76 Squadron of the Royal Army Service Corps Fleet (later renamed HM Army Vessel *Agheila*) carried the advance party of thirty-five RAF technicians from Lochboisdale to St Kilda on 16 April. In their wake came Magnus Magnusson, then a reporter for the *Scottish Daily Express* which had chartered a boat to cover the landing in Village Bay. Because the expedition also included two scientists sent at the behest of the Nature Conservancy Council to keep an eye on the RAF, the *Express* dubbed it the Mousetrap Armada. Kenneth Williamson, the Conservancy's representative, had taken a stock of catch-alive mousetraps – 'not to kill the creatures, but to protect them from the Servicemen' he was quoted as saying.

The tasks ahead of the men of 5004 Airfield Construction Squadron were formidable; and right from the start they ran into trouble. Once the landing craft had ground hard on the sand all personnel available were formed into a human chain and the tedious job of ferrying 37 tons of stores across the beach and over the slippery, weed-strewn rocks began. Meanwhile the cooks had their fill of trouble, trying to prepare the first hot meal on the island; one of their field kitchen petrol burners exploded, but fortunately no one was injured. The very first night ashore the men bedded down as best they could in the manse and the Factor's House, but the following day lines of tents were erected on the more or less level ground between the village and the storm beach. The second night ashore was a nightmare for the airmen, unaccustomed to the savagery of St Kilda's unpredictable weather. Driving rain, compounded with spindrift as the beach was relentlessly pounded by a severe south-easterly, drenched anyone foolish enough to venture outside to adjust the guy-ropes, but as dawn broke the ferocity of the wind intensified.

Within the space of an hour the gale became a hurricane which ripped up the tents and deposited them on the far side of the bay. Airmen and officers alike scrambled frantically to save bedding and furniture that was being hurtled all over the place, and all but the heaviest stores were hurriedly stowed away in the nearest cleits. The Great Storm of 19 April 1957 was probably one of the worst ever recorded on an island which has notched up some pretty frightful weather. It was the RAF's baptism of fire, but somehow they survived the terrifying ordeal.

Within a fortnight, the Task Force had swollen to over three hundred men – far more people than Hirta had probably ever sustained before. By that time the advance party had come to terms with St Kilda's awful spring weather and had taken steps to combat it. Tent pegs had assumed the proportions of pit-props and poles were anchored with hawsers to prevent a recurrence of the 'airborne camp'. One of the features of St Kilda was its beach – ideal for landing craft which could run ashore at high tide; when the sands dried out at low water the bow doors could be opened and the ramp lowered. At the end of April the first vehicles came ashore by this method, the first petrol-driven wheeled vehicle of any kind on the island being a bulldozer whose immediate task was to clear a pathway through the boulders of the storm beach above and behind the sand in order to lay down the hard standing and the approach to the proposed road. This turned out to be a much harder task than originally envisaged, and in fact, work on this vital element in communications had to be continued the following year.

In these inhospitable surroundings, bewildered by the wildness and desolation of the island and the claustrophobic effect of the lowering hills and towering cliffs, these airmen, many of them teenage National Servicemen who had never been outside a city in their young lives before, must have felt as though Fate had consigned them to some Devil's Island. It says much for the forceful personality of the Commanding Officer, Wing Commander W.M. Cookson, that before long the three hundred servicemen who made up the task force were welded into a happy and hard-working team. Some people would say that Cookie was a slave-driver, as he often kept his men at it sixteen hours a day, seven days a week; but he worked every bit as hard as any of them, and had the brilliant knack of knowing just how much his men could take, so that when he declared a holiday, everyone thought he was being remarkably generous.

Cookie was a rough diamond nevertheless. I have been told that his language on occasion would have shocked even the most vocal of sergeant-majors, and when he conducted an argument with some staff officer back at Benbecula by means of the VHF radio link, the ether would be sizzling with his violent obscenities. On one occasion at St Kilda an Army driver who had only just arrived by ship that very day, did not pull off the road to let the Wingco's car pass. Cookie stopped and ordered the unfortunate driver to get back down the road, pack his gear, and get aboard the ship before she sailed off. He was a strict disciplinarian and brooked not the slightest waywardness in his men; but, like George Cooper, he was a bonnie fechter as well as a benevolent despot, and those who served under him held him in affectionate regard. Not surprisingly, the task of building the road and other installations was accomplished well ahead of schedule and in due course the next Honours List intimated that Cookie had been awarded the OBE, the most appropriate award in view of the fact that this decoration is popularly known as Other Blokes' Efforts.

A general view of the RAF's tented camp in the summer of 1957 when more than 300 men were under canvas. In the foreground can be seen the Manse and the Church with the first Nissen huts behind

Gradually, the island was tamed and some semblance of civilisation began to

A refrigerated meat container about to be unloaded from a tank landing craft. The tractor has AM (Air Ministry) number plates which places this picture in the summer of 1957

take effect. By June the first generators were up and running and electric light had been installed. A rudimentary NAAFI canteen was established, although its store of chocolate was rapidly taken over by the St Kilda field-mice. By July showers and washing machines were providing some basic creature comforts, though the cookhouse was primitive and the dining facilities consisted of a draughty marquee. Even the spiritual needs of the Task Force were not entirely overlooked. Although the old church was in a state of disrepair, a few pious souls gathered there regularly each Sunday for an impromptu service. By midsummer and the arrival of better weather it was even possible to stage the occasional cricket match in the Minister's Meadow.

Within six months, the construction of the road and the other installations had advanced considerably and the Hardrock Task Force was able to hand over the island to a Care and Maintenance Party from Fighter Command, for the winter months. In mid-September, therefore, the officers and men of 5004 Squadron left St Kilda and returned to their base in England. Compared with the armada which had been there all summer, the winter party was quite small, consisting of twenty-three RAF and eight Army personnel, commanded by Flight Lieutenant A.N. Johnstone.

The Factor's House, which had been used during the previous months by the Nature Conservancy and National Trust officials, was now converted into the officers' mess. Johnstone and the medical officer, Flying Officer Peter Saundby, occupied the two upstairs rooms which had been redecorated and had water installed. The three senior NCOs at first used the hut which had been the summer officers' mess, but they too moved into the Factor's House downstairs, when their mess was taken over as a detention room to accommodate two prisoners undergoing punishment for burgling the canteen. Apart from the three generator operators, who had to work night shifts and were consequently housed in one room of the old manse, the remainder of the detachment lived in two Nissen huts erected near the church. Thus they passed the winter, painting and renovating the church, looking after the radar installations and repairing the road and the slipway which were already beginning to show signs of wear and tear.

In their spare time they read endlessly (with 1,200 books to choose from in the library), wrote letters home (mail deliveries and collections averaging one every five weeks) and photographed the island's incredible scenery and wildlife. The doctor even embarked on a study of St Kilda's fauna and contributed a great deal to our knowledge of the Atlantic grey seals whose breeding and other habits he observed in detail.

Life must have been pretty monotonous for them, but occasionally things livened up, as when they had a visit from a Spanish trawler one day in late October. The Spaniards had been accustomed in the years following the Evacuation to call in at Village Bay, perhaps to mend their gear or salt their catch, or just take shelter from a north-westerly gale. They probably also trawled illegally round the island, or even came ashore to raid the sheep. This particular trawler came in and tied up to the mooring buoy without permission, and then sent a party ashore, all armed with rifles. Before the airmen could stop them they had shot a seal pup which had been basking on the rocks in front of the ruined Store House, and carted it off. They were about to turn their attentions on the sheep when Johnstone and some of his men came down from the camp to intercept them. He pointed out to them that they had landed without his permission and under no circumstances would be allowed to touch the sheep. The leader of the Spaniards reacted in a high-handed manner, declaring in broken English that they had always come ashore at St Kilda, that they had always killed some sheep for their own use, and that no one was going to stop them. The others showed their approval by ominously fingering the triggers of their rifles.

What was Johnstone to do? Obviously the only answer to this show of force was to take a bellicose attitude also. But how? He could not bluff them with threats of the naval gun; they were bound to have seen it before and knew that it had been rendered useless, and he was painfully aware that the .38 revolver locked in his desk in the office was hardly sufficient to deal with the marauders. Suddenly he had a flash of inspiration. Putting on a bold front, he addressed the Spaniards: 'I will give you five minutes to leave here and get back to your ship. If you refuse I will call on my artillery on the hill up there,' and he waved to the quarry on the hillside half a mile away, 'and they will blast your ship out of the bay.'

'But you have no artillery here,' scoffed the Spaniard.

'That is where you are wrong, amigo, and just to prove it to you I shall order a practice shot to be fired to warn you.'

With that he picked up his field telephone, rang up the quarry and asked the NCO in charge to fire off a shot. The NCO prepared a charge of plastic explosive which was speedily detonated. The explosion rang out across the bay and reverberated from cliff to cliff, scaring off countless thousands of seabirds. It had the desired effect all the same, and a boatload of very frightened and panic-stricken Spaniards scurried back to the trawler. In a matter of minutes the ship had cast off from the mooring buoy and steamed off as fast as her engines would take her. The word must have gone round the fishing fleets of Bilbao and San Sebastian after this incident, for over a year went by before another Spanish trawler dared to venture into Village Bay. As a result, the Air Ministry decided, like the Admiralty forty years earlier, to provide arms for the defence of the island. In due course a consignment of twelve obsolete Lee-Enfield Mark IV rifles and 600 rounds of ball ammunition was despatched to St Kilda.

Conditions improved gradually over the winter of 1957-58. By December a supply of films had been sent to relieve the tedium of the long winter nights. A screen was rigged up at the back of the church and the projector was mounted on the pulpit. The ancient church had now been wired for electric light, re-panelled and re-roofed, and in the pews where the former islanders had sat through interminable hours of divine worship every Sabbath, the airmen of Fighter Command watched interminable repeats of George Formby and Will Hay comedies of 1930s and early 1940s vintage. Radio reception was poor, being pretty well limited to Radio Luxembourg on 208 metres and those exotic North African stations which always seem to come over loud and clear when the BBC is faint and distorted. Television, which would have been a godsend to the men of this lonely garrison, was totally non-existent.

In the summer months mail had passed between St Kilda and the mainland through the LCTs which plied regularly between the island and Cairnryan near Stranraer, but these flat-bottomed vessels with their very shallow draught were quite unsuitable for winter operations. As the fish that frequented the waters round St Kilda was the variety esteemed by the English fish and chip industry trawlers from Fleetwood frequently sheltered in the bay, either going to or coming from the Iceland fishing grounds. An ad hoc arrangement with these trawlers to take the mail rapidly developed into a regular contract with vessels of the Boston Deep Sea Fishing and Ice Company and, as a result, St Kilda acquired a new postal address care of P.O. Box 99, Fleetwood, Lancashire. If mail was landed on the voyage out, the letters might only be two or three days old, but if the weather was unfavourable several weeks might elapse before the mailbag would be dropped off. Conversely getting mail off by trawler was an uncertain business, and finally the system broke down altogether when the trawlers, in search of cod and dogfish, ceased to frequent that part of the Atlantic. Of course, neither the General Post Office nor the Air Ministry were informed of this change, and while mail continued to accumulate at Fleetwood the boys on St Kilda went without news from home.

The arrangement with the Fleetwood trawlers was sporadic and infrequent at best during the winter months. The men of the Care and Maintenance party had been promised a regular mail service but during their first two months on the island they only got one mail call. T.G. Griffiths, the Head Postmaster of Fleetwood, had handed over a sack of mail on the morning of Sunday 29 September to the skipper of the *Boston Seafoam*, but he refused flatly to take it and the bag was returned to the post office the following day. By chance, however, Griffiths learned that HMS *Hound*, a fisheries protection destroyer had berthed in Wyre Dock that very day on completion of a NATO exercise, and was due to sail for Iceland on Friday 4 October. Griffiths contacted the Home Mails Branch in London which phoned Squadron Leader W.P. Scott at the Air Ministry who got on to his opposite number at the Admiralty, and as a result HMS *Hound* took the mailbag which was delivered on 6 October. The ship took on board the island's outgoing mail which was landed at Reykjavik a few days later and thence flown to England for onward transmission.

The intransigence of the Fleetwood trawlers is difficult to understand, other than their ingrained wariness of being trapped at St Kilda by a sudden change in the weather; but matters took a new turn early in November when the trawler *Julia Brierley* diverted to St Kilda to put ashore the bosun, Michael Quinn, who had suffered a perforated ulcer 24 hours after leaving Fleetwood. At first the skipper, Jim Port, made for the mainland, but a severe gale sprang up and the trawler spent two days in the Atlantic, riding it out. All the time Quinn's condition continued to deteriorate and it was in sheer desperation that the vessel made for Village Bay. The ship's lifeboat was lowered and the mate, Dan Cossey, with five crewmen, rowed ashore with their ill companion. After a nerve-wracking trip through raging surf the little boat reached the jetty and Quinn was soon tucked up in the Medical Centre where Peter Saundby diagnosed acute appendicitis. Unable to operate, the doctor plied his patient with penicillin and morphine. After a week Quinn was well enough to get out of bed, but a further five days elapsed before the *Julia Brierley* returned from Iceland and he had to undergo another ordeal of a surf ride to the trawler. On arrival in Fleetwood he was rushed to hospital for an emergency operation.

Interviewed by the local and national press, Michael Quinn sang the praises of the RAF doctor and the men who had looked after him so well, but he took the opportunity to publicise their grievance about the lack of mail. The *News Chronicle*, in particular, pursued this matter relentlessly. A spokesman for the RAF said that an agreement had been reached with the trawler firm, but when the newspaper spoke to Sir Basil Parkes, the company chairman, he denied that any assurance had been given, saying that he had merely offered to look into the matter. Pending a resolution of the problem, mail for St Kilda was diverted to Aberdeen where it was put aboard HMS *Orestes*, bound for Iceland but diverted to the island to deliver 218 private letters, 42 pieces of official correspondence and two registered packets. The private mailbag weighed 32 lbs whereas the official mail was a hefty 45 lbs; one wonders what 'bumf' the detachment commander was bombarded with on this occasion!

The next ship to call at St Kilda was the *Turquoise*, a vessel chartered by the Air Ministry which left Ardrossan on Tuesday 10 December. Four days earlier Griffiths made up a mailbag at Fleetwood and sent it to Ardrossan by train.

On Wednesday 18 December Parkes relented and permitted the island's Christmas mail to be taken on board the *Fleetwood Lady*, a brand new diesel trawler under the command of Jack Drennan. The mailbag, containing 137 letters and cards, plus a parcel of recent newspapers, was delivered the following Sunday morning. On the voyage north the trawler had run into exceptionally foul weather which delayed her progress, but during a brief lull Drennan had taken a chance and managed to get the mail ashore. The chief concern of the trawlers, apart from the loss of fishing time, was the constant hazard of launching their lifeboats and getting to and from the tiny jetty in Village Bay.

On 15 April 1958 the Care and Maintenance Party left St Kilda and returned to RAF North Weald, to be succeeded by the Hardrock Task Force again. In their wake came the usual party of scientists and naturalists sent out under the aegis of the Nature Conservancy and taking full advantage of the transport and amenities provided by the RAF. In turn, they were closely followed by a shipload of tourists when the MS *Meteor* of the Bergen Line was chartered by the National Trust for Scotland for its annual Islands Cruise. Then, as now, the visit to St Kilda was very much the highlight of the voyage, while the visit of dignitaries from the National Trust and over a hundred tourists was probably the high point in the St Kilda social calendar.

More enterprising and at far less cost were the people who, seeking an unusual holiday 'away from it all' joined the Trust's work parties which came to St Kilda in July and August. For about £25 the more adventurous and energetic could have two weeks' holiday on the island, under canvas. They spent a few hours a day repairing cleits and dry stone walls, but the rest of the time was their own, to roam the island and study its birds or sheep, or ancient structures, or whatever took their fancy. There were even girls in these work parties, and at least one of them, an assistant to some professor of archaeology, caused havoc among the sex-starved servicemen on account of the brevity of the shorts which set off her bottom to great advantage.

The summer of 1958, with all this varied activity and a population in excess of three hundred, marked the high-water mark of hustle and bustle on St Kilda, but by this time the Air Ministry had decided to leave the Range project to the Army. Originally the Range was to have been primarily a matter for the RAF, with the Army and Navy participating to a much lesser extent; but as the costs soared well over budget (£25m in 1957) wrangling between the services erupted. In the end, the RAF pulled out of the deal, while the Navy had never really got fully committed in the first place. Consequently, as soon as the work of the Airfield Construction Branch was completed, St Kilda was handed over to the newly formed Royal Artillery Guided Weapons Range, and the small band of Army technicians and surveyors who had been on the island since July under Captain George Langford formed the nucleus of the Army garrison which was left behind when the RAF departed at the end of August. On 11 August Major Tony Riach arrived with the main party of soldiers from Troon, and the hand-over was completed on 28 August.

Militarily speaking, St Kilda had come a long way from the days of Frank Athow and his naval signallers with their primitive wireless transmitter. Yet there was a link with the past in the giant surveillance radar which had been installed by Marconi technicians, the technical descendants of Dudley Miller and his men, and it was perhaps symbolic that the RAF should have filled in the hollow centre of the old concrete base with their own leaded inscription. Still, I wonder what Greenhill, Davies, Kerr, Paton, Pirie, MacLean and those other stalwarts of the First World War would have thought of the vast army of servicemen who wrought such dramatic changes on their island forty years later.

6. THE ARMY TAKES OVER

THE day that LCT *4074* arrived at St Kilda late in August 1958 was a very inauspicious beginning to the Army's sole occupation of the island. After an uncomfortable journey all the way from Cairnryan, the ship was unable to beach in Village Bay on account of a south-easterly gale which blew up suddenly. The landing craft, with Colonel Cooper and David Boddington on board, had to make for the uncertain shelter of Glen Bay till the storm subsided. For thirty-six hours they rode at anchor within sight of Hirta but unable to land. With nothing to do but sit in the wardroom, reading paperbacks and the extremely dog-eared hardbacks supplied by the Seamen's Mission, the colonel champed at the bit with impatience. Eventually the wind dropped and the skipper brought his vessel round to Village Bay again. Even then, the beaching was not without mishap. When the ramp was lowered the tide had still to ebb for another hour, but in his impatience to be ashore and get on with the hand-over, Colonel Cooper ordered the Landrover on the tank deck to drive off with him and David. They drove down the ramp and stuck fast in the swirling sand and water, well-nigh inundated at waist level, and it was all they could do to scramble back aboard the LCT.

When they did manage to drive ashore, the colonel conducted the fastest hand-over on record; in little more than twenty minutes he had driven to the top of Mullach Mór, down again, popped into the Mess, and was ready to go back to the ship, satisfied that the RAF had left everything as it should be. After donning a suit of dry clothes and having his first solid meal in two days, David felt a lot happier. Already he had spotted several interesting birds and noticed the wild sheep; St Kilda was going to be a pleasant station for him after all. In fact David soldiered on the island for almost a whole year, with only one short break at Easter 1959, and it was probably the thought of the ghastly sea voyage which deterred him from leaving oftener or sooner.

For seven months Tony Riach ran the show with the happy informality of Popski's Private Army. Safe in the remote fastness of his island command, he

LCT 4062 running up on the beach

A view of Village Bay with Oiseval in the background, taken from the pinnacles of Mullach Sgar, showing a landing craft anchored and waiting for the tide to go out

waged a constant battle with the chairborne warriors in Whitehall and Edinburgh Castle, a battle which was second only to the grim struggle against the weather and the mud. On one occasion a storm tore the cutter from its moorings and threw it up on the rocks, completely reduced to matchwood. On another occasion the roof was rolled right off one of the Nissen huts as if it had been the lid on a can of sardines. On many days it was impossible to drive a vehicle past the Bailey Bridge owing to the hurricane force of the wind. There was a constant struggle to combat the loneliness and boredom which was inevitable on such a small, remote island. David organised photographic competitions and tried to interest the men in nature studies.

Unfortunately this interest in ornithology took the wrong course. There was a terrible scandal involving Sergeant Court and Bombardier Harris in November, when George Langford was in command during Tony's leave period. This was so great a scandal, in fact, that, like all good scandals, a faint whiff of it had eventually reached Major McGregor at Troon. Hearing that two soldiers had been involved in some frightful business on St Kilda, Mac immediately feared the worst. Impatiently he waited for George's return to Troon at the beginning of December and tackled him about it straightway.

'I hear that there has been some, er, trouble involving Court and Harris,' he began. 'I want you to tell me all about it.'

'Oh, I don't think anything need be said about it now,' replied George hastily. 'It's all over and done with. Very serious business, though – could have been a court martial affair, and that's the last thing we want to happen out on Kilda.'

'For God's sake, George, come out with it, man!' cried Mac. 'It wasn't, er, buggery, was it?'

George stopped shuffling his feet umcomfortably and looked up sharply. 'Oh no! It wasn't that. Good heavens!'

'Well then, what was the matter?' Mac, somewhat relieved, was still exasperated at George's diffidence.

'Oh well, you see, it was like this,' George explained. 'It seems that Court and Harris were out for a walk round the cliffs one day when they spotted a Solan Goose – a Gannet – on the rocks below them They wondered what the bird would taste like – if it would be like a common-or-garden domestic goose, and Harris's natural poaching instincts came to the fore. Apparently they had not gone unobserved, for McLennan the cook saw them and immediately went and told David. They were in the middle of plucking the bird when they saw David coming across the rocks at a great lick, so they stuffed the goose under a boulder. "What's this I hear about you two killing a gannet?" asked David, to which they replied in all innocence that they didn't know what he was talking about – this, in spite of the fact that they were absolutely covered in feathers! Well, of course, the fat was really in the fire then, for not only had they contravened Unit Standing Orders by molesting the wild life, but seemingly these wretched birds are protected by Act of Parliament. Old David was in a real paddy about it, and no mistake. Threatened to report them to the Nature Conservancy and that would really have stirred things up. Anyway, I managed to pacify him and the whole affair was hushed up. I was a bit sorry for Court and Harris, though. David made them take the bird and bury it, so they never found out what it tasted like after all. The funny thing about it all was the film we had that very night – Will Hay in *The Goose Steps Out* – and that just about brought the roof down.'

ONE of the more interesting specimens of the island's fauna was a young ram called Larry who had been orphaned the previous spring and adopted as a two-day-old lamb by the RAF. The airmen had nursed and fed him, so much so that Larry was ostracised by his own kind who had very strict ideas about sheep fraternising with the humans. Still, Larry was very content to be the camp mascot and could always be found hanging about the cookhouse when there were scraps in the offing. Larry the Lamb, however, grew up to be Larry the Ram, a great hulking, stinking one at that, who had no compunction about scattering his droppings in the dining hall or the barrack rooms. It was this particularly unsociable habit of his which, quite naturally, earned him the opprobrium of the servicemen who, with kicks and blows and curses, tried to drive him away. Eventually there was only one person who had any time for poor Larry, and that was David who fed him and showed him a moderate amount of kindness.

It so happens that one of the customs of the Soay sheep is that, like the people of some primitive societies whose young men learn the practical aspects of sex from the older women, young tups learn the rules of sexual behaviour from the older, more experienced ewes of the flock. This is done by the young tup following an older sheep. If the sheep turns out to be a ram, the young tup is butted and kicked to show him the error of his ways. Should the sheep be a ewe, then he is accepted and may follow that ewe with impunity. One thing further, however, and that is that the tup must keep a constant look out to ensure that he himself is not being followed by some other young hopeful whom he, in turn, must butt off. To this end, therefore, while following his ewe, he must constantly be turning and looking over his shoulder to left and right to ward off any undesirable suitors. Thus it was that when Larry followed David all over the island, he instinctively looked to left and right over his shoulder. David, the only person who did not kick him and chase him off, was his ewe – so the men always used to say.

All this Nature in the Raw around them had a devastating effect on the libido of the soldiers, as the following signal from Tony to Mac at Troon, dated late October 1958, bears out:

STK 1300/31. Originator's Number – Funny.

DUE TO LARGE NUMBER OF RAMS SHEEP SHOWING ABNORMAL TENDENCIES (.) DOCTOR SUSPECTS MICE WILL ATTEMPT TO EMULATE (.) REQUEST YOUR ADVICE OR CAN I CHARGE A SHEEP (.) OTHER INHABITANTS NORMAL BUT WATCHING BIRDS CAREFULLY (.)

Back came the answer by tele-printer on the same day:

TRO 1600/31. Originator's Number – Haha.

IN ABSENCE OF CO SUGGEST OBSERVATIONS BE DISCONTINUED FORTHWITH (.) MIGHT LEAD TO UNCONTROLLABLE BIOLOGICAL URGE AMONG INHABITANTS AT PRESENT ALLEGEDLY NORMAL.

I am relieved to add that Tony's fears in this respect were unfounded.

AT this early period the only immediate form of communication between St Kilda and the outside world was a tele-printer of Second World War vintage, and because it was not a secure line and there was naturally the probability that the Russians were eavesdropping, all messages, no matter how trivial, were supposed to be encoded at one end and laboriously deciphered at the other, using a primitive and time-consuming system called Slidex which probably dated from the days of Mata Hari. It is easy enough to make an error while simply typing out a message, but the scope for mistakes when codes are involved is seemingly infinite. A tiny glitch in decoding almost cost the Army a very embarrassing situation which, if the tabloids had got wind of it, would have severely dented the reputation of the service. At that time the popular press was for ever running stories about senseless Army 'bull', such as scrubbing barrack-room floors with toothbrushes or painting heaps of coal white. But the story of the St Kilda beer cans would have far exceeded anything that had been published before. Now, more than forty years after the incident, the story may be told.

Some time in November 1958 George Langford sent a signal off to Troon requesting fresh supplies of beer, and in it he listed 250 cans of Guinness. Somehow or other this got garbled slightly to 250 cases. Mac promptly ordered this fantastic amount from the brewers and in due course a heavily laden *Mull* sailed out to the island with some six thousand cans of Guinness packed in cardboard cartons. When George came back to Troon at the end of that month he confronted Mac with his problem. The demand for Guinness was really very small, and he could not see how thirty men (of whom only a dozen were drinkers of stout) could possibly get through that amount of it.

'We'll just have to send most of it back to the brewers,' said Mac finally, 'and hope that they will overlook this dreadful mistake this time.'

'There's just one thing though,' said George gravely, 'and that is that the cartons got bashed a bit in the dory when we were bringing the stuff ashore.'

'Not to worry. Get it shipped back here somehow, and I'll fix it.'

'Are you sure it'll be OK, sir?'

'Yes, of course. The brewers will understand,' Mac re-assured him.

'Well, I don't know,' said George hesitantly. 'But if you say so…'

The matter was left at that in the meantime, and in due course Tony Riach had the bulk of the Guinness consignment returned to Dundonald Camp. Mac got a shock when it arrived. Instead of in cartons, the cans were packed in hessian sand-bags, and on opening these sacks it was found that the cans had likewise suffered severe mishandling, either in going to St Kilda or in leaving again. Many of them were dented and scratched, and most of them were incredibly rusted owing to exposure to the humid atmosphere of the island.

'Good God!' exploded Mac. 'What an unholy mess these cans are in.'

'The brewers'll never accept them, sir,' said Sergeant Watson flatly. 'At most, we might be able to claim a purchase tax rebate on them from the Inland Revenue,' he added knowingly.

'Never say die, sergeant,' Mac reproved him. 'Anyway, I'll get on to the brewers and see what can be done.'

As it happens, Mac was right, and the consignors agreed to take back over five thousand cans, as canned beer was guaranteed for nine months after sale. Nevertheless Mac felt that he could not possibly return the cans in their present state.

'We'll have to clean up this mess a bit before we send them back, he said.

'Only one thing for it, sir,' said Sergeant Watson.

'What's that, sergeant?'

'Brasso, sir,' replied Watson promptly. 'And steel wool – plenty of it. Me and the lads'll get down to it right away.'

Thus it was that Watson and five men sat down in a cold, draughty hut in Dundonald Camp in February, and polished cans and cans of Guinness until they were sick of the sight of them.

ST KILDA was not all play and no work either, during those first few months of the Army occupation. One of the objects of the detachment was to acquire some practical experience in operating the two radars, and to do this a number of small rockets were launched to enable the radar technicians to track them. These rockets were of the Starling type – about five inches in calibre and fifteen feet long, fired from a small steel ramp which had been erected on the ridge not far from the Decca site. Most of these rockets took off perfectly when the blue touch paper (or whatever) was ignited. Others, however, proved to be temperamental and either refused outright to take off in the approved manner, or merely slid cautiously up the ramp, hesitated, and slid back down again, spouting flames feebly from the exhaust.

One rocket unfortunately behaved even more unpredictably than that. When it was ignited it shot off the ramp all right, but instead of arcing over Mullach Bi and heading harmlessly out to sea, it changed its mind and curved in the opposite direction. A gasp went up from the onlookers on the ridge. 'Christ!' yelled one. 'It's heading towards the Camp!' Sure enough, the wayward missile had turned over the bay and began a rapid spiral descent towards the Nissen huts. As it plunged through the roof of the Other Ranks' billet, more than a mile from the launching site, everyone on top of the hill ran wildly down the steep heather-clad slopes after it.

Meanwhile Signalman Dryden, having a surreptitious snooze on his bed in the barrack-room, suddenly had his slumbers rudely shattered. The rocket tore a hole in the corrugated roofing and crashed to rest behind Dryden's steel locker which toppled over on top of him with the force of the impact. There he was, pinned to the bed by his locker, when his mates burst in seconds later. Anxiously they dragged him out of the debris and David frantically examined him for injury. Dryden, though he had personally escaped with only minor cuts on his forearm, was on the verge of tears.

'Me guitar!' he wailed. 'That fucking rocket's clobbered me bleedin' guitar!' and he held up the mangled remains of his musical instrument.

The Army camp of 1959-61 viewed across the Minister's Meadow. The semi-circular buildings were Romney huts (a bigger version of the famous Nissen hut) while the square tower in the background denotes the generator sheds

'Never mind, mate,' one of his friends consoled him. 'That was an act of Providence, that was. We was beginnin' to get chocker with you beatin' hell out of Hound Dog.' But this unsympathetic approach only provoked Dryden to further outbursts.

'No bloody right to do that! I'll write to my MP, so I will,' he threatened darkly.

Fortunately there were no Parliamentary Questions, far less a Ministerial Inquiry, into Dryden's guitar. In the interests of justice and a quiet life, Tony got a grant of £20 from Regimental Funds to purchase a new guitar to replace the one his rocket had smashed, and the whole regrettable matter was hushed up. This incident had a fateful sequel, nevertheless, several months later when Dryden was stationed at Benbecula. He and his pals went on a 'recreational' trip to Lochboisdale for a booze-up in the hotel. On the way back, however, the truck in which they were travelling swerved off the narrow road and struck a telegraph pole. Although no one was hurt in the crash, the only

The Factor's House. The OC's quarters were on the right. Note the flight of steps at the side leading to the upper floor and the MO's quarters

casualty was Dryden's new guitar, now reduced to a mass of tangled strings and splintered wood. I have never known anyone who had such an accident-prone guitar. Perhaps Dryden learned a lesson from this and concentrated in future on something less adventurous, like a piano for instance.

THE other main task facing the detachment at that time was to keep the slipway and approach to the jetty clear of rocks. This was a never-ending labour since, no sooner did the men clear the rocks off the slipway, than the tide and south-easterly gales brought them crashing in again. This was no mean feat as many of these boulders were as tall as a man and ten times as heavy. Tony rigged up an ingenious device for hauling these rocks clear. A large crane was constructed out of several telegraph poles filched from the Signals section, and the winch on the Scammell recovery vehicle was used to pull the cable which lifted the obstruction off the slipway. The remainder of the detachment, like a bunch of slaves in a film epic of ancient Egypt, hauled and strained on the end of a guide rope which directed the jib of the crane. Corporal Denham, looking for all the world like some overseer from the same epic, stood with feet outstretched on top of the rock and directed the efforts of the others in lifting the boulder. The disadvantage of having the easy job was that every so often a big wave would sweep in and inundate him, so that he was lifted unceremoniously into the water. But Denham did not mind the occasional ducking. Although it was the depths of winter the water was surprisingly mild – and, besides, a ducking meant a free issue of rum afterwards.

As well as the slipway, the concrete ramp on the beach where the landing craft came aground had to be maintained. When the RAF constructed it in 1957 it was Cookie's proud boast that it would outlast the old stone jetty. The jetty, which had been built in 1901, was still almost as good as new sixty years later, but the ramp, after the severe pounding of only two winters, was now in a sorry state. Boulders cast up by innumerable gales broke its surface, while the relentless action of the tide undermined it by eroding the shingle and sand on which it was built. Consequently, by the spring of 1959, not much was left of the original RAF ramp. When Colonel Cooper, accompanied by the Brigadier Royal Artillery at Scottish Command, Peter Henderson, DSO, visited St Kilda on 10 April, they not only made a thorough inspection of the damage but even rolled up their sleeves and got down to the job of clearing rocks along with the squaddies. This was 'hands on' leadership with a vengeance – but St Kilda tended to have that effect, even on the most senior visiting officers. Only one man refused to soil his hands. Geoffrey Hutton, the Brigade Major, declined to join the Brigadier and the Colonel playing at navvies, and contented himself with standing at the side offering such well-meant advice as 'Use a little more purchase here' to such of the sweating soldiery as would pause to listen to his clipped tones. At any rate, with the combined efforts of the Top Brass and the detachment, a first class repair job was effected and the ramp was sufficiently serviceable to allow the first LCTs of the 1959 season to beach without undue difficulty.

On this occasion I not only accompanied my CO but had the doubtful privilege of sharing a bedroom with him in the Factor's House. Colonel George, as broad as he was tall, was an unnerving sight to behold naked as the day he was born. This time it was the Brigadier who had the tiny single room on the ground floor, and I imagine that the Brigade Major had to double up with Will Warner. What I mainly recall about this three-day visit was the splendid dinner which David Boddington laid on. Not only did he persuade Gunner Wathall to wait table, thus sparing the Top Brass the traumatic indignity of queuing up at the hotplate with the hoi polloi, but also to don a white mess waiter's tunic. The pièce de résistance, however, was the first course. While we lesser mortals had standard Army issue mulligatawny, a rare treat was reserved for the Brigadier. It so happened that Tony Riach, who enjoyed the finer things in life, occasionally brightened the rigours of the winter on St Kilda by ordering a gourmet hamper from Fortnum & Mason. When he left the island for good in March, he left behind the remnants of his last self-indulgence, in the form of a pot of turtle soup. David could easily have been tempted to consume this himself, but instead he held on to it for that special occasion. And now that time had come, he arranged that the lucky recipient would be the Brigadier. We sat silently, with bated breath, as Peter Henderson tucked into the soup set before him, awaiting, if not unstinted praise, at least a grunt of appreciation. But nothing happened and the Brig continued supping. At length David could contain himself no longer.

'How is your soup, sir?'

'Oh' – slurp, slurp – 'not bad.'

'It's turtle soup, sir. From Fortnum & Mason.'

The Brigadier took a final slurp, thought for a moment and then said, 'I think Fortnums are a trifle over-rated.'

Here we were, on tiny, remote, wild St Kilda, with a Force 10 gale howling outside and a spring shower (i.e. torrential rain) thundering down on the tin roof of the Romney – and all he could comment was that Fortnums were a trifled over-rated!

The main outcome of the BRA's inaugural inspection was that more professional hands were needed to get the ramp back to its former state, and accordingly in May 1959 a small party of Territorial Army Engineers, led by Captain Robin Ward, and including a petty officer from HMS *Adamant* to give advice on underwater demolitions, arrived on St Kilda to take part in Operation Bird Watch. Robin Ward, a Scotsman from Renfrewshire, heralded his arrival by playing the bagpipes as the landing craft on which he was a passenger entered the bay.

He and his party stayed on the island for about a week and did a lot of valuable work in that short time. Not only did they carry out extensive repairs to the ramp but they eliminated most of the larger and trickier rocks blocking the approach to the jetty by attaching charges of plastic explosive to them and blasting them to pieces. One charge, however, whether on account of its size or because of the way in which it was placed, had the unexpected effect of blowing far more rock out of the bay than was intended. The whole camp shook as a gigantic column of water shot skywards and for several seconds afterwards a shower of rubble spattered down on the roadway and the roofs of buildings. One huge lump of granophyre shot clean over the roof of the cookhouse and buried itself in the meadow behind. When I visited St Kilda three days later I found that the boys had roped off the 'crater' with stakes and tape. But an even greater wonder was the lump of rock which hurtled through the roof of the manse, now the Sergeants' Mess, dislodged a number of slates and came to rest on the Battery Sergeant-Major's bed. This was regarded by the men as nothing short of miraculous, a judgment on the BSM and the answer to their prayers. Be that as it may, the offending lump of rock was removed and placed reverently on the top shelf of the cocktail cabinet in the Officers' Mess where it was pointed out to visitors over the ensuing years as 'an original Ward', and the story of how this curious piece of sculpture got there was repeated ad nauseam.

7. HERE COME THE GIRLS

I MADE my third trip to St Kilda in May 1959, this time aboard a tank landing craft, the *Arromanches* commanded by Captain John Leach, RASC. In spite of her unprepossessing box-shape and ungainly superstructure aft, she was a very comfortable ship and run on strictly naval lines in the best tradition of the Senior Service. We were even piped aboard when we drove up the ramp, in the South Ford where she lay beached, waiting for the tide.

There were five of us, travelling first class: Major Bob Allday, RA and Captain Nobby Hall, REME, who were to conduct a Board of Inquiry into damage sustained by one of the island's generators, a Mr Scott who was going out to superintend the gang of civilian labourers who had been sent out earlier by the Garrison Engineer in Inverness to carry out various constructional tasks, Captain Douglas Upton from the School of Artillery at Larkhill, and myself. Doug was to relieve Captain Warner as Officer Commanding the detachment for four weeks while Will had some leave, and I was sent along to give him a helping hand and also to give me some experience in the running of the place, in preparation to going out as relief detachment commander at some later date.

The voyage was extremely pleasant; a beautiful sunset silhouetting the rugged outline of Hecla and Ben More on South Uist contrasted with the vivid turquoise sea, reminding Bob Allday of the Aegean. Although I had never been there myself, I could well imagine that we were on some Mediterranean cruise, as we lolled on deck chairs on the Officers' Deck, basking in the sunshine and listening to the strains of pop music from a tape-recorder, relayed over the ship's tannoy system.

We had not turned Barra Head when we retired to our sleeping berths for the night. When I awoke next morning, Doug was shaking me and motioning for me to get up and come out on deck. It was only five-thirty, but already the hot sun was streaming through the open port-hole. I looked out and beheld St Kilda, scarcely three miles ahead. I jumped down to the deck and pulled on my trousers and open-necked shirt. Up on deck, the morning air was crisp and clear. Before us we had a wonderful vista of Hirta, the glorious emerald of its hillsides rising out of the pale blue sea.

'We'll be there in half an hour,' said Peter Jones, the First Lieutenant, wrapped in his duffel coat, who was just leaving the bridge. By six o'clock we had dropped anchor in the bay, and waited for the cutter or dory to come out and take us ashore. No sign of life materialised until almost eight o'clock when the first figures straggled across the roadway from the Nissen huts to the cookhouse. Shortly afterwards the OC himself appeared and eventually the boats were launched and came out to us. Rather than wait till high tide at eleven, when the LCT could run up on the beach, we were rowed ashore in the dory.

After a hurried breakfast Bob immediately assembled his Board, of which I was, reluctantly, a member, delegated the task of taking down the proceedings. I was itching to get out and explore the island more fully than had been possible on my previous visits, but for six boring hours I had to sit in the ward of the tiny hospital while ten witnesses were sworn in and all the facts relating to the damage of a Meadows generator were gone through. Ultimately the Board broke up and I was free. David Boddington helped me up to the Factor's House with my trunk, and we chatted about all the recent doings on the island.

'We've had a bit of a tragedy,' he said rather forlornly.

'Oh. What was that?'

'Larry,' he said simply. 'We had to do away with him, poor darling. I'm afraid he was getting to be a bit of a nuisance around the camp… Anyway, some of the chaps loaded him into the truck and took him up the hill. They were going to chuck him over the cliff – seemed the best way – we couldn't have eaten old Larry.'

'Oh, I don't know. He wasn't that old, surely.'

'It wasn't that,' David answered reproachfully. 'He was almost one of the family, y'know. Anyway, they took him up the hill, and damn me if they didn't bring him down again. They hadn't the heart to kill him either.'

'Well then, where's the tragedy?'

'Some other rotten swine who had no feelings whatever took him out and did it instead. Knocked him on the head and threw him over the cliff, after all.'

'How did Willie Stewart get on while you were away?' I asked, changing the subject hurriedly.

'Poor Willie! He lived in a little triangle: the Factor's House to the dining-room, to the Medical Centre, and he never strayed out of it. He just wasn't interested in anything except getting off the island and back to his young bride. He got a bit of a shock one day, though, when he had to go out to a Fleetwood trawler and give medical assistance. Nearly died of fright I believe. He wasn't all that keen on boating, I hear.'

We went into the house.

'I haven't quite got your bed made up yet,' he apologised. 'I was washing sheets this morning and they're not dry yet. Hope you don't mind sleeping in creased sheets, by the way. We never bother to iron them. No one sees them anyway except ourselves.'

'Aye, right enough,' I replied. 'This place needs a woman's touch.'

'I couldn't agree more,' said David earnestly. 'Will Warner was told by his Postings Branch that he would get a quarter for his wife and baby out here on St Kilda. Ridiculous, isn't it? I mean to say – fancy telling anyone that there were married quarters on Hirta. It just shows how little these War Office people really know or care about us.'

'That's nothing, David,' I said. 'Mac told me the other day that some staff officer – a colonel no less – got up at some War Office conference when the idea of occupying St Kilda was first mooted, and proposed that in the interests of economy the troops should be billeted on the civilian population.'

'Oh, I know,' said David resignedly. 'Only the other week I got a letter from my Medical Branch in Edinburgh saying that I was authorised to recruit suitable women from the local population to act as chaperones in the Medical Centre, to look after my female patients.'

'I didn't think that would be necessary in the lambing season,' I quipped.

'It's not as funny as it might seem on the face of it,' he said. 'Did you know that we are expecting some women ashore here tonight?'

'Women?'

'Yes. There's a party of holidaymakers coming from Harris in a fishing boat. They're due here some time this evening. The National Trust organised it, you know.'

'Ah yes, I remember now. I saw a bit in the *News of the World* a few weeks ago about it. "Want a holiday on Ghost Island" it said. A load of guff about them missing the spectacle of rockets screaming by, high overhead, on the Queen's Birthday. There won't be any missiles launched until the end of June, as the schedule stands at the moment.'

The *News of the World*, eh? Might've known you'd be reading that!' David laughed. 'Anyway, I've got to get their tents ready for them. Come and give me a hand.'

'My goodness! It's like working at Butlin's.' The notion of a highly qualified medico, and scion of one of the country's leading brewery families at that, acting as charlady to a bunch of tourists on a desert island suddenly struck me as surreal.

While we were preparing the tents, their present occupants were moving out; Robin Ward and his party were packing up their Commando gear, and Morton Boyd and his Nature Conservancy team were likewise getting ready to depart. At 8pm the departing officers and men were lined up on the jetty to commence the tedious business of ferrying out to the LCT which was now off the beach and tied up to the mooring buoy a thousand yards out. Suddenly, a very diminutive vessel came into sight round the point of Dùn and chugged into the bay.

A dozen pairs of field-glasses eagerly swept the little craft as she came to a halt. I made out the name *Maighdean Hearrach* painted on her wooden bow. 'The Harris Virgin,' I chuckled. 'What a pretty name.' A boat had been lowered, and with keen interest the soldiers watched as her passengers were rowed ashore. A bombardier in front of me, his binoculars glued to his eyes, cried excitedly, 'Boy! There's a smasher there!' One would have thought that the top of the jetty was the front row of the Windmill Theatre, judging by the comments and whistles which the appearance of three young ladies in the boat evoked. At least one soldier was seen to be subconsciously slicking back his unruly mop of hair…

'It won't be a bad thing to have some women around the place,' I thought, 'if it has a civilising effect on the men.'

Will Warner's last duty as OC before leaving the island had been to write out an appendix to Unit Standing Orders:

As there will be females among the National Trust Party, the attention of all ranks is drawn to the following points:

The area of the tented camp is strictly out of bounds.

Shorts or trunks will in future be worn at all times when swimming.

The practice of urinating in the stream behind the Canteen will cease forthwith.

The use of obscene language will be avoided when in the vicinity of the National Trust Party.

Meanwhile the passengers from the *Maighdean Hearrach*, a small wooden fishing boat from Scalpay, were being helped ashore by any amount of willing hands. Foremost among the hosts was David who was last seen escorting the young ladies with 'Come this way. I'll show you to your tent.'

'Listen to Casanova there,' called out Robin Ward who was about to get into the dory. 'Keep an eye on David! He's far too young to be going into girls' tents.'

'Leave him alone,' said Will. 'The poor lad hasn't seen anything in skirts since March.'

As far as I could see, however, skirts was a misnomer, for all three girls wore jeans, ski sweaters and wind-cheaters. Still, I had to agree with Will that after a spell of enforced celibacy on St Kilda one would be only too happy to have some women – any women – around the place. Not that these girls could be considered as 'any women'; without exception they all appeared very easy on the eye. The eldest was an attractive brunette, then there was the petite blonde and finally the fair-haired girl with the quiet voice. As for the men of the party, they were a mixed bunch, ranging in age from about thirty upwards; but, like the soldiers, I must admit that I did not pay very much attention to them at that early stage.

By ten o'clock the landing craft had sailed, and shortly afterwards the *Maighdean Hearrach* also departed. The work party had settled down in their little camp in the paddock above the Minister's Meadow, and all was quiet on the western front. In the Mess, David was being ragged unmercifully by Bill Ellis, a Signals officer who had been on the island for several weeks, carrying out trials with new equipment.

'Which one have you got your beady eye on? Or is it all three that you're trying to get off with? You're a randy young devil and no mistake!' David blushed hotly but refrained from rising to the bait.

'Take your time, David,' said Doug. 'You've got a whole fortnight…'

St Kilda sheep were not sheared, only plucked. Here Captain David Boddington gives a demonstration of 'rueing' the fleece while James Mackay holds the sheep's horns

'I'm off,' said David. 'I'm going to get some of my mouse-traps. Are you coming, Jim?' He got up and I followed him out of the room. Behind us, Bill called out, 'Watch that you don't trap something else instead!'

We went up to the Factor's House and there I left him to collect his traps. He rejoined me a few minutes later and we set off up the Street, carrying a dozen aluminium Longworth catch-alive traps. David stopped at a cleit and, taking a handful of grain from a pouch, poured it into the bottom of the trap which he then set and placed inside the doorway of a cottage. The process was repeated along the Street until all twelve traps had been baited and set.

'We'll come back here in the morning and see what we've found.'

'What d'you do with the mice when you've caught them?' I asked.

'First of all I weigh them,' he said. 'You'll be surprised how much they weigh – anything from forty to seventy grams. Oh yes, they're big brutes, the St Kilda field-mice – big as rats in fact. *Apodemus sylvaticus hirtensis*,' he reeled off the imposing Latin name, 'is quite a lad indeed.'

'He sounds like it,' I commented. 'I am looking forward to seeing one up close.' Hitherto I had only caught fleeting glimpses of them as they scurried across the Mess carpet or heard them rattling round the Factor's House in the dead of night. 'But what then? Do you let them go again once you've weighed them?'

'Yes. But before I release them I mark them – for identification – same as ringing a bird. I clip off one or more digits of their fingers or toes. You can get innumerable combinations of clips with twenty toes and fingers to play with. Quite harmless, really – doesn't harm them a bit. And if I trap the same mouse twice, I can always identify him again.'

'Ugh. It sounds positively barbaric.'

We had reached the middle of the village and were just turning back when we ran into the two younger girls, Liz and Mary. They had gone for a stroll up to the far end of the village and were now walking back to their camp. David and I fell in with them and accompanied them as far as the Factor's House. They told us that they worked at the National Institute for Research in Dairy-farming at Reading. They had read the National Trust's press release in the *Daily Telegraph* and decided to try an unusual holiday in this out-of-the-way place.

'You've made us very comfortable in the tents,' said Liz. 'We never expected anything like this. Why, we didn't even know that the island was inhabited, far less did we expect we'd find electric light laid on in the tents. And to think I brought a supply of candles!'

David had been very hospitable indeed, having made arrangements for the men to use our wash-house and the girls to use the washing facilities in the Medical Centre. The sight of Sergeant Tutt, the quartermaster-sergeant, putting up curtains in the hospital bathroom windows raised a chuckle. 'Just in case we get any Peeping Toms, sir,' he said grimly.

Next morning Doug and I spent a couple of hours in the Detachment Office, sorting out the mail which had come by *Arromanches* the previous evening and filing reports. Doug was to deal with the 'discipline' side of things while I dealt with all matters pertaining to messing, canteen, welfare and general administration. Doug was appalled at the state of the OC's office and our first task was to give it a spring-clean. I borrowed a broom from the storeman and swept out the floor while Doug busied himself with a duster. I was rapidly learning that on St Kilda the pips on one's shoulders did not count for much. Having cleared the clutter off the desk we tried to get to grips with the detachment accounts which were, frankly, almost as much of a mess as the office had been. The rest of the morning we toured the camp, inspecting the billets and installations. Doug was horrified by the casual atmosphere and particularly the untidy appearance of the men.

'I understand that one has to relax the usual discipline a bit,' he grumbled, 'but I do think that the men should shave occasionally…'

After lunch I was free, so I set off on a walk round the village. I met David behind the Factor's House, examining the results of the previous night's trapping. He had one mouse squealing and protesting in a small wire cage attached to a pair of scales.

'Forty-seven grams. Not bad for a young buck, eh?' He lifted the mouse out of the cage and held him on his outstretched palm.

'Here you are. What d'you think of him? Big, isn't he?' The mouse lay quietly on David's palm. He looked just like a large golden hamster with the addition of a long scaly tail like a rat. I stroked his soft tawny fur.

'My. He's quite a size.' David held him firmly and with a pair of clippers deftly cut off the tip of a toe and a finger. The mouse squirmed momentarily and then scurried off as David released him. Taking out a notebook he jotted down the mouse's particulars – weight, age, sex, where trapped and the combination of clipped digits.

'Good. That makes the ninetieth I've trapped this year. I'm learning an awful lot about their habits and movements from this now.'

'And what good is that to anyone?' I asked sceptically.

'Well, it advances the frontiers of human knowledge,' he said portentously.

'Seems a waste of time to me,' I said, unconvinced.

'Have you seen the stone cross yet?' he asked, a minute or two later.

'Ah! D'you mean the ancient Celtic cross? I've read about it in one of the books about St Kilda. Where exactly is it?'

'Come on and I'll show you.'

He led me to the far end of the Street. The National Trust people had beaten us to it, for they were all grouped round the end cottage while their leader, Alec Warwick, pointed it out to them. Set in the wall, below the right hand window of the cottage, was a dressed stone about two feet square. Traced on its surface was a cross of simple design, having an outline incised about the central arms. It was very faint and obviously worn down by centuries of exposure to the elements, but it was a Celtic cross nevertheless, and believed to date back to the period of the sixth to ninth centuries. Apparently there had been three small churches on the island in medieval times, though why three churches were necessary I could not understand, as the population had never been more than two hundred at its peak. Of these churches – St Brendan's, St Columba's and Christ's – no obvious trace now remained, and even the sites of the first two were a matter for conjecture. Undoubtedly this old stone cross had come from one of them, probably Christ's Church which, in Martin Martin's time (1697) was still intact and stood within the precincts of the burial ground. Perhaps the last ruins of the old church, believed to have still been in evidence about 1815, had been plundered to provide a ready supply of building materials for the cottages when they were built in 1860. Now these houses themselves were in a pitiable state, their roofs gone and their gables crumbling away. I thought that, as the cottage itself disintegrated, the National Trust would remove this precious stone to some place of safety; but in 2001 I was heartened to see that not only was the cross still in situ, but also that the cottage itself, though still unroofed, had been carefully pointed and preserved from further ravages of the weather. A second incised stone cross was discovered some years ago in the wall of a cleit.

Wednesday developed into a warm and sunny morning, just the day to get out of the stuffy office and go exploring the old village again. I found it the most fascinating part of the entire island; to wander through these old ruined houses and speculate what manner of people had once dwelled in them. House number two was still quite well preserved. I stepped inside and carefully examined the rubble in the centre of the floor. Something bright green caught my eye. Stooping down I picked up a dessert-spoon, crusted with verdigris. Whose mouth had this once fed? Looking round the interior of what had once been the bedroom, I tried to picture how it must have looked when still inhabited. There was the fireplace, still with its rusty iron grate and hook dangling from the chimney. To left and right of it were shallow recesses where the St Kildans had had their presses, those cupboards

The author, with the late Alec Warwick, Master of Works of the National Trust for Scotland and leader of the first work party of 1959, examining a St Kilda fieldmouse.

NTS volunteers disembarking from a 15-cwt Army truck, June 1959. I have forgotten the name of the man on the left, but next to him is Peter Scola who married Mary 'Steve' Stevens (right, front). Beside him is Liz Evans, the friend (and later bridesmaid) of Mary Jackson (bottom left) who became my wife in September 1960

which were once a feature of Scottish houses all over the country.

The faded wallpaper with its floral pattern had all but vanished from the walls, revealing the original plaster which covered the masonry. Scraping off a piece of this wallpaper from the corner beside the right-hand press, I suddenly found some writing, scratched in the plaster when it had been wet. 'N. McQueen' read the large scrawly lettering in the plaster and below it was a hand print, like the fossilised footprint of some prehistoric creature, where the builder had leaned on the plaster to leave his autograph. N. McQueen? Why, Neil McQueen, to be sure. He was the elder brother of the famous Finlay McQueen who, in his prime, had been the champion fowler of St Kilda, credited with catching six hundred fulmars in a single day. The same Finlay (born in 1858) had been one of the island's three old age pensioners at the time of the Evacuation, and had been presented to Their Majesties King George VI and Queen Elizabeth at the Glasgow Empire Exhibition of 1938. He was three years old when these cottages had been built (Neil being two or three years his senior); he died several years after the Second World War, having spanned almost ninety years. And now here were his brother's fingerprints, a poignant reminder of that other St Kilda a century earlier.

At lunchtime David announced, 'I've planned an expedition round Oiseval this afternoon. Anyone care to come?'

'You can count me out,' said Doug. 'I can't stand heights. I even get dizzy standing on the cherrypicker when we are erecting a missile.'

'I'll come with you,' I said. 'Who else will be going?'

'There'll be you, me and most of the National Trust party,' said David. 'Why?'

'Oh, nothing,' I answered hastily.

'I expect the girls are game, anyway,' he added with a smile, 'if that's what's interesting you.'

We assembled at the tented camp at two o'clock, suitably dressed for the occasion. David wore his anorak and rubber-soled Commando boots. I was not so fortunately kitted out as he was, having to make do with my standard issue ammunition boots which my batman had polished to perfection before I left Benbecula – even buffing the studs on the soles! The eight campers, including all the girls, joined us and we set off along the top of the head dyke which ran above the camp towards the cliff of Oiseval. We gained height steadily, making for the edge of the wall which ran straight up the side of the hill and had been designed, we conjectured, to prevent any sheep from falling over the edge.

At the top of this low dyke the hillside broke off abruptly, a thousand feet above the sea. We dropped over the edge into a steeply ridged gully forming the entrance to the path which led round the cliff about three hundred feet from the summit. At this point three of the men of the party, having made a preliminary inspection of the terrifying drop below, declined to go any farther and decided to sit on the lip of the gully to await our return. Alec Warwick, Peter Scola and the three girls decided to continue, ably guided by David who gaily skipped ahead, oblivious of the sickening drop on to the boiling surf and the extremely narrow ledge we were traversing.

For about a mile we wound slowly round the cliff on this narrow grassy ledge which jutted out over the ocean and then receded into the face of the cliff several times. At one point we slithered down a hundred feet and then had to climb the same height again in traversing a buttress. Four hundred feet above us towered the jagged cliffs, and twice that distance fell sheer below us to the raging waters of the Atlantic. I was speedily realising that my boots might be splendid on the parade-ground, but were totally unsuited for promenading round the cliffs. I had my heart in my mouth many times during that afternoon, and eventually I began to fall behind the main body and bring up the rear. Fortunately I was able to disguise my clumsiness by pretending to keep company with the two girls from Reading who likewise were finding the going a bit difficult. My only consolation was that I could have a conversation with Mary, the youngest and prettiest of the trio, and occasionally give her a helping hand over the trickier parts.

At one point we had to slither across an overhanging rock, wet with mud oozing from the cliff face, and drop in a series of great steps to another ledge. David had christened this nasty stretch the Organ Loft, and indeed it did resemble the high vaulted loft of a Gothic cathedral. All about us, thousands of fulmars nested on the ledges, courting, squabbling, fighting, incubating eggs and fluttering around. We passed too close to one sitting on her egg, and the poor bird, obviously frightened, shot a stream of repulsively smelly oil from her nostrils and hit Peter on the head as he ducked. Once you get fulmar oil in your hair no amount of shampooing will eradicate the dreadful pong which lingers for weeks.

Eventually we clambered over a wall of rock and came round the next ridge to behold the most impressive sight of the whole island – mighty Conachair, whose seaward side drops cleanly thirteen hundred feet into the ocean. Just to look at it made me dizzy. All over its face, speckled variously with strata of red, blue, yellow and brown rock, and interlaced with small patches of scurvy grass, were studded the homes of countless sea birds – fulmars, puffins, razorbills, kittiwakes, guillemots and little auks – while at the very foot, on a wide ledge washed by the surf, basked a score of young seals, belly upwards, enjoying the sunshine.

'Look down there,' said David, indicating a ledge halfway down the face of Conachair. 'Can you see anything on that ledge?' We peered intently with binoculars at the solitary patch of grass. There, grazing peacefully, was a brown ewe, all on her own. 'She fell over the cliff last autumn,' David told us. 'How she managed to survive I don't know. She's imprisoned on that small ledge there, and can neither get up nor down. Of course, she has plenty of pasture, but it must be a very lonely life for her all the same.'

Gingerly we retraced our steps along the cliff path, but after a quarter of a mile, David led us sharply downwards, descending two hundred feet in a pebble-strewn ravine, on to the lowest of the three paths which slash the face of Oiseval. The going was a lot easier though we were still four or five hundred feet above the water, and eventually we came back on to the hill slopes overlooking the camp. With a great feeling of relief I stumbled behind the others, down the hillside to the Factor's House.

'No more jaunts round the cliffs for me, David,' I said when we were relaxing in the Mess afterwards. 'That little trip you organised today was quite enough for me.'

'Oh, come now! It wasn't as bad as that!' he scoffed. 'Goodness sake! That girl Steve had you licked. In fact,' he laughed, 'she even asked me if we weren't taught this sort of thing in the Army. She was surprised to see you scrambling around on all fours like that.'

'It's these damned boots,' I explained testily. 'They're no use for that kind of work. And anyway, it's no disgrace to be a bit scared of these cliffs. Look at Doug here, he was a wise man in not coming. And what about Will Warner? Does he come round the cliffs with you? He's a paratrooper after all, so he must be used to that sort of caper.'

'Who – Will?' David chuckled. 'I took him down the Carn Mór once and he actually fainted. He's far worse than you, I'll give

The author in 'mufti'; you wore your oldest clothes for expeditions such as this as clothing sprayed with the foul-smelling fulmar oil was fit only for burning. The ground on which I am standing is riddled with puffin burrows and the whole hillside seemed in danger of collapsing

David Boddington creeping up on an unsuspecting bird with his fowling rod. Birds were snared with a running noose mounted on the end of the pole

David Boddington disentangling a fulmar from the noose prior to ringing its leg

you that.'

'There you are,' I returned triumphantly. 'No one but a bloody mountain goat would traipse around the cliffs the way you and Alec Warwick did this afternoon.'

'Well I am only doing what Colonel Cooper told me to do,' said David. 'He told me you were to be taken all over the island and shown all its finer points, as you were so keen to learn as much as you can about the place.'

'He said that?' I was incredulous.

'Yes, he did,' said David. 'And tonight I have planned another expedition, down the Carn Mór to ring petrels. 'You simply must come.' I groaned and Doug laughed. 'Yes,' he chimed in, 'you'll have to go with him. Good for you – all this nature study and all that.'

So it was that shortly after eleven o'clock I changed into my oldest flannels and thick woollen jersey and complete with a fur-lined parka and climbing boots borrowed from David, I set out with the rest of the party. There were ten of us altogether as we plodded along to the end of the Street, crossed the Amhuinn Mhór, and tramped up the road to Am Blaid, the saddle which divides the Village from the Great Glen. At the road junction we cut off westwards across the rough, boulder-strewn moorland, past the wreckage of the Sunderland, and came to the ridges and tumbled rocks of Mullach Bi. Here we slid on our bottoms down an almost vertical grassy slope until we had reached a ledge hanging above the sea. We turned northwards and clambered over gigantic boulders, some as big as a house, at the foot of the Carn Mór. We gradually went upwards over these rocks and ultimately came to a broad grassy bank whereon stood a cleit, from which David retrieved his bird nets and long bamboo poles.

He proceeded to erect a device not unlike a huge badminton net, but much higher and having loose folds in the netting. In the poor light (it was now past midnight) the poor birds fluttering bat-like in from the sea to their burrows would fly into the net and become entangled in its meshes. Excitedly David and his helpers would disengage the storm petrels and ring them before releasing them again. In this manner David also caught three Leach's Forked-tailed Petrels, which looked to me like swallows with webbed feet. After a while we had a picnic of oranges, washed down with flasks of coffee. One of the National Trust party had thoughtfully equipped himself with a hip flask of whisky which he liberally passed around. We sat there on the bank, huddled together for warmth, and watched the sky gradually getting lighter again as a new day dawned.

On our way back we caught a Manx shearwater and a puffin and ringed them both. Deep underground, in the vast recesses of the boulders, we could hear the rumbling groans of contentment from the puffins and shearwaters in their burrows, sometimes as much as thirty feet below our feet. All around us the little petrels were rushing out to sea again, with a great beating of wings, to avoid being found on terra firma in daylight by the black-backed gulls who regard them as a tasty morsel.

It was well after four o'clock when we staggered wearily down into the camp again. As I was Orderly Officer, one of my duties was to visit the generator attendant at some time during the night and check that he was not asleep on the job. I found Gunner Davis on the point of infusing a pot of tea and I joined him in a mug before retiring to bed. As I made my way up the Meadow to the Factor's House, I was amazed to see the hardy Mr Warwick having an early morning swim in the bay.

'WELL,' queried Doug, when David and I came down to lunch, 'did you find any of your Peach's Forked-tailed Kestrels?'

'Leach's Forked-tailed Petrels, please,' said David, giving him a pained look.

'Honestly, I can't for the life of me see what all the fuss is about, chasing after some crummy little bird at your age,' Doug wound him up.

'Some day I may write the definitive monograph on this bird and its nocturnal habits,' David prophesied. 'Just you wait.'

'You'd do just as well to make a study of the sexual life of an Ammunition Boot. In fact, that would probably be very rewarding!' Doug chortled and took a hefty slug from his beer can.

David kept a diary, writing in long-hand in a large, leather-bound volume. Occasionally he would leave it lying around in the Mess and I frequently dipped into it to see how he chronicled the day's doings. There were wonderfully evocative descriptions of the wildlife and the scenery, as well as long, reflective passages documenting his feelings about life on such a wild, desolate spot. His prose was elegant, if a trifle mannered. I hoped that one day he would publish it, but he never did. His knowledge of nature in general and of the birds in particular was prodigious. Over the years I have met other naturalists who were woefully ignorant beyond their narrow specialisation, but David was a veritable Renaissance man of the natural world. I was confident that he would become one of the great figures of natural science. He had a happy knack of infecting others with his enthusiasm. Like Willie Stewart, I could scarcely have distinguished a crow from a seagull before I went to St Kilda, but I learned a great deal from David Boddington, and by the time I left the Hebrides in 1961 I could discuss the melanistic tendencies in the tail coverts of Leach's Forked-tailed Petrel with the most avid ornithologists. I might add that David's enthusiasm would later pass to both my son and daughter. On leaving the Army, however, David settled down in general practice in deepest Herefordshire where he remains to this day. So far as I can ascertain, he has never published anything, but has been content to pursue bird-watching solely as a hobby – and there are far worse things one could do with one's spare time.

David Boddington shows the finer points of Apodemus sylvaticus hirtensis *(the fieldmouse).*

AS well as being our doctor, David was in over-all charge of catering. He was honorary Nature Warden, meteorologist, postmaster, dentist and barber. He took all of his multifarious duties very seriously and did an excellent job, except in one respect. I have to state that he was a terrible barber, although, mindful of the medieval traditions of the barber-surgeons, he tackled his tonsorial tasks with his customary panache. Shortly before we left St Kilda, Doug remarked that my hair was on the wild side and that I should set the men a good example, so I submitted to David's scissors and clippers with some trepidation. My fears were wholly justified and I was horrified when I beheld the resultant mess. Shortly after returning to Benbecula I was sent on a course at New College, Oxford and the first thing I did on arriving in the city of dreaming spires was to visit a barber to mitigate the worst of the St Kilda haircut.

'Oh my!' shrilled the barber with horror as he surveyed my head. 'I've never seen such a mess! Did you do this yourself?'

'No. As a matter of fact, my doctor did it.'

PHOTOGRAPHS 1959 TO THE PRESENT DAY

Conachair and Oiseval on Hirta rising out of early morning mist

Cleit on the edge of the world. Looking north from Conachair to Boreray. (Alastair Mackay)

Fulmars in Village Bay, St Kilda. (Alastair Mackay)

The island of Dùn and Village Bay

The Cambir, with the island of Soay beyond

High noon on the shortest day of the year, December 1959 following heavy rain

Soay sheep grazing in the Minister's Meadow. Church and Manse in the background and a Nissen hut on the right

The village from Mullach Sgar, with the islet of Levenish beyond, mid-winter 1959

A closer view of the village showing the 1830 'black houses' alternating with the houses of 1861-3. Six of the latter have now been restored by the NTS

The north-east coast of Hirta showing the Cambir and Soay stacks

The Amazon's House, a cluster of Stone Age dwellings in the Great Glen

Oiseval from Mullach Sgar showing the Army camp and the old village

Ruin of the Store House, destroyed by German submarine, May 1918. In recent years it has been fully restored by the NTS.

Looking along the barrel of the gun at the Church, 1959

The Factor's House (officers' quaters); background wreathed in mist. Note the officers' toilet block across the footpath.

Boreray, viewed from the bows of the Nature Conservancy launch Fulmar. *Stac Lii and Stac an Armuinn on the left*

Captain Bob Breadnam, RA and Captain Richard Hudson, RAMC on the jetty. Mr. Cox at the top of the steps with trousers rolled up to prevent soaking while boarding the dory.

A Spanish trawler Virgen de la Merced *winter of 1959.*

LCT 4061 beached in April 1960. Soldiers swimming and playing beach ball

Loading lobster pots on to the dory in the slipway

Medical orderly posing with RMS Rocketeer, *the most sophisticated of the Army's 'mailboats', posing outside the Medical Centre which doubled as the unit post office. Note the bilingual post office sign, in Gaelic as well as English*

Various aerial views of St Kilda and Boreray, including several in snow!

Laying out the markers for an airdrop. Private Duckworth and Captain Harry Chester RAMC

Wreck of the Beaufighter near the summit of Conachair

Wreckage of the Sunderland strewn across the Great Glen

Captain Desmond Williamson RA and orderly recovering the mail on the summit of Mullach Sgar. Mobile radars in background.

Nerve centre of the military base: the OC's office, QM stores and Medical Centre

Soldiers burning sheep, June 1960

Humping 40 gallon diesel drums, the life blood of St Kilda

Public transport, St Kilda style: soldiers in a ten-ton trailer towed by a Scammell tractor

Soay sheep crossing the road at the sharpest, steepest bend in the British Isles

Hauling a mobile radar unit by Scammell to the summit

Setting demolition charges to blow up the huge boulders that clutter the landing area in the winter storms. TA Engineers at work

Explosions in the approach to the jetty

Soldiers posing with mailbags on top.of a cleit

Bailey bridge over the Dry Burn

Summer increment under canvas on the banks of the Dry Burn, 1960

Approaching the Decca and Marconi radar stations on the summit of Mullach Mór

Examples of souvenir covers, 1971-81, along with a National Trust mailboat cover, recovered in Lewis, and an American aerogramme addressed to 'the Mayor or Governing Authority' of St Kilda, which completed its journey on the first official airdrop on August 19, 1960

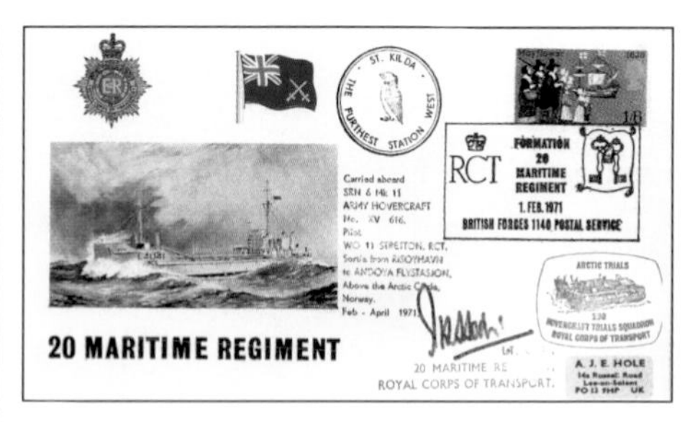

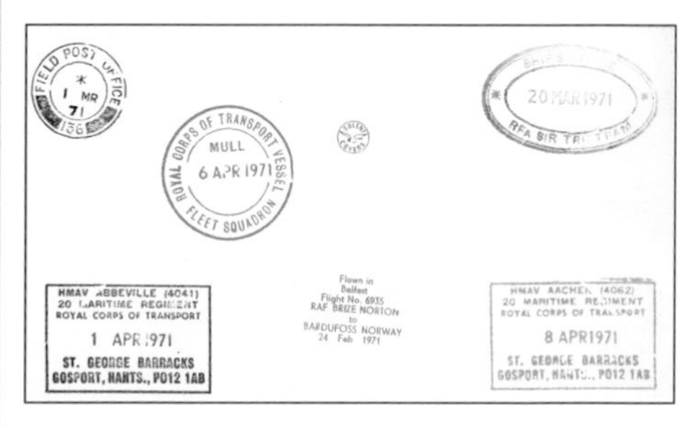

Dùn viewed across the back of a ruined house.

NTS on cliffs, David Boddington in the foreground. Mary Jackson, Peter Scola and Mary Stevens.

NTS on the summit of Conachair with Boreray in the background. Alec Warwick in the red sweater. The pole on the summit was the mounting for the coastwatcher's telescope in 1915-18.

"Steve" and a cooking pot.

THE VILLAGE TODAY

NTS work party outside no. 6.

House No 5, the former residence of Neil Ferguson the postmaster from 1906 till the Evacuation in 1930.

The most westerly pillar box in the British Isles stands at the roadside near the summit of Mullach Sgar and was erected as a spoof in 1972. For many years mail posted in it was collected once a year and put into the post at Christmas time. Nearby stood a spoof zebra crossing and a London bus-stop

8. ST KILDA SUMMER

I SPENT an idyllic month on the island that summer. Military duties were relatively light, Doug and I taking it in turns to act as Orderly Officer. In an ordinary military unit this duty might come round once every two or three months, when one was expected to be on call for a full period of 24 hours; but in St Kilda the OC was technically on duty right round the clock, seven days a week, without any leave. Apart from periodic checks on the generator shed to ensure that everything was operating smoothly, this duty entailed an inspection of every installation at least once in 24 hours, from the radar stations on the hilltops to the cookhouse and the Other Ranks' ablutions. Last thing at night, the OC made a final tour of the camp, ensuring that all unnecessary lights and appliances were switched off, but before turning in he had one last duty to perform. Some time in the previous year a soldier had been sleepwalking and apparently in this somnambulant state had walked off the edge of a cliff. Although he was not badly injured this was regarded as a very serious business indeed, and the board of inquiry which examined this incident concluded that, henceforward, it would be the duty of the OC to check that every man was nicely tucked up in his own little bed. I do not recall that this required a check on the Sergeants' Mess – after all, they were all big boys well able to look after themselves – but as I went round the darkened barrack rooms and shone a torch over each recumbent form I could never help thinking that this was just about the daftest duty ever inflicted on a commanding officer. What was to prevent a man sleepwalking after OC's rounds?

While Doug devoted all his spare time to reading or writing endless letters to his young wife (then expecting her first baby), I was keen to explore the island. The whole of Hirta fascinated me and every day I hiked over the hills and explored the Glen, in many respects the most beautiful, yet tragic, part of the island, so very different from Village Bay. Despite the efforts of the RAF fifteen years earlier, strips of duralumin sheeting and huge, jagged struts from the Sunderland flying-boat were still strewn all over the valley. These poignant reminders of the Second World War vied with the Amazon's House, a strange cluster of semi-underground structures with little rooms interconnected with a maze of tunnels. In fact there were several buildings fairly close together, believed to be the earliest human settlement on Hirta and perhaps three thousand years old.

From the flank of Conachair I descended towards Glen Bay. I scrambled over the rocks on to a promontory twice as high as Hell's Mouth in Cornwall and much more impressive, then came round a ledge on the surf-lashed rock to behold the most startling sight that Hirta could offer – a cliff face six hundred feet high which was pierced by a natural archway over a hundred feet high and almost as broad at its base. The great sea tunnel of Gob na h-Airde must have been gouged out by the sea over countless centuries and even now the torrents of white-flecked green water rushed back and forwards endlessly through the archway. A broad ledge along one side enabled us to traverse it quite easily. Over the next two years a trip to the sea tunnel opposite Soay would be one of my favourite outings. At different times of the year it was crowded with birds or a trysting place for grey seals in the mating season.

Often I would clamber to the summit of Conachair to admire the view of Boreray and the stacks, or scramble over the rocks round Village Bay, examining the pools left when the tide receded. Apart from interesting specimens of marine life, I once found a bottle with what appeared to be a message inside. On breaking open the bottle I was astonished to find a mock parchment from King Neptune, permitting the House of Guinness to launch the said bottle as a way of celebrating the bicentenary of the famous brewery, and enclosing a special bicentenary label to acquaint the finder with the hobby of 'labology'. I had heard of the St Kildans finding strange things washed up on the beach, including the Caribbean bamboo which they used to make the reeds in their hand-looms, and on one memorable occasion a buoy from New York harbour which had broken from its mooring and drifted all the way across the Atlantic on the Gulf Stream.

A subsequent enquiry of the brewery's London office elicited the fact that Guinness, founded in Dublin in 1759, had recently launched thousands of these parchment bottles off the American coast as a publicity stunt. At least two of these bottles crossed the Atlantic to find a landfall on Hirta. Checking the bar accounts I totted up the stout which had been consumed and – notwithstanding the unfortunate business with the beer cans the previous spring – I wrote to the public relations officer of the brewery claiming that enough Guinness had been consumed on St Kilda to sink the island, and was this a record worthy of inclusion in their *Book of Records*. By the next ship came several crates marked with the famous toucan logo. They contained thirty copies of the book – one for each soldier on the island – together with thirty bedside lamps (with the same toucan on the shades), several dart-boards, scorers, jugs, an assortment of glassware and sundry other items of bar equipment, including posters proclaiming in Gaelic that Guinness was good for us.

OF all the aspects of St Kilda, I was endlessly intrigued about the vestiges of human settlement. I filled numerous notebooks with sketches and later photographs of the more interesting cleits and all of the structures that predated the village of the 1830s. One of the first sites I examined in considerable detail was the Earth House, sometimes referred to as the Fairy House. This was a thirty-foot long underground chamber, roofed and lined with huge slabs. In the middle of the nineteenth century about a hundred iron and bronze axeheads had been discovered there, although the chamber had never been excavated in the archaeological sense. A good part of my time over the ensuing weeks was spent in this and Tigh Calum Mór ('Big Malcolm's House'), a circular, semi-underground structure with an intricately corbelled roof, giving the impression of a stone igloo. The stones were so neatly and intricately overlapped and balanced until they met in a single slab in the centre of the roof. Considering that no mortar was involved, it never ceased to amaze me that this structure had stood intact for centuries, perhaps thousands of years. Nearby stood one of the larger cleits with rounded gables which betrayed the fact that it had probably been a dwelling-house in the fifteenth or sixteenth centuries.

Another structure was Tobar Childa (Gaelic for Kilda's Well), although keld is a Norse word for 'well' – as in such placenames as Threlkeld, Salkeld and, of course, Roskilde in Denmark. The interior of this structure, however, contained the slimiest, most revoltingly yellow-green mess of stagnant water I had ever seen. I hoped that the St Kildans maintained it in a much better state back in the days when it was their principal source of drinking water. In 1959 the Army tapped the very same source, a deep, natural underground reservoir, by means of pipes and a pump which raised the water up into the screening plant whence it was transported by gravity to the camp. I wished that the detachment were allowed to keep a cow on the island, for I could not stomach the evaporated milk diluted with chlorinated water. In fact, it was during this sojourn on St Kilda that I gave up milk in tea or coffee.

From Alec Warwick I borrowed a pamphlet about St Kilda compiled in 1877 by John McDiarmid, Clerk to the Highland & Agricultural Society of Scotland, and spent several days making a fair copy of it on the office typewriter. Here were fascinating snippets about the islanders, and this brought to life the old ruins in which the work party were toiling every morning. They cleared the rubble and repaired the walls in the very last house of the 1830s. It had been used as a byre and outhouse in the post-1900 period and consequently the soil in it had been well-manured. In this rich loam the workers had found a large wooden rake and a scythe whose blade was paper-thin with rust.

For most of that month the weather was uncommonly fine. After a week of brilliant sunshine heavy, low-lying clouds rolled in from the west, forming woolly caps on the summits of the hills and gradually rolling down the steep slopes towards the bay. In spite of this, a rising humidity and a falling barometer, no rain fell that day or, indeed, on succeeding days either. We were now in our fourth week without rain and the Minister's Meadow was looking decidedly parched. David and I went up to the Gap between Oiseval and Conachair one afternoon and anxiously inspected the water situation. The Gap was formed at the end of the last Ice Age by a glacier scooping its way out of the surrounding hills. Its rounded sides were covered with screes and its flat bottom was dotted with huge grotesque rocks deposited by the ice. Down the middle ran a dried-up shingly water-course, and here David (by what scientific means I knew not) could judge how bad the water situation would be in the wells farther down.

There were four enormous drystone sheep-folds in this moraine valley; but when they were used is a mystery, for even as far back as the 1690s, when Martin Martin wrote his account, the St Kildans never herded their sheep and let them roam around at will. David concluded that the water levels were dangerously low. A long discussion with Doug impelled him to contact Benbecula, a laborious business at the best of times, and recommend that it might be advisable to send out a landing craft fitted with emergency water tanks. It seemed ironic that an island which was apparently known to the Vikings as a source of water (hence its name Skilda) should run dry. It was the first time I appreciated just how much our modern civilisation depends on water, and just how profligate we are with nature's greatest treasure.

Fortunately, before an emergency supply could be shipped in, the rains came. And oh, how they came! After dinner a few days later the sky suddenly darkened and Dùn on the far side of the bay vanished behind a thick, swirling mist. Within an hour you could not see the jetty from the camp. Enveloped in thick cloud, the village area was then subjected to a torrential downpour which lasted right through the night. We remained in the relative comfort of the Mess, reading and listening to Radio Luxembourg. The work party huddled and cowered in their tents, desperately trying to keep dry. This was high summer, with the longest day of the year approaching, but a more dismal scene was hard to imagine. What must St Kilda be like in late December, on the shortest day of the year, when the sun never got above the ridge? I thought of the St Kildans, cut off from the outside world for seven months each year, and I shuddered.

The following day the rain abated slightly but kept up a steady drizzle. Despite this the weather was surprisingly mild and we continued to move around in shirt-sleeves. We were constantly soaked through, but the remarkable thing was that the warm wind dried our shirts between showers. This weather pattern was something we got used to eventually and old hands on St Kilda soon became quite oblivious to the weather and its frequent caprices. David explained that what we experienced was a 'pelagic' climate – in other words, small islands that poked their jagged heads into cloud all the time must expect the weather to change every five minutes. The only thing predictable about St Kilda's weather was that it was so damned unpredictable. While David positively revelled in it, Doug became increasingly morose. Like Willie Stewart, he had no

A National Serviceman who was a sign-writer in Civvy Street painted the interior of the Puffin Bar (later the Puff Inn). Sergeants Grant and Marsham behind the bar; Major 'Uncle Arthur' Morrall at the counter

head for heights and his world was bound by the little triangle of Factor's House, Mess and Office. His despondency was compounded by the fact that the canteen ran out of beer. Bill Ellis, on the other hand was far too absorbed in his work installing the new VHF signals equipment which would enable us to communicate by radio-telephone with the Rangehead on South Uist. In his spare time Bill took numerous photographs which he developed and printed in the former ammunition store. One of his better efforts was a panorama of Village Bay, a sequence of frames which, when joined together, gave a completely circular view of our little world.

The one bright moment in this unseasonable gloom was an invitation to attend a party in one of the larger cleits adjoining the work party camp. Each of us officers received an invitation, beautifully hand-written on cards bearing the portrait of a puffin: 'You are most cordially invited to spend a few hours in the only – and most exclusively – inhabited Hirta cleit, from 2000hrs this evening. Refreshments by kind permission of yourselves. NB: Strictly no swimming before 0400hrs.'

At eight o'clock prompt, the four of us made our way up to the tented camp where the party was in full swing. One of the nearby cleits had been renovated for the occasion. It was a fairly large one – about twelve feet long and slightly over seven feet high – but to enter one had to go through a hole three feet square and then down four large, uneven steps. But what a transformation inside. The work party had suspended their customary labours on the 1830 house and lavished all their skill on the cleit. Two chandeliers, cunningly fashioned from spars of driftwood with candles stuck in tobacco-tin lids, hung from the ceiling and provided the main illumination, augmented by other candles on ledges all round the walls and reminding me of a religious shrine. The interior was decorated with several vases (or should I say tin cans) filled with golden irises and primroses which grew in great profusion along the banks of the streams. Several posters, drawn or painted and stuck to the drystone walls with sticking plaster, provided the appropriate decoration.

Seating was provided by two long benches, formerly pews filched from the church and now cushioned with Army blankets, which ran along the walls. At the far end of the cleit was a low table stacked high with liquid refreshments, and under the benches were plates of savouries, sticky Scottish tablet, sausages on sticks and all the usual paraphernalia of a cocktail party. The party was a true Highland ceilidh in which, over the course of five hours, we did our party pieces, cracked jokes and sang songs, between tucking into the trifle and jelly, and quaffing vast quantities of (David) Boddington Special Brew – a mixture of port, orange squash, golden syrup and medical alcohol! All the while we did our best to avoid the streams of hot candle-grease which shot frequently and disconcertingly from the chandeliers in all directions. Corporal Coghlin, the cook, had baked a birthday cake and after Mary blew out her candles we drank her health in tin mugs. The party broke up some time after one o'clock. Needless to say, Bill Ellis made a complete photographic record. Considering that the candle-lit interior was not of the brightest, and he forgot to remove a cloud filter from his camera, the results came out surprisingly well.

Some of the lads whooping it up in the Puffin Bar on a Saturday night. Note the cans of Wee Willie, a very popular beverage on St Kilda in the late 1950s

Sunday mornings were a time of rest and long lie-ins. After a late breakfast I sauntered across to the Medical Centre where David was already hard at work on a model of St Kilda on the scale of six inches to the mile. For the past seven months he had been labouring on this plasticine masterpiece, continually refining the details. When he tired of this self-imposed task he would turn to the more congenial exercise of revising and up-dating his share portfolio. It was my introduction to the world of high finance, and as he explained the intricacies of working out the exact state of his fortune I mentally questioned yet again what he was doing in the medical profession, let alone ministering to a bunch of soldiers in such a god-forsaken spot.

One evening we invited the work party to the Other Ranks' Mess Room for a party which included contests at darts, table-tennis and billiards: the National Trust for Scotland versus the Army. Surprisingly, the NTS beat the Army hands down, but the soldiers were not the least downhearted as they milled around the three girls and vied with each other for their attention. Alec Warwick whipped Sergeant Tomes, the reigning St Kilda indoor sports champion, in three straight wins at billiards, three-ball and snooker. Even Doug, who had been getting more and more downcast as the days dragged by, cheered up quite a bit in the company of the young ladies. His mood lightened when a signal came one day to say that the *Mull* would soon be on its way.

The return of the *Maighdean Hearrach* was also imminent as the work party's fortnight drew to a close. Another big party was planned to coincide with the arrival of the second group of volunteers on the Thursday, which just happened to be Gunner Wathall's twenty-first birthday. He was our mess steward and the garrison comedian, a great favourite with all the men. It was noticed that beer consumption had dropped sharply that week, as stocks were running low. Then Doug learned from Sergeant Court that the men were deliberately abstaining in order to have a really good piss-up to celebrate Wathall's coming of age – just in case the *Mull* (with a promised consignment of beer) failed to arrive in time.

Around 11.30 on Tuesday night, however, a howling wind suddenly got up. I was awakened by the rattling of the windows, but that was nothing. In the morning we discovered that one of the NTS tents had blown away about 5am, much to the discomfiture of the work party who spent the rest of the night trying to retrieve it from the slopes of Mullach Bi. Fortunately it had been dry at the time, but by the middle of the following morning the force eight gale was accompanied by heavy showers which lashed down with terrifying suddenness at irregular intervals.

About ten o'clock a small seine-drifter chugged groggily into the bay and anchored off Dùn. Through David's telescope I identified her as the *Swiftsure* of Lossiemouth, soon joined by her sister ship, the *Spinaway*, and shortly after mid-day a third drifter, the *Fair Wren*, came in as well. They remained there till the following day, riding out the storm, bobbing up and down, pitching and yawing in the waves. If the water in the bay was decidedly choppy, the full force of the storm was venting itself on the far side of Dùn and now and again a column of spray would shoot up over the jagged ridge, a startling sight. The boat crews made no attempt to come ashore, and we thought it wiser not to risk one of our precious dories on a trip out to them; so there they lay, within sight of warmth and civilisation, but bobbing uncomfortably in a storm-tossed sea. We wondered whether they might have some freshly caught fish going a-begging, but through the telescope we could see their nets and gear neatly stowed on otherwise empty decks, obviously on their way to the fishing grounds.

Then we got a signal to say that the *Mull* was storm-bound at Rhu near Helensburgh on the Firth of Clyde and nowhere near the Hebrides, far less St Kilda. A landing craft might come out at the weekend, but everything would depend on this awful weather abating, and as we stared despondently out of the rain-lashed window that seemed extremely remote. Moreover, the *Maighdean Hearrach* could not possibly attempt the trip in such a storm. I stared out of the window at the hideous aspect of Dùn. Towards the extremity of that island there is a tunnel which runs right through from side to side. Today the sea was blasting through it with such violence that columns of water were shooting straight out of the cliff face, high into the air, every few seconds. It was like some gigantic artery sending out enormous gouts of blood with every heartbeat. Beyond the point of Dùn, the open ocean was churned into demented waves, great white-crested columns of water which obscured the uneven horizon, conveying the disquieting impression that Hirta itself had broken free of its moorings and was afloat.

'This cannot last,' said Doug morosely; but as if to prove him wrong, the wind suddenly rose another notch or two and the wailing rose several decibels. By now David estimated that it was above force ten, almost as bad as anything he had experienced the previous winter.

'The worst storm we had,' said David in his matter-of-fact way, 'occurred on the 27th of December. Force twelve it was, a full-blown, rip-roaring hurricane. It lashed us for fully three hours. What a sight that was! You can still see the end of Dùn, right? Well it was completely enveloped in spray, although it's 320 feet high. You have to live in a place like this to appreciate the fury and violence of nature at her worst.'

We must have been at the very edge of the storm, for when we awoke the following morning the sky was bright and clear and the wind had dropped to a stiff breeze. By mid-afternoon the three drifters had departed, their place being taken by two large Norwegian trawlers, painted bright green over all. Three of our NCOs, Denham, Pare and Harris, launched a dory and went across the bay and were very cordially received aboard the *Reform* (registered at Stavanger). Over coffee and little cakes the skipper told them that they had taken shelter because the forecast on Norwegian radio was for severe south-westerly gales. David, on the other hand, maintained that the BBC's shipping forecast was for fine weather with an anti-cyclone fairly stationery over South Iceland. Shipping forecasts were probably the most important things we listened to on the radio and the weather was an endless topic of conversation.

Mary Stevens (the future Mrs Scola) launching the Army's first tin can mail from the Point of Coll, June 1959

Two of David's traps had been sprung overnight and contained a pregnant female and a young buck who had made a neat little nest out of the grass in the trap and was fast asleep when David came to clip his toenails. They were lovely creatures, with enormous black eyes and silky dark brown fur. The members of the work party came up and took several photographs of me holding the female on the palm of my hand. They had spent the day tidying up houses 9 and 13 and among the debris had found a cut-throat razor, an enamel candle-holder (with stump of candle still intact), several fish-hooks, a file for cutting glass, a roll of late-Victorian floral wallpaper and three leather straps from somebody's trouser-braces.

Doug and I climbed Mullach Geal to inspect the radar beacon for any damage it might have sustained during the storm. On the way back I stumbled across an instrument from the cockpit of the Sunderland. I must have lost it in one of my many moves some years later, but fortunately I made a sketch of it in my diary at the time. It had a horseshoe dial upper left with a pointer below. A little plate bore the inscription:

> IMPORTANT
>
> Spacing dial must be set when pointer is at H.
>
> Pointer must be rewound slowly.

Towards the right of the panel was a small spring-loaded button, and below this was an inner dial marked on one side in MPH from 100 to 350. It was surrounded by a fixed outer band marked on one side in feet from 20 to 70, and on the other in seconds from 45 to zero. I had never come across anything like this in my own flying experience and wondered whether it was some sort of bomb-aiming device, the button being perhaps the one which released the bombs. I was rather surprised to find it, as I assumed that all instruments and gadgetry would have been removed from the scene of the crash for the subsequent court of inquiry.

With the weather improving, we decided to launch a St Kilda mailboat. In my diary I commented that this must surely be the most scientifically constructed mailboat to leave the island, but it paled into insignificance beside the extraordinarily elaborate contraptions produced in later years, although whether they were any more efficient remains a moot point. On the occasion of this, the Army's first attempt to emulate the St Kildan method of communicating with the outside world by relying on the Gulf Stream, the letters were put in polythene bags inflated and hermetically sealed. They were then stuffed into a stout hard-tack biscuit tin, the lid of which was sealed with soldering metal. Two large flat stones were put in the bottom of the tin to act as ballast, and a stout little mast with a Puffin flag was lashed to the can. The sides were inscribed in luminous red paint: ST KILDA MAIL – PLEASE OPEN. It contained sixteen letters in all and was launched at 7.15pm, half an hour after the tide had turned, from the Point of Coll on the rocks below the base of Oiseval where, traditionally, Finlay McQueen had set his sheep's bladder, wooden-hulled toy boats adrift sixty or seventy years earlier. We watched the tide bear the tin can steadily away, out of the bay and round to the north-east. It was recovered on the beach near Doune Carloway on the west coast of Lewis eleven days later and the letters posted at Stornoway, none the worse of their unconventional voyage. A photograph of the tin can itself graced a story about it in the *Stornoway Gazette*. Subsequently the story was picked up by the *Scottish Daily Express* which expanded it under the heading 'Rocketmen's Mail Goes Faster by Tin Can'.

Actually, by this time there had been a decided (if temporary) improvement in our communications with the outside world, thanks to the efforts of Bill Ellis installing the new VHF equipment. By this means I was able to send off the first telegram from St Kilda, via Benbecula, to Boots the Chemists in Glasgow, ordering photographic materials for our darkroom. Even more remarkable was the reply, only two hours later, querying the sizes of the paper required. A confirmatory copy arrived from Nunton, Benbecula a fortnight later.

Despite the heavy rain our drought was as bad as ever. In fact the water situation was now so critical that water was only to be used for drinking. Baths were strictly forbidden and washing reduced to the bare minimum. As the barometer rose again, our hearts sank at the prospect of another prolonged spell of fine weather.

One day David and I, with his medical orderly Private Rhodes and Corporal Riley, R.Sigs, took advantage of the good weather to climb to the top of the ridge to carry out some work on the radar beacon, while Doug and his party were at the Decca radar station. Riley had to shin up a twenty-foot pole swaying in the wind and remove the radar cone, then replace it again, while Doug watched the process on the radar screen. The exercise was highly successful, proving that the beacons and scanners were in perfect working order. On the way back to camp David and I took a long detour in search of the probable site of one of the island's three ancient churches. One side-effect of the drought was the emergence of crop-markings – dry patches of vegetation

The radar stations on the summit of Mullach Sgar viewed from a passing aircraft

The interior of the radar station; Sergeant Tomes is the one with the dark hair, Captain B.K. 'Will' Warner is the chap with the lighter hair in the foreground.

where they barely concealed a stone structure. We fancied that we had spotted a regular pattern from the ridge, but as we got closer it became impossible to distinguish one dry patch from another. The trouble was that, as Martin Martin had shrewdly observed 260 years earlier, the whole island was one hard rock. Giving up this quest as hopeless, David spent the rest of the day building a hide close to an oystercatcher's nest and was rewarded with some fine photographs of the hen incubating her eggs. I improved the shining hour by sun-bathing behind the Factor's House, frantically revising for a forthcoming exam.

In the evening Mary and I climbed to the summit of Oiseval with the express purpose of scanning the sea for any signs of the *Maighdean Hearrach* which was expected. After a fruitless search of the sea with the telescope – there was no sign of the boat although visibility was perfect and we could clearly make out the Sound of Harris, North Uist, Ruaival on Benbecula, Hecla, Ben More and other hills of South Uist and even Heaval on far-off Barra – we came down again, to discover that the little fishing-boat had already arrived and was now disembarking her passengers. She had been circumnavigating the islands while we were up on Oiseval, and had slipped into the bay while we were looking out to sea. Inevitably I took quite a bit of ribbing about being too pre-occupied to notice the boat; a year later, when Mary and I announced our engagement, David wrote to me:

I now quote from an ancient, often criticised, archaic journal which lies in front of me... Jim and Mary had gone for a walk and by 19.20 had not returned. They had previously announced that the purpose of the walk was to look for the boat, Aesop's fables are more credible... So it seems that courting fulmars on a Thursday evening can even influence the minds of boat seekers! How you nearly missed the boat then, even if you are apparently ready now. May I remind you that 'A ship is sooner rigged by far than a gentlewoman made ready'.

The second work party had had a terrible crossing and staggered ashore and straight into their sleeping-bags, deeply fatigued, soaked to the skin and suffering the effects of sea-sickness. They had left Tarbert, Harris at 6am and endured a terrifying thirteen-hour voyage, pitched and thrown about all day long without respite and nowhere to lie down or protect themselves from the spray. Originally the plan had been for the boat to remain in the bay overnight and embark the first party in the morning; but the skipper announced that they would leave almost immediately as a south-westerly gale was forecast. There was a frantic bout of packing but at last Alec and his party were down on the jetty with their bits and pieces, looking remarkably like the scene of August 1930 when the St Kildans were evacuated. We four officers were on hand to wish them bon voyage; after hurried handshakes all round they clambered into their rowing boat. At eight o'clock the diminutive fishing-boat weighed anchor and headed out of the bay into the uncertainty of the Atlantic.

Wathall's birthday party that evening was an all-military affair, the first party having left and the second dead to the world. Wathall was a veteran of the RAF occupation, one of the handful of soldiers who had been on St Kilda since the previous summer. Sandwiches of lobster and crab were neatly laid out on trays, and for liquid refreshment there was port, whisky and rum (the beer having run out two days earlier). Wathall came through to the Officers' Mess halfway through the proceedings and we four stood and drank his health and wished him luck now that he was officially a man. In truth there was actually precious little of the 'hard stuff' either so as birthday parties went it was a pretty decorous affair and ended well before midnight.

The following day I put in almost thirteen hours final cramming for my exam, interrupted only by a signal from Major McGregor regarding details of men and stores coming out by LCT. On the subject of signals, a very strange telegram was relayed from Stockholm that afternoon, via Nunton. Addressed simply to 'Boddington, St Kilda, Atlantic Ocean – telegram at sender's risk' it contained birthday greetings from Klas Eriksson, a Swedish ornithologist whom David had met at Skokholm, Pembrokeshire two summers previously. It had been despatched three days earlier but the Swedish telegraph service had been doubtful as to the correct method of sending a telegram to St Kilda, if indeed that were possible at all.

One of the Norwegian trawlers was still in the bay that evening, the other one having disappeared at dawn, and Doug was getting rather apprehensive about it and not a little suspicious at its prolonged stay. Accordingly the dory was launched and I, with four lusty oarsmen (our outboard motor having packed up) set out on the perilous task of boarding her to find out the reason for her delay. At Doug's insistence I was carrying a side-arm and feeling very self-conscious about the cumbersome revolver on my hip. Once afloat, we discovered that a heavy sea was running and our little boat rose and fell awkwardly as the great Atlantic rollers hit her on her port bow. Even launching the dory proved a very hazardous operation during which we shipped a considerable amount of water. After a twenty-minute delay we succeeded in clambering aboard and pulled away from the jetty. Fully half an hour elapsed before we passed the buoy and veered round to approach the trawler. It was very exhilarating as we lurched forward on the crest of a wave and pitched downwards into a trough, the spray whipping our faces. I held the tiller to keep the dory headed into the wind and called the strokes to the oarsmen. Eventually we came alongside the trawler and her crew made our dory fast. One by one we climbed over the gunwhale, to be greeted with apprehensive stares. Doubtless the appearance of an officer (and an armed one at that) conveyed the impression that this was not just a social call. I addressed one of the crew in English and asked to see the captain, but when I got a blank look I spoke to him in Norwegian (a relic of a student summer job in Scandinavia) which got an immediate response. I was ushered up an iron ladder, through a hatchway and on to the bridge. In the wheel-house I met a stocky, fair-haired man, the skipper, who spoke no English. The engineer had been called in to interpret and he spoke a peculiar brand of English ('I were mit Royal Navy i' last war').

On being asked why they were still in the bay, they said that they were expecting a south-westerly gale. I pointed out that they had been expecting that weather two days earlier and anyway the other Norwegian ship had left. They replied that they had salting and deep-freezing gear and had to process their catch at sea; thus they required at least ten days' run of clear weather, whereas the other ship was just an ordinary trawler. I then warned them that a 'warship' was coming into the bay some time early in the morning and the trawler would be in the way, so they would have to move round to Glen Bay on the other side of the island. They promised to move out as soon as possible. Actually I was more worried about them seeing the LCT unload, in view of certain large and very sensitive pieces of radar equipment which would come trundling down the ramp in the morning. I noticed the ultra-modern equipment on this vessel: her highly sophisticated radar, powerful transmitter and sounding device for detecting shoals of fish. She was the *Skallagrim* from Maløy, one of the islands off the north-west coast of Norway.

The return journey was an absolute nightmare. In the hour and a half since we had left the jetty the wind had risen considerably and the tide was flowing. Consequently we got to the buoy, a hundred yards offshore in fifteen minutes, but then overshot it and missed the stout rope along which we should have pulled the dory in to the jetty. We were now running the risk of being hurled on to the rocks by gigantic breakers and only a superhuman effort of desperate rowing pulled the dory round towards the jetty again. I made a mental note never to attempt such a foolhardy trip again without an outboard engine. God knows how the St Kildans managed, with their clumsy rowing-boat.

We got a rope ashore to Doug who was standing anxiously on the jetty, and he made it fast to a stanchion; but before any of us could get on to the iron rungs at the side of the jetty we were overwhelmed by an enormous wave, and then another and another, which left us gasping, drenched and sprawling on the bottom of the boat in a tangle of bodies, arms and legs. This was my baptism, and it left me with a healthy respect for the unpredictable violence of the sea. We jumped into the water before the dory was totally swamped and guided her round the jetty and into the slipway where other soldiers were now on hand to haul her up on rollers. Water restrictions were momentarily relaxed as Doug ordered hot baths and a generous tot of rum all round. I swotted for a couple of hours before turning in for the night. The LCT was due to arrive at 0230 hours and off-load at dawn (4am), so Doug would be up all night with the unloading party. The Atlantic and the forces of nature had evidently never heard of the Army's 44-hour week.

Needless to say, all our plans and preparations were confounded by the weather. The LCT *Arromanches* arrived at 3am but a rip-snorter of a storm had suddenly blown up and the ship did no more than poke her nose into the bay. Beaching was impossible in such atrocious weather. Even to attempt to anchor in the bay would be extremely dangerous with the wind howling in from the south-east. During later stints on St Kilda I frequently saw vessels at anchor in the bay in calm weather, hastily weighing anchor as a south-easterly sprang up. In fact three vessels were caught on a lee shore in such conditions and were wrecked on the boulders of the storm beach. The landing craft steamed round to Glen Bay and rode out the storm in comparative shelter. I could appreciate the frustration of the men on board, so close to the island yet unable to land, for the Glen Bay was beset with treacherous reefs and a high cliff which only a skilled cragsman could have negotiated. Aboard were Colonel Ronnie Winfield from the School of Artillery (in over-all command of the Range during the missile-firing) and two Signals officers, along with a very expensive Mobile Radar 4 Mk VII, the accumulated mail and the long-awaited beer.

We were up till 4am the following night due to the pandemonium of trying to get the LCT into Village Bay. To make matters worse, the *Skallagrim* was still there, but not showing her lights, so that she was almost rammed by *Arromanches* in the thick dawn mist. We fired three rockets to warn the trawler which upped anchor and steamed out of the bay as if the hounds of hell were behind her. As luck would have it, the landing craft was unable to anchor in the bay, owing to yet another caprice of the weather. So she sailed off for a second night in Glen Bay...

I grabbed a few hours sleep before reporting at the Medical Centre at 9am to sit my exam. Already preparing for my return to Civvy Street, I decided to practice what I preached and had therefore embarked on a correspondence course of study set by the Chartered Institute of Secretaries. I had some half-baked notion that a professional qualification which included some accountancy and law as well as company secretarial practice might come in useful should I enter the world of commerce. Normally I would have had to travel to Glasgow or Edinburgh to take the ACIS examination at an approved centre, but because of the exigencies of military duties I had been granted a special dispensation to take the examination on St Kilda, provided that I was properly invigilated by a university graduate. I still have my exam admission ticket whereon was stated my candidate's number (Hebrides 1) and the venue as the Medical Centre, St Kilda. David supervised my three-hour examination very conscientiously, nay rigorously, while I sat at a desk in the tiny hospital ward, distracted only by the bleating of the sheep and the cries of the sea-birds outside. The paper turned out to be much easier than I had expected and I tackled all of the questions. In due course I passed with flying colours and Colonel Cooper tipped off the *Daily Telegraph* which made quite a story out of the first examination ever taken on this remote island.

It was almost midnight before *Arromanches* came into the bay and had to run straight up on to the beach. As high tide was due at 3.30am we had barely three hours to unload, resulting in some furiously concentrated work for everyone. While Doug showed the colonel over the new radar installations and Bill Ellis handed over the new VHF link-up to Alan Earl, I sorted the incoming correspondence and despatched replies by return. My life-long habit of dealing promptly and rapidly with letters was thus inculcated during these hectic visits of ships at St Kilda.

As dawn broke the landing craft departed with the colonel and all three Signals officers. The Mess was now down to three of us, plus Dr David Jenkins from the Nature Conservancy Council, a 'hairyologist' as Colonel Cooper put it, on the assumption that visiting scientists were invariably bearded and, of course, they all had an 'ology'. He was, in fact, clean shaven, but in truth he was an ornithologist, intent on spending a fortnight doing some research into the snipe which had begun breeding on St Kilda in recent years.

A letter which I had written to *Stamp Collecting* about the new St Kilda postmark had duly appeared in the issue of 2 June and two complimentary copies of the magazine were in the mail – along with several sacks of mail from philatelists from all over the British Isles with requests for specimens of the postmark. Some had sent as many as a dozen stamped addressed envelopes to be postmarked, and I feared that Neil Campbell, the postmaster at Nunton, would have a fit when he got all this lot to frank. Successive ships, in fact, brought us a deluge of mail from every part of the world.

On Tuesday 9 June 1959 I made history – the first telephone call to the outside world from St Kilda. For the previous fortnight we had been able to speak to the Rangehead by VHF radio-telephone but from this morning the new telephone exchange at West Geirinish on South Uist enabled us to link up with the GPO lines. I made the cardinal mistake of telephoning Major Simmons, RAEC, the GSO II at Scottish Command Headquarters, Edinburgh to inform him that I was about to submit a lengthy report on the educational, welfare and recreational amenities of St Kilda, together with my recommendations for improving them. He was very surprised to hear me as he had been told that I was incommunicado on St Kilda. When I told him that I was, he was too flabbergasted to ask the pertinent question, what was I actually doing out there. It would be a very different matter a few months later when I was in the same place but in a rather unusual situation.

The following day Doug and I spent the entire morning dealing with administrative matters arising from the ship's visit and were just coming out of the office for lunch when we heard an unusual noise droning above the normal hum of the generators. Then suddenly, round the flank of Ruaival, came a Shackleton aircraft flying quite low. She rounded the point of Dùn, banked sharply and came in towards the village at less than a thousand feet. I could clearly make out the number 204 painted in red on her fuselage and WR 961 on the underside of her wings. She flew overhead, climbed over Am Blaid and re-appeared five minutes later round Oiseval and repeated the process. In all, she flew over us, from every angle, five times before heading out to sea and back to Ballykelly in Northern Ireland whence she had come. All work ceased and everyone dashed out to wave to the aircrew – quite an event.

Later in the day I had a look round the village. The new work party seemed to have a very different approach from the first group. Under Alec Warwick, the National Trust's Master of Works, they had concentrated on repairs to walls and gables to prevent further damage. The second group, however, had a blitz on the 1860s houses and 'tidied' them up. Huge bonfires of rubbish smoked all week as the contents of the cottages were ruthlessly cleared out. By the end of the fortnight the houses were completely bare inside, just as houses do when tenants leave and before the next crowd moves in. I was dismayed at this operation. The volunteers reminded me of the citizens of Berlin clearing up the rubble at the end of the war, vigorously applying rakes, picks and shovels where a true archaeologist would have worked slowly with a small brush and trowel. Not surprisingly the only 'finds' were iron fireplaces, a blacksmith's anvil, the cast-iron wheel of a barrow and other large, solid objects of that nature.

I consoled myself with pottering about in House 3 which, according to Robert Atkinson who had spent some time on St Kilda in the summer of 1938, was still in a reasonable state of preservation although even then the roof was giving way. Now, one wall had collapsed, heaping the floor high with rubble and fallen masonry, preserving its contents from the over-enthusiasm of this work party. My patience was eventually rewarded by the most intriguing find yet recovered. It was a clay-pipe, the bowl absolutely intact, as well as most of the stem. The bowl was embossed with the regimental badge of the East Surrey Regiment. Now, what

NTS volunteers repairing the gable-end of one of the 1830 houses; Alec Warwick with pole on the roof.

A rear view of the houses of the St Kildans, about 1900, with cleits dotted all over the place

was that doing here, I wondered. Surely no St Kildan had served in the infantry, far less an English county regiment. It seemed more probable that one of the St Kildans, who were forever cadging tobacco off the tourists, was presented with the pipe along with a plug of baccy.

For the second work party, however, the undoubted highlight of their sojourn was the telegram sent to their leader Renee Waterston from her husband George, one of the big-wigs in the NTS. It jubilantly informed her that an osprey had successfully hatched a chick at a secret location near Boat of Garten and urged her to tune in to the BBC the following morning when this news of immense ornithological importance would be broadcast to the nation. I recall the euphoria which naturally engulfed the two Davids at this exciting news. Now, more than forty years later, ospreys are common all over the Highlands and they have even been sighted at Possil Loch on the outskirts of Glasgow, but back in June 1959 this was tremendous news indeed.

The latter part of the second party's fortnight, however, was blighted with a dense sea fog which shrouded Hirta for several days and left a pervading sense of gloomy dampness. It was quite chilling to see the thick mists rolling down from Conachair towards the bay and swirling among the ruined cottages. The mist gave way eventually to heavy rain which did nothing to dispel the gaiety of the social evening laid on by the work party. Two of the men, Hamish and Scottie, played the bagpipes and contributed largely to the success of the evening with their skirling duets which ended appropriately with Pipe Major Ross's slow march 'Leaving St Kilda' inspired by the evacuation of 1930. This party was held in a large tent and thus lacked the ambience of Mary's birthday party two weeks earlier.

Fortunately, the rain dispelled the fog and the following day was gloriously sunny again. Doug and I took advantage of the change in the weather to check the geophysical references, plotting the precise location and elevation of the radar stations for the benefit of the launch base at South Uist. This was quite a complicated trigonometrical exercise, but eventually we agreed that we could see the Flannan Isles at 83 degrees, Benbecula at 120 degrees and Barra Head at 154 degrees, with most of the Outer Hebrides in between.

I had a great ambition to land on Dùn which, though it is the nearest of the lesser islands to Hirta, was extremely difficult to land on, as its sheer, smooth sides made landings extremely dangerous. Even in the calmest weather there was always a large swell to reckon with. Just after dinner one evening, however, David decided at last that it might be possible to land, the bay being very calm with the ebbing tide. We lost no time in mustering the crew of the cutter who had intended checking their lobster pots anyway, and at 8.10pm we pushed off from the jetty. A fifteen-minute trip brought us under the cliffs of Dùn. The swell, which had been barely discernible at the jetty, now appeared really frightening as the wash rose and fell ten feet every other second.

David, perched in the bows, timed his jump nicely and leaped on all fours on to the slippery rocks. I came next and got off on the crest of the wave, but David Jenkins misjudged it, sprawled on the rocks, and was overwhelmed by a huge wave before we could haul him to safety. By now the cutter was away, and we were marooned for three hours, the crew having agreed to return at 11.15pm, at slack water when the swell would be minimal.

We set off up the steep rocks, an easy climb in our plimsolls, and came on to the grassy slopes. No sheep had been on Dùn since 1930 and the ungrazed land was waist high with rank vegetation into which we sank at every step. When we reached the ridge we were on bare rock again and could move more easily; but soon we ran into the fulmar colonies and had to run the gauntlet of nesting birds which squirted the most obnoxious oil at us. At one point I was caught in the crossfire of four birds. The worst of it was that, the terrified bird, having expelled about half a pint of vile, stinking oil, then attacks a second time by giving you the contents of its stomach for good measure. Not for nothing is the fulmar known as the skunk of seabirds. I had to admire the tenacity and fortitude of David Boddington who was vomited on four times by one bird as he struggled to put a ring on its leg.

The St Kildans used to catch the birds with a long pole which had a wire running noose at the end. This they slipped round the bird's neck and then strangled it by yanking it up into the air. David tried a gentler variation of this method of catching fulmars, using a twelve-foot bamboo pole for the first time. He snared seven birds which he ringed and then released, none the worse of their ordeal.

Past the fulmar colonies we came on to what appeared to be firm, grassy slopes; but countless thousands of puffins had decided to nest there, with the result that the entire hillside was honeycombed with their burrows and it was quite nightmarish treading gingerly along, with the ground crumbling under one's feet as angry puffins squawked around our ankles and flapped out around our legs. It was our intention to push on towards the very point of Dùn to examine the drystone structure at the end, marked 'Castle' in Gothic script on the Ordnance Survey map. It might have been a Viking outpost or a Pictish fort, or even of much earlier vintage; no one knew for certain, for it had never been properly examined. To the St Kildans it was known as *Dùn Fhir Bolg* – the fort of the pygmies. Fewer than a dozen people who had not been born on Hirta had ever visited this strange island, far less had the chance to inspect the ramparts at its extremity. Only one person had been twice on Dùn and that was David Boddington, but this was likely to be his last, as he was due to leave St Kilda for good in eight weeks' time. Over the two ensuing summers, however, I visited Dùn several times, on one memorable occasion taking a party of American soldiers; and nowadays it is an easy task, facilitated by chains and handrails that enable the more agile and adventurous to cross the narrow Passage from Ruaival on Hirta at low spring tides.

On this occasion, however, the ground was so heavily riddled with angry puffins that we were forced to give up trying to reach the fort. Instead we clambered upwards to Am Bioda Mór, the highest pinnacle, at an altitude of 600 feet above sea level. Once there, we got an astounding view of the other side of the island which does not drop sheer into the ocean so much as slant inwards, so that on looking over the edge we could not see any rocks at all, only the deep blue-green Atlantic – a most alarming prospect if you had no head for heights.

On the way down we came across an interesting mass of huge stones methodically built up into a flat-topped pyramid. This was not the Altar which was marked on the map (the so-called Altar, in fact, turned out to be nothing more than a large rocky outcrop on the ridge, roughly resembling an altar but of no human significance whatsoever). This strange structure seemed to have no purpose. Superficially it resembled a cleit but was completely solid. There are, in fact, no cleits as such on this island.

By eleven o'clock we were scrambling and slithering over the rocks to keep our appointment with the cutter. The tide was rising by the time we reached the shore, and getting aboard our little boat was a nasty business, involving a drenching and several bruises apiece before we tumbled to the bottom of the cutter. The lads had got three large lobsters and a dozen crabs in their pots, so everyone felt satisfied with a good night's work. When we returned to the Mess we were oblivious to the awful stench which permeated our clothes, but poor Doug had to stand with his head stuck out of the window. I had a long hot soak in the bath before going to bed to get rid of the stink of fulmar oil; but the old pair of flannels, shirt and sweater I had worn were beyond redemption and had to be consigned to a bonfire.

The *Maighdean Hearrach* arrived about 4.30pm one afternoon and without further ado the work party hurried aboard and sailed off without any warning. They neglected to scavenge their camp-site, return their bedding to the Army store or fill in their grease-pits, far less take their leave in a civilised manner. They left their camp-site in a shocking mess, so much so that David Jenkins fired off a stiff complaint to Morton Boyd about their conduct during their sojourn. This left a rather sorry impression, all the more regrettable as the first work party were paragons by comparison. Poor Mrs Waterston seemed to have little or no control over her party who were altogether of a different stamp from the first party.

As our month on St Kilda drew to a close Doug and I completed the radar survey and tidied up the administrative details for the hand-over to Will Warner on his return from leave. In the afternoon I made a farewell tour round the deserted village and finished off a watercolour sketch of the camp, with Dùn in the background. When LCT 4062 arrived the following morning the bay was like a mill-pond and after early mist had burned off it proved to be a day of absolutely perfect weather. The return voyage to South Uist via the Sound of Harris was, indeed, just like the Aegean cruise Bob Allday had described and Hirta and Boreray remained in sight until we entered the Sound of Harris. Already I was overcome with St Kildaitis, a strange affliction akin to homesickness which assails many visitors to the island. Noting my downcast expression, Doug enquired if I was feeling all right; but when I explained the reason he snorted, 'You must be mad. I hope to God I never set eyes on that place again!'

9. OFF AND ON THE ISLAND

I VISITED St Kilda early in July and August 1959, on both occasions spending a week there at a period when landing craft were calling relatively frequently. These visits were ostensibly on educational duties, but these consisted largely of ensuring supplies of knitting wool, crochet tools, embroidery and rug-making kits, for suddenly a craze for textile pastimes swept through the detachment. It was quite comical to see the 'brutal and licentious soldiery' totally absorbed in threading thrums through canvas or knitting shapeless sweaters. A few of the more independent spirits ordered kits for painting by numbers. Photography was another hobby that was ardently pursued. The scenery and wildlife of St Kilda simply cried out 'Snap me!' and as there was an endless supply of 35mm black and white film (used in the radar stations), it was a simple matter to cut oneself off a strip of film and load a cassette. The dark room in the old naval powder magazine must have been in operation right round the clock. Apart from ensuring that the men were kept fully occupied in such wholesome recreations, I organised correspondence courses for several of the technicians, keen to improve their qualifications before returning to civilian life, and this also entailed supervising them and encouraging them to stick at it. Of all the methods of acquiring an education – full-time, part-time (evening classes) and by correspondence course – the last-named was by far the hardest. Benbecula had too many distractions, but St Kilda positively encouraged study.

An important part of my educational duties was to ensure that both Benbecula and St Kilda were kept well stocked with books. Paperbacks were non-accountable and, in practice, the men could do what they liked with them. On one memorable occasion eyebrows were raised when I indented for thirty copies of the Penguin edition of *Lady Chatterley's Lover* which had just been published and was already hitting the headlines. Hardbacks were sent out to us by Mary Hutcheson, the Command Librarian in Edinburgh, and had to be returned after three months when a fresh supply would be despatched. Once a consignment of books was returned from St Kilda in the cargo-hold of the *Mull*, along with a number of supposedly empty diesel drums, but during a tempestuous voyage drums and books rolled around together and the latter became badly soiled and had to be written off.

I also dealt with an outfit in leafy Buckinghamshire which rejoiced in the name of the Army Kinema Corporation. Presumably the archaic spelling was deliberately chosen to avoid a confusion of the AKC with the Army Catering Corps (which was jocularly referred to as the Ashington Coal Company). The films supplied to St Kilda were as archaic as the AKC's title. On one occasion I wrote to the AKC saying that if they could only spare their very oldest films for the hazardous voyage to and from St Kilda, why could we not have some of the real old classics, such as *Hell's Angels* and *All Quiet on the Western Front*? But more often than not, what we actually got were prewar British comedies and B-feature thrillers. In keeping with the quaintness of our movies, our film-shows were styled the Puffin Bioscope.

At Benbecula I was also responsible for St Kilda's requirements, both general and personal. I would get signals from the island requesting all sorts of odd personal items, from tortoiseshell spectacle arms to a rubber idler pulley for a Phillips Stella three-speed automatic record player. One soldier developed a passion for Scotch eggs and ordered this dubious delicacy by the dozen; had I not been certain of his sex I would have supposed that this peculiar craving arose because of pregnancy! I would write to the various firms on the mainland to have these articles sent to the island direct. The bills were sent to Benbecula and debited against individual soldiers' pay or the detachment's imprest account, whichever was applicable.

In the first operational year of the Rocket Range I liaised with Bill McStay, the Public Relations Officer at Scottish Command, as well as the British Army News Unit and *Soldier* magazine direct, organising trips for selected journalists and invariably accompanying them when they journeyed out to St Kilda. As the unit strength built up and the firing of the first missiles became imminent, life became more and more hectic.

One form of light relief in this period came from an unexpected quarter. In my first year at university I had been a cadet pilot in the air squadron (RAFVR). I went solo after eight hours and would probably have become a competent flier eventually, but in September 1955 I came in to land at Scone aerodrome one evening, approaching the field on the heading I had been given by the control tower but oblivious to the fact that the wind had suddenly changed direction by almost ninety degrees. Thus, although I thought I was moving forward, I was actually crabbing sideways. As a result, my starboard wingtip struck a fence post at 100mph and an altitude of five feet. The impact ripped off the wingtip, somersaulted the Chipmunk a couple of times, detached the starboard wing, telescoped the fuselage somewhat and left me pointing in the opposite direction with the aircraft tilted over on its side. Fortunately for me, I had had the presence of mind to close the fuel cock and flick off the switches, so the plane did not burst into flames and I escaped with little more than severe bruising.

The subsequent board of inquiry concluded that the accident was largely due to pilot error (I should have checked the wind-sock before making my final approach) which explains why I ended up in the Army and not the RAF. As luck would have it, however, the Rocket Range had a contract with Airworks of Perth which sent an Airspeed Consul, a twin-engined aircraft, to Benbecula twice a week, to stooge around the sky between the Rangehead and St Kilda and give the radar technicians practice in tracking, although there was a world of difference between an elderly aeroplane, trundling around at 120 knots and a supersonic missile. I was familiar with the pilots who performed this task. Although civilians, they were all ex-RAF types and, indeed, Bob Critchley, a recently retired squadron leader, had been one of my flying instructors a few years previously. The Airworks contract began early in May 1959 and from the outset I flew in the Consul, sitting in the co-pilot's seat and getting some useful (but quite unofficial) instruction in flying a twin-engined job with variable pitch propellers and retractable undercarriage – a big step up from the Chipmunk trainer I had been used to.

Ostensibly these flights came under Tony Riach's control, and sometimes he accompanied us. At first we confined these Air Co-operation exercises to the area immediately west of the Rangehead but inevitably on clear days we were acutely aware of St Kilda and this drew us like a magnet. One of the pilots, in particular, had a devil-may-care approach to flying. Bill Hamilton would go down in Range history as the pilot who actually landed the Consul on the launch pad and even more miraculously got it back into the air without mishap. His next stunt was to effect a landing on the South Ford Causeway, the long, narrow road bridge that linked Benbecula to South Uist, and on another occasion he could not resist 'beating up' a landing craft as it threaded its way through the Sound of Harris. So when I suggested to him one day that we take a closer look at St Kilda, he was game. It was a beautiful day in July and for once there was not a cloud in sight; but as we descended to 1500 feet and made our first pass over Hirta we were suddenly buffeted by clear air turbulence. Being chucked around the sky was something you got used to when flying through great banks of cumulo-nimbus, but when you suddenly drop several hundred feet in a clear sky it is extremely disconcerting. In fact, on this particular flight, we narrowly avoided hitting the Gap between Conachair and Oiseval and I have a vivid recollection of the terrible sinking feeling in my gut as we flashed past at cleit-top level and could clearly see the individual blades of grass on the roofs. Although the general perception is that the three aircraft that crashed on St Kilda during the war had flown into it in thick fog, I have a hunch that one or more of them may actually have come down to take a look, and had then got caught in one of those terrifying down-draughts. But Bill Hamilton had nerves of steel, for he banked over Dùn, turned and flew back over the village and up through the Gap.

'There, now,' he said evenly. 'That wasn't so bad this time, was it?'

In the summer of 1958 an experimental airdrop was carried out by the RAF when a parcel of newspapers was dropped over St Kilda, but the experiment was considered too risky and was never repeated. In August 1959, however, the detachment's bakery ran out of yeast and on 20 August a three-pound parcel of the stuff was successfully dropped by Tony Riach, sitting in the back seat of the Consul, with his left foot braced against the open door as he chucked out the package done up in a hessian sandbag with a bandage streamer attached.

The success of this mission encouraged us to contemplate dropping the mail, now that St Kilda was back to the vagaries of the *Mull's* winter service. With the agreement of the detachment, we decided to try dropping the mail. On 3 September the Consul took off for St Kilda with Don Pow at the controls and Tony sitting up front in the co-pilot's seat. Mike Barling, a National Service second lieutenant in the Artillery (and later a vicar of the Church of England), and I were seated at the back of the plane as air despatchers. On taking off we flew first of all south to the Rangehead. After one low-level pass to waken up the radar crew we climbed to 2000 feet and did three circuits at a radius of about five miles of the launch pad, then headed in a north-westerly direction for St Kilda. It was a perfect day for it, with a ten-knot wind and very good visibility. As we neared Hirta we dropped to 1500 feet and flew a triangular course from the north-east, heading south-west across the Gap, then diving towards the village and hard to port over the bay, left past Levenish and climbing towards Boreray, then back across the cliffs on the eastern flank of Conachair. Don performed this exercise a couple of times, but on the third pass he throttled back, put down some flap and skimmed over the Gap, down the slope and aimed for the camp. At his command I turned the handle to open the door. You would think that this was a very risky thing to do but in fact it took quite an effort to push it open into the slipstream, then hold it open with a boot braced against the side. Don gave me a count down, 'Three, two, one, go!' at which I lobbed out a couple of sandbags. As we banked over the bay we had the satisfaction of seeing figures on the ground swarming towards the precious bundles. Mission accomplished, we roared over the point of Dùn and headed back to Benbecula.

Loading an aircraft at Benbecula to carry out an airdrop: 2nd Lieut Mike Barling and Capt Alec Byrne, RAMC.

Over the ensuing months we perfected our technique. The triangular course around Oiseval was preferred when the winds were blowing from east or west, but when there were winds from the north or south we opted for a much more elongated course. Approaching from the south-east, we would fly along the west coast of Dùn and Hirta, turn to the north-east and fly across the strait between the Cambir and Soay, then head in a south-easterly direction up the Glen, past Mullach Geal and drop the mail on the plateau of Mullach Sgar. In practice, this was the course usually adopted, although the actual direction, clockwise or anti-clockwise, would be dictated by the

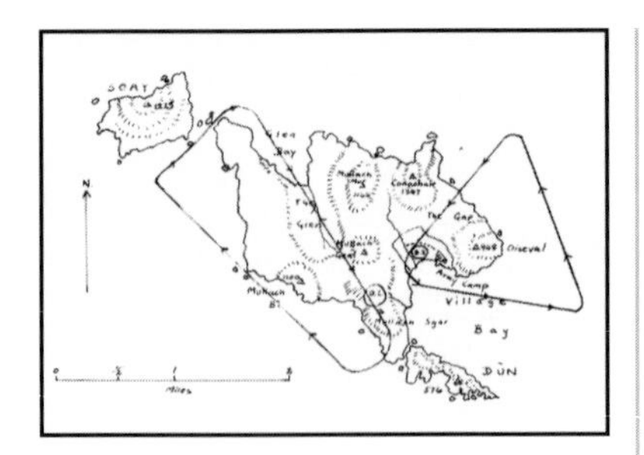

Map of island showing circuits and dropping zones for north/south and east/west winds

wind. Radio communication between the aircraft and the detachment would alert the pilot to the wind strength and direction which would thus determine the course and dropping zone. Then the doctor and his medical orderlies would lay out a triangle of hospital bed sheets to indicate the target, and be on hand to recover the parcels.

There were advantages and disadvantages to both dropping zones. Over the camp was easier for the men on the ground and the risk of loss or damage was minimal, but the Gap was a tricky feature to navigate and we were always conscious of the remains of the Beaufighter on the summit of Conachair. The dropping zone on Mullach Sgar was safer from the pilot's viewpoint but this called for great precision in getting the parcels smack on target. On two or three occasions parcels missed the DZ and went over the cliffs. I am proud of the fact that when I was air-despatcher we never lost a single parcel, but invariably when things went awry I was at the receiving end, and then had the tricky job of organising parties to go down the rocks to salvage light stores and the ever-precious mail.

One of the most dramatic incidents in the early years of the Army base took place on Monday 7 September 1959 when St Kilda received a signal from Benbecula bearing the grim news that Barbara Mackenzie, wife of one of the civilian labourers then working on the island, had been rushed to the Royal Northern Infirmary, Inverness in a critical condition. An appeal had gone out just after nine o'clock on Sunday evening when the hospital authorities asked Inverness police to inform Colin Mackenzie of his wife's illness. The police contacted Benbecula immediately, only to be told that St Kilda's only link with the mainland, the VHF radio-telephone, did not operate after 6pm. After an agonising night, the relief operation swung into motion at dawn the following morning. Frantic phone calls between Benbecula and Scottish Command resulted in the Navy being alerted via the Northern Rescue Co-ordination Centre at Pitreavie in Fife.

At 1.40pm on Monday a Dragonfly helicopter piloted by Lieutenant Anthony V.Rowed, RN took off from Lossiemouth for Benbecula. Less than half an hour later a twin-engined Percival Sea Prince, acting as escort to the helicopter, took off with Lieutenant Bryan Neave at the controls. The Sea Prince landed at Benbecula at 3.15pm and the helicopter touched down just before four o'clock to refuel – an exercise that was carried out manually and involved several forty-gallon drums of aviation gasoline. I was lucky to thumb a lift in the chopper with a sack of mail and newspapers for the island hurriedly put together at the last moment. The helicopter flew at barely a hundred feet all the way out to the island, with the Sea Prince keeping watch high above. We came down on the level ground beside the manse, where the doctor and his orderlies had laid out some bed sheets in the form of a large H, and picked up a very distraught Colin Mackenzie. It was the quickest visit I ever paid to St Kilda, for we paused for less than three minutes, just long enough to exchange greetings and mail and dash off again. It was terribly turbulent coming low into the bay, though there was scarcely any wind on the flight from Benbecula, and we had kept a close watch on the waves. God knows what it would have been like in the normal blustery weather. There were only a handful of letters to come off and Richard Hudson had put them in a large OHMS envelope with 'Mail by Helicopter' printed in large letters across it, and embellished with both the unit stamp (the Puffin cachet) and the Tin Can Mail mark suitably endorsed for the occasion.

At Benbecula Mackenzie was transferred to the Sea Prince and flown to Dalcross where he boarded another helicopter which landed on the Bught Park playing fields at 7.30pm. A police car then rushed him to the hospital where he was able to spend about forty minutes with his wife before she expired. Writing home that eventful day I commented, 'It shows what can be done when the Army want to'. The pity was that such speedy and efficient communications were only possible in the direst emergency. The entry in the St Kilda Unit Diary concerning this incident is worth quoting:

At approximately midday informed from Sunray Minor Benbecula [Major McGregor] that a helicopter airlift operation was in hand to evacuate a civilian labourer, Colin Mackenzie, from the island to Inverness where his wife was on D.I. list at the Royal Northern infirmary. The landing strip on sea wall was cleared, "H" and arrow indicating wind direction were laid, supply of Avgas laid on and fire fighting apparatus positioned to hand. Helicopter reported by R/T (whilst still out of sight) "landing in two minutes". Time 1708 hrs came in over Village Bay, over the Sgts Mess, landed on "H" at 1710 hrs. Mail collected at Benbecula was dropped off, St Kilda mail put aboard, Mackenzie put aboard and helicopter was airborne and heading towards Levenish at 1714 hrs!! "Nae bother at a'." Weather conditions 4/8 cloud at 4000 ft. Wind SSE 10 knots gusting about 18 knots. All personnel on the island were greatly impressed with this demonstration of what can be done in an emergency.

On 8 October 1959, the *Daily Mail* chartered a De Havilland Rapide biplane with the intention of dropping a bundle of the newspaper on St Kilda with the results of the General Election. A small quantity of mail was also dropped. The Rapide left Stornoway at 0700 hours with the newspapers and a *Mail* photographer, and landed at Balivanich two hours later. On this occasion Captain Alan Earl, R. Sigs and I were the despatchers and we bundled several packages of light stores on to the plane. Among my souvenirs is the pilot's flight plan, jotted on the back of a sheet headed 'Instrument Approach Procedures (Manchester)', which included the comment 'Time of delivery at KILDA is not crucial to the charterer as no rival outfit is delivering there'. The notion of several newspapers having the same bright idea and jostling each other to carry out such stunts over St Kilda raised a chuckle.

The airdrop of 8 October had a serious side to it, for St Kilda had been suffering prolonged bad weather which delayed the sailing of the *Mull* for several weeks and as a consequence the morale of the tiny garrison was at an all-time low. Although the Consul had carried out airdrops on 11 September and 2 October, ensuring that mail reached the St Kildans, there was no way that mail could be taken off the island. Even more seriously, the canteen ran out of beer. Consequently, part of the mission on 8 October was to carry out a 'beer-drop'. To this end, I tried to lob a pack of two dozen Younger's Wee Willie beer cans into the boggy ground on the summit of Mullach Sgar, but unfortunately the carton struck a rock instead. I was later told by those on the receiving end that it exploded with the impact of a mortar shell. The *Weekly Scotsman* of 30 June 1960 ran a story entitled 'Beer Supply Ran Out – So The Soldiers Made Their Own!' which was very loosely based on this incident. 'A few weeks ago' ran this highly coloured work of fiction, 'a minor crisis arose when beer supplies ran out on St Kilda'. The only element of truth in the ensuing story was the explosion of the beer cans, although this had actually happened nine months earlier, but the story went on to relate how a subsequent flight had airdropped a 'do it yourself' brewing kit, a story which was the figment of the overheated imagination of the reporter who concocted this nonsense. The paper even ran a picture of Bob Critchley at the controls of the plane which allegedly carried out this humanitarian mission.

Not only were seaborne communications severely disrupted in October 1959 but even the Consul had difficulty in getting to St Kilda. Cyril Sweetman attempted an airdrop on 15 October but had to turn back on account of atrocious weather over the island. A week later he made a second attempt but had engine failure on take-off, and it was not until 24 October that he successfully carried out the airdrop.

By and large, however, these airdrops were a great success and, more importantly, gave a tremendous boost to the morale of the detachment. In September St Kilda should have reverted to the winter adddress, PO Box 99 Fleetwood, Lancs, but personnel were asked to tell their family and friends to continue using the summer address via Nunton, Benbecula which ensured that their personal mail would be transmitted by air at least once a week. The only people who were not informed of this were the War Office and Scottish Command Headquarters. In fact, the airdrop system continued for a full year on a purely *ad hoc* basis, and it was not until 19 August 1960 that Airworks received a formal contract which put this procedure on an official footing. On 12 February that year, however, the

Brigadier Royal Artillery, having got wind of what we were doing, came up to Benbecula to see for himself. On that occasion a demonstration flight over St Kilda was carried out by Bill Hamilton and a bag containing only nineteen letters was dropped. It was presumably after he had seen the success of this ploy for himself that Peter Henderson set in motion the paper-work that led eventually to the airmail contract.

David Boddington left St Kilda for good on 6 August 1959, his place being taken by Captain Richard Hudson who had been the medical officer at Dundonald Camp when I was there the previous winter. At that time, it should be remembered, St Kilda was a year-long posting for the OC and the MO, with three months' leave in that period. Later the posting was reduced to nine and then six months for these two key officers; for certain other key personnel the posting varied from three to six months, and ordinary soldiers night expect to do several periods of six weeks in the course of a two year stint at the Rocket Range. Apart from David Boddington and, later, Estlin Waters, I have a feeling that the doctors posted to St Kilda were not volunteers. Richard may have volunteered; his father Hubert Hudson had accompanied Shackleton on his expedition to the Antarctic in 1914-15 and was one of the five men who made the incredible journey of 800 miles from Elephant Island to South Georgia in an open boat, so he felt that he had a lot to live up to. In any normal situation he would have been all right, but St Kilda was an exceptional place at the best of times, and it was his misfortune to arrive there at one of the worst of times.

He had been quite bullish about his new posting when I accompanied him on the landing craft that August, but when I saw him a month later he had become querulous, and quite little things were niggling him. He was particularly annoyed that none of the welfare wireless sets provided in the Rec Room and the Sergeants' and Officers' Messes were working, and he found the want of news, especially about the election campaign, particularly trying. In my capacity as Welfare Officer for the Range as a whole I should have taken his grousing and griping more seriously. The next time I saw him, in mid-October, matters had clearly taken a turn for the worse.

The autumn of 1959 saw some of the worst weather ever recorded on St Kilda. Old St Kilda hands from the Army will doubtless remember the *Mull* with mixed feelings. We were utterly dependent on her, and there was never a more welcome sight in the long winter months than the ship coming round the flank of Oiseval into the bay. But she could be maddeningly frustrating at times (plenty of times) because of the undue caution of her skippers who would not venture out of Loch Carnan if the slightest breeze was blowing. The awful weather in September and early October that year meant that her sailing was considerably delayed and, as a result, the voters of St Kilda were denied their rights to take part in the General Election. I doubt very much whether the bulk of the garrison would have bothered to vote in any case, but Richard took this disenfranchisement very badly. Early in October he composed a very long report, running to three closely typed foolscap pages to which were attached sworn depositions from nine soldiers complaining about the poor communications, the exorbitant cost and hopeless inadequacy of the VHF radio-telephone link, the impossibility of sending telegrams or remittances of cash. Even the *Daily Mail* airdrop came in for criticism: the newspaper contained nothing of interest to the island's personnel.

I fully empathised with Richard, for I was also suffering as a result of the prolonged bad weather. Ever since the end of September I had been standing by to embark for St Kilda, and every day since the beginning of October I had driven from Balivanich down to Loch Carnan to sail, and on each occasion the trip had been postponed 24 hours because the weather forecast was bad. Actually, the weather had nearly always turned out glorious, which only made matters worse, and in the end Major McGregor more or less forced the skipper (a new man who had never done the St Kilda run before) to put out to sea – and of course at long last the weather had turned foul. We weighed anchor at 8am on Sunday 11 October, and 24 hours later had been forced to shelter in West Loch Tarbert, Harris. After a thirteen-hour voyage we had actually got within sight of St Kilda when a force seven south-easterly had sprung up. It would have been suicidal to try to enter the bay under those conditions, but why we did not sail round to the Glen Bay I cannot understand. Instead the new skipper, Donny Ross, headed back into the open Atlantic and fled before a wind which ran right off the end of the Beaufort scale. I will never forget the forty-foot waves that pursued us and threatened to engulf us; it was the most terrifying trip I ever made.

On this occasion I was travelling with the new REME chief of staff at Scottish Command Headquarters, Brigadier Rabagliatti. 'Rag-bag' was a Maltese of extremely volatile temper which was certainly not improved by the discomfort of sea-sickness. We huddled together in the tiny wardroom and at some point in the night one of the crew popped in with a garfish which had been washed up on deck. I examined this fine specimen of marine life with considerable interest. It was about two feet in length and looked like a swordfish in miniature, with a four-inch blade on its snout. The ship's mate told me that its backbone was bright green in colour and glowed in the dark. The brigadier might have been on the point of expiring from *mal de mer*, but I was feeling quite peckish and naturally enquired whether the garfish was edible. On being told that it was esteemed as a delicacy in Cornwall I gave orders to the galley to cook it for my breakfast, and I kept the luminescent backbone as a souvenir. Apparently Cornish lasses regarded it as a love token.

When we took refuge in West Loch Tarbert and the anchor was dropped, the Brigadier insisted that the crew lower the ship's lifeboat and take him ashore to the comforts of the Harris Hotel. The skipper demurred and stood on his rights to determine what was best for the safety of his ship, but he sadly under-estimated the mettle of the Brigadier. Rag-bag claimed that it was within his remit to demand a demonstration of the crew's efficiency at hoisting out a lifeboat, and the bunch of squaddies who had been heading for a spell on Hirta instinctively formed up on deck behind the Top Brass, their collective body language leaving the skipper in no doubt that if there was a showdown the *Mull* and her crew would come off second best. The skipper's diffidence about lowering the boat was well-founded for almost an hour passed before the crew succeeded in getting it slung out on its davits, and even then they clumsily dropped one end so that the bow was almost swamped.

Eventually the boat was in the water and everyone piled in behind the Brigadier. On the short trip to the jetty, however, the boat's engine conked out and we began drifting, lashed by wind and rain, toward the rocks before the Brigadier could organise the soldiers to get the oars into the rowlocks and head for the shore. Forty years later, watching BBC's super-soap *Castaway 2000*, I was forcibly reminded of the relative luxury of the Harris Hotel, whither some of the more reluctant castaways had fled when their accommodation on Taransay was not yet ready.

Two days later, the storm died down and we headed out to sea again. It was quite late at night before we anchored in Village Bay and were ferried ashore in the

RASC-V Mull *anchored in Village Bay, 1960. In the background the narrow gap between Dùn and Hirta can clearly be seen.*

RASC-V Mull*, St Kilda's winter life-line.*

island's cutter. What a sight greeted us! A loudspeaker had been rigged up on the jetty, relaying pop-music from the Rec Room's record-player. As Rag-bag and I stepped on to the raft and climbed the rungs of the jetty it was perhaps unfortunate that the record that greeted us was 'Lipstick on Your Collar', which the red-tabbed Brigadier took as a personal affront. The REME inspection in particular, and the state of the St Kilda garrison in general, were thus condemned out of hand before the Brigadier had taken a single step ashore. Somewhere in the Ministry of Defence files in the Public Record Office at Kew there must be a copy of Rag-bag's report. I have never seen it, but I can imagine its vitriolic tone. The deplorable state of the St Kilda detachment reflected badly on everybody, all the way up to Colonel Cooper himself. I had the misfortune to share the wardroom with the Brigadier on the return voyage as well and got a tremendous ear-bashing as he recited the short-comings of the worst garrison he had encountered in his thirty years in the Army.

Despite the frenetic jollity of the pop music on the jetty, St Kilda was in a sombre mood. One need not have studied the Army handbook on man management to appreciate that morale was at an all-time low. No one had had a haircut since the Demon Barber had retired and there was a general air of sullen slovenliness. But it was the condition of Richard himself that gave me the gravest cause for concern. I went up to the stores to help him check the incoming supplies, including the much-needed consignment of canned beer. I have a vivid recollection of him standing there, tears welling in his eyes, continually fumbling with the wooden peg-buttons on his duffel-coat as he launched into a long litany.

'Oh, God! This is an awful place!' he cried, unconsciously paraphrasing Scott at the South Pole. I was shaken by his obvious distress and wished that I could take him back to Benbecula, but I had no authority to do so and had no wish to draw the Brigadier's attention to the state he was in. Moreover, a doctor in distress was surely better than no doctor at all, and St Kilda needed him, come what may. Before I reboarded the ship, Richard pressed on me a bulky package which he insisted I should deliver to Colonel Cooper in person.

'It is a report on conditions here,' he said, adding darkly, 'and I've put a copy in the mailbag for the Deputy Director of Medical Services at Scottish Command. This place ought to be closed down.'

In due course I handed the packet over to Colonel Cooper. Later he called me into his office and thrust the bundle at me. Before I read it, I told the colonel that I was extremely worried about the doctor who, I feared, was on the verge of a nervous breakdown. The colonel robustly pooh-poohed this.

'Read this,' he said. 'It all makes good sense to me.' By now he would have had an interim verbal report from the Brigadier on the low morale of St Kilda and had formed his own opinion that vastly improved communications lay at the heart of the trouble. 'Take this away and rewrite it. Get the salient points down on one side of a sheet of paper. No more. These wallahs in the War House have a very low threshold of boredom. What we need are ship-to-shore rocket lines. It's not just the *Mull*, you know; it's these damned Fleetwood trawlers. They get an obscene amount of money to collect and deliver the mail, yet they will hardly stop if the weather is not completely perfect and then bugger off up to Iceland for weeks on end before trying again to deal with the mail. It's just not good enough.'

Among the papers attached to the report was a statement from one of the signalmen who had served on Gan in the Maldives. Even on that remote Indian Ocean island they got their mail regularly every week – and St Kilda was supposed to be a home posting! In due course a condensed but considerably beefed up report on the deplorable lack of communications went off to Scottish Command, and after a decent interval a response came from Major John Burrill, RA to the effect that a recommendation had been sent to the War Office requesting the installation of rocket equipment. Later, however, we received another letter from Major Burrill stating that the trawler company was endeavouring to obtain long-range rockets and lines 'by which it is hoped that they will be able to deliver mail satisfactorily'. The second paragraph was unconsciously ironic: 'As you may be aware, the only boat carried by the trawlers is very small and suitable only for use in the calmest weather. It will thus be almost invariably necessary for the mail to be delivered by rocket line.'

While the War Office and the Boston Deep Sea Fishing and Ice Company dithered over the provision of the rocket lines and argued over who should foot the bill, the garrison whose very existence was tied up with rocketry of another kind continued to suffer.

Then Providence stepped in.

In November I went out to St Kilda to take over from Will Warner as Officer Commanding. On my previous stints, I had served as second-in-command but now I was in full command. In light of the REME Brigadier's visit, however, it was decided that what St Kilda needed most was a spell under the Regimental Sergeant Major. Bert Jessup was not like other WOIs I had previously encountered and, in fact, he and I were good buddies. We shared a passion for messing about in small boats, or more particularly the cabin cruiser which the Nuffield Foundation had purchased for the Range. I had even chosen a name for the trim little vessel which was christened *Kirstag*, after Christina Mackay of Embo, a Nora Batty lookalike who worked as a cleaner at Dornoch Hotel when I was the night porter. It had been one of my more congenial tasks to go to St Monans in Fife to attend her sea-trials, and early in May Major McGregor and I, accompanied by Major Jim Brunker and Captain Tony Spackman, keen yachtsmen from the School of Artillery, had gone to Mallaig to take delivery of the boat at the railhead and then sail her across the Minch to Loch Carnan. Thereafter Bert Jessup and I were enrolled as trainee skippers under Tony Spackman and together we spent all our spare time afloat.

About 10.30pm on 22 November 1959 the Fleetwood trawler *St Botolph* came into Village Bay and sounded her hooter, the signal that she had mail on board. It was a filthy night, black as pitch, with a heavy sea running. In hindsight, it was the height of folly to launch a dory in those conditions, but the prospect of letters from loved ones overruled any objections. On this occasion Lance-Corporal Denis Hodgson, RASC, our Seaman Military, had no difficulty in mustering a crew of six, including Bert Jessup who decided to go along for the ride. The *St Botolph* was anchored about 800 yards offshore, but before the dory had covered a tenth of that distance she was making very heavy weather. Several waves broke over her bows and she was shipping water badly. Too late, Hodgson decided to turn back, but the dory capsized, pitching the crew into the water. God knows what might have happened if the RSM had not been in the boat, but he kept a cool head and had the crew hanging on to the rat-lines and 'swimming by numbers' as they slowly propelled the upturned boat back to the jetty. Meanwhile Denis swam for the shore to get a line out to the stricken dory.

At the time it seemed like a minor mishap. No one was injured and the dory was not damaged. A routine accident report was sent off to Benbecula the following day, but Colonel Cooper seized the opportunity to press his claim for the rocket lines which had not yet materialised. The report was rewritten and eventually this masterpiece of creative writing went off to Scottish Command. Brigadier Henderson was so impressed by this that he decided to recommend Jessup and Hodgson for decorations. When I queried this with Colonel Cooper later on, he coolly replied that Jessup, nearing the end of his 22 years' service, deserved the MBE anyway. In fact the medals to both men were gallantry awards, distinguished from the run-of-the-mill decorations by the addition of silver oak-leaf clusters. The true hero of that awful night was Denis Hodgson and I regretted the military caste system which made the distinction between the RSM and the Lance-Corporal who only got the British Empire Medal. Denis was another close buddy of mine. He and I joined the unit at the same time and he was with me on that memorable trip to St Kilda the previous March, but he had been there more or less continuously ever since. He readily fell in with my hare-brained schemes to visit all the islands of the St Kilda group and the following summer we succeeded in landing on both Soay and Levenish, regarded as the most difficult of the entire archipelago. I later had the opportunity to remedy the defect of the awards system to some extent. On the expiry of his National Service Denis applied to join the Hong Kong police. Not only did I endorse his application but attached a letter of personal recommendation. He eventually reached the rank of Chief Superintendent.

The annoying thing about the mail aboard the trawler was that it went all the way up to the Iceland fishing grounds, and it was not until 1 December, on her homeward voyage, that she succeeded in landing the mailbag. When it was opened, however, it was found to contain only seven pieces of mail – all emanating from Scottish Command or the War Office (oblivious to the airdrops, the only organisations still using the official winter address). Thus seven men had risked their lives for a bunch of red tape.

We never got those damned rocket lines. By the end of 1959 the system of sending mail to St Kilda by Fleetwood trawlers had completely broken down. The last mail despatched from Fleetwood was carried aboard the *Boston Firefly* which left her home port on 26 December. The trawler went straight to the Iceland fishing grounds and five weeks later dropped off the mail at Lochboisdale, South Uist, on the homeward voyage. The mail was eventually airdropped on 4 February 1960.

10. ST KILDA WINTER

I SPENT much of November and all of December 1959 on St Kilda. Not only was this my longest spell there but I was actually in command, and lest anyone imagine that this highly irregular situation had arisen purely because the Baron of Benbecula had thus ordained it, I should add that on the trip out to the island I was accompanied by both Colonel Cooper and Brigadier Henderson. Doubtless the latter had been impelled by his superiors at Scottish Command to see for himself the deplorable situation that had confronted Brigadier Rabagliatti a few weeks earlier. Mercifully things had improved in the interim, not the least being in the provision of a new medical officer. Lieutenant David Woodward had only been in the Army a fortnight when he was hastily summoned from Birmingham and sent out to St Kilda to replace Richard Hudson. Despite the trauma of moving from the very centre of the kingdom to the outermost edge, David was remarkably cheerful about it all and I soon discovered that in his short tenure he had already outdone his predecessors in attending to the regimental duties required of him on the island.

The Officers' Mess was spotless for a change, and the dining table lavishly set out with a silver service, no doubt in honour of the Brigadier. On this rare occasion our food was served to us by our new orderly, Gunner May, but after the VIPs departed next day we reverted to the usual practice and queued for our grub with the squaddies.

Once more I shared a bedroom with Colonel Cooper but we were up very early the following morning. The BRA, the colonel and Will Warner toured the camp, inspecting the buildings and the radar stations, examining the slipway and the thousand and one other items which invariably catch the attention of visiting Brass, while I got on with the mundane business of checking the cash and the canteen stock. Already the RSM was in his element, supervising the loading party which ferried stores to and from the *Mull* in the dory. By 10.20am the last boat-load had left the jetty, amid the usual cries of encouragement or derision from those left behind. Ten minutes later, the *Mull* had vanished round the Point of Coll in a flurry of dirty black smoke, and we were on our own. A sudden feeling of desolation swept over me as I realised that I would be marooned on this desert isle for the next few weeks.

Better dwell in the midst of alarms
Than reign in this desolate place.

But the shouts and laughter of the men coming up from the jetty were reassuring and comforting. As I glanced up at the towering mass of Conachair and Oiseval that dominated the bay I wondered how the coast-watchers who maintained their solitary vigil in the opening months of the Second World War had fared on this grim little island.

Fortunately there always seemed plenty to do, even in the depths of winter, and I found that the time passed remarkably quickly. I had acquired yet another job, being the only trained projectionist on St Kilda after Sergeant Gearing, the manager of the Puffin Bioscope, left on the *Mull*. The AKC had finally heeded my pleas, for the films we had that winter were a vast improvement, and included some Hollywood productions of the 1940s and early 1950s, quite a few of which were in technicolor.

After the terrible weather in late November, early December favoured us briefly with clear blue skies and hardly a breath of wind to ruffle the turquoise waters of the bay. To crown everything, the *St Botolph* which had so spectacularly failed to deliver the mail in November, called in on Tuesday, 1 December. On this occasion Bert Jessup, David and I accompanied Denis Hodgson in the dory and went aboard the trawler. Hodgson discovered that one of the crew was a fellow scouse, from a neighbouring village, and it was all we could do to get him back to the dory. When he heard that the trawler would be back in Fleetwood in two days time he felt like stowing away.

After a brief spell of really fine weather, however, St Kilda reverted to form and we were subjected to one of those force ten storms for which the island was so rightly famous. Fantastic steel-blue clouds of cumulo-nimbus piled themselves in nightmare shapes and outside the bay the mountainous waves crashed against Levenish, sending columns of spray high into the air. The wind was almost due south for several days, and so the bay itself was fairly well protected, yet we could see the clouds of spray over the Dùn Passage and the spouts of boiling surf jetting out of the tunnel under Am Bioda Mór. Occasionally, an exceptionally huge wave hitting Dùn's Atlantic side broke right over the ridge of the island, a good two hundred feet high, and cascaded down the rocky slopes into the bay.

In the midst of this storm two fishing vessels staggered into the bay. Their rakish bows and high sterns proclaimed them to be Spaniards, and with binoculars we could discern their serial numbers, low on the bow water-line, which identified them as being from San Sebastian. In the afternoon they were joined by four others, all six being part of a large syndicate, the Alvamar Company. At sunset a Fleetwood trawler came in, and anchored some way to the east of the Spaniards. The storm had abated considerably by nightfall but the boats remained there all night. In the dark their many lights twinkling and bobbing on the water was a comforting sight.

Bert Jessup worked wonders on St Kilda that winter. Although he was not a martinet by any stretch of the imagination he was largely instrumental in eliminating the slackness and slovenliness which had been so evident in the autumn. He certainly made my job infinitely easier. I think that an outcome of this was that thereafter the St Kilda detachment always had a WOII to instil a bit of discipline; a good Battery Sergeant Major was worth his weight in gold. Bert and I fell into a routine, making a point of touring the entire camp area every morning and dealing with the myriad of mundane matters that cropped up; but after lunch, unless the weather was unbelievably bad, we would go for long walks. A favourite ploy was beach-combing, which turned out to be very profitable; in one week alone we recovered more than two dozen jerry-cans and several fire-buckets, and located a number of empty diesel drums. Although these were stored in their respective dumps the high winds of Hirta soon dislodged them. Later on, when the weather was incredibly foul on two days out of three on average, we organised search parties to recover lost stores from the bay area or the hillsides behind it.

One day Bert and I stumbled across a baby seal. It looked such a pet with its huge, liquid dark eyes and its beautiful silver coat flecked with bluish grey spots; but when the RSM went up close to touch it, it lunged at him, snapping its jaws and displaying a fine set of sharp little teeth. Bert gingerly poked at it with a driftwood spar and the seal left savage tooth marks on it. After photographing it from every angle, we carried on across the storm beach towards the RAF slipway which had been used by the LCTs in the summertime but which was now completely unusable. Here we made an interesting discovery, a lifebelt with SS JAGA inscribed on it. A few days later, after another angry storm, we came across some spars which bore the tell-tale marks of a ship's lifeboat but without a name and surmised that this might have belonged to the same vessel. I later ascertained from Lloyd's that this ship had vanished without trace in mid-Atlantic during one of the great storms in late November. Another strange find amid the debris littering the beach were two mooring buoys, enormous hollow iron balls weighing a couple of hundredweights each, both of identical pattern but otherwise unidentifiable. What a mystery it was to conjecture whence such flotsam had come.

We found many fragments of the detachment's cutter and one of the dories which were smashed in one of the October storms. The twisted propeller shaft of the cutter was a graphic reminder of the terrible power of the angry ocean which we had always to treat with the greatest respect. On another occasion we disturbed a huge flock of black-backs and ravens which were demolishing some large creature washed up on the beach. At first we could not identify it and thought that it was a cow; but a closer examination revealed that it was a horse, stinking and decomposing rapidly, its belly bloated and distended to fantastic proportions. Where had it come from? Was it washed off a ship? Unlikely. Had it floated up from the Caribbean on the Gulf Stream? The distance seemed improbable, but the currents were not such as would have brought it from the mainland of Britain. The likeliest answer was that it had come up from western Ireland, from Galway or Donegal perhaps. A few weeks later I read in one of our out-of-date newspapers that some ship had lost or jettisoned a cargo of Irish horses bound for England, so this hideous corpse must have been one of those wretched beasts.

Up on the edge of the scree at the base of Conachair, amid the jumble of what were then regarded as very large cleits but which we now know were the remains of the medieval village, we found the middle section of what had been a thirty-foot boat, sawn off to form the roof of one of those buildings. Bert, whose ambition it was to have a ketch of his own, was quite annoyed at the wasteful prodigality of the former St Kildans. I later discovered that they had been given this boat by the generous citizens of Glasgow and Edinburgh, but this generosity was misplaced, for the boat was far too heavy and cumbersome for the islanders to manhandle over the rocks, and so, like many other boats presented to them, it had ended up as firewood. Perhaps some of this fine oak was utilised in the little 'mailboats'; we certainly made good use of it, and for a time everyone in the detachment seemed to be busy fashioning model boats from this timber.

Close-up of a bull Atlantic Grey Seal lazing on the beach [photo: Estlin Waters, 1961]

One of the morale-boosting exercises that had recently been inaugurated was a unit newspaper. Will Warner was the founding proprietor of the weekly *Gannet Gazette* which consisted of about six foolscap pages of pin-ups and cartoons culled from various magazines and newspapers, and another half-dozen pages of poems, articles, jokes and short stories – some contributed by the men but largely the handiwork of the editor. This was a task which I tackled with relish, the results being pinned up on a large board displayed on the Rec Room wall. I remember that I was particularly pleased with my reviews of forthcoming films (which I had already seen back at Benbecula).

A major problem at this time was the field-mice which had taken over the role of house-mice and overran the camp. Under the benevolent gaze of David Boddington, the little perishers had been fruitful and multiplied, and now we were reaping the benefit. They had the ability to cut their way through armour plate and we were powerless to protect our precious food stores from their rapacity. Furthermore, it was disconcerting to be awakened in the dead of night by mice holding a square dance on your pillow. Bert Jessup and I discussed this matter at some length, then I remembered that the Nature Conservancy had a number of catch-alive traps. A brief search of their storeroom revealed nine traps which were quickly doled out to the men. One soldier, however, had returned to St Kilda from leave armed with a break-back trap and was reputed to have caught no fewer than fourteen mice in a single hour. Within a matter of days the slaughter of the mice was in full swing. Having trapped them alive there arose the problem of how best to despatch them. The first one I caught was a big fat buck which I threw over the jetty into the turbulent waters but I was amazed to see him swimming strongly and scurrying off over the rocks! Another time I examined my trap and found two mice in it. One must have followed close on the other's heels for them to be so trapped. It was impossible to get one out without immediately releasing the other, so eventually I popped both trap and mice into a bucket of water and drowned them. In the Medical Centre, Sergeant Grant got the surprise of his life when he opened a trap and its inmate immediately shot up to the roof, giving the onlookers quite a shock. It turned out to be a St Kilda wren which had crawled into the trap out of curiosity and had been caught by mistake. David Woodward's treatment of his captives was humane, swift and painless; he popped half a dozen mice at a time into a tin whose lid had a hole bored in the centre through which he dropped some nitrous oxide, then dumped the bodies into the bay.

Dedman, our REME WOII, had a macabre sense of humour, dressing the corpse of a buck in a little cardboard stetson, with cowboy boots, spurs and gunbelt fashioned from plasticine and a pair of tiny six-guns in the paws, then photographed the mouse on its back, snout in the air. The resultant picture, captioned 'Mexican Pete, Flour Rustler of St Kilda Gulch – he died with his boots on' duly appeared in the next edition of the *Gannet Gazette*.

Apart from film shows the social highlight of the week was the Saturday Night Tombola (a pastime now better known as Bingo) conducted by Bert Jessup who had a nifty line in patter and called out the numbers in quick-fire staccato, 'Royal Salute, twenty-one, all the crutches, seventy-seven, blind eighty, doctor's chum, number nine, never been kissed, sweet sixteen –' and so on, at great speed, while the players, either lone-wolves or in the syndicates which many preferred, huddled intently over their boards till a frenzied 'House!' from some lucky individual halted the round and Sergeant Wacey doled out half a crown to the winner. And so it went on, amid boos and cheers and much banter, till eleven o'clock

Sunday was officially a rest day and when the weather was poor there was little incentive to venture forth. One dull, blustery afternoon in mid-December Reilly, Bailey and MacLeay joined the RSM and me for a jaunt to the summit of Oiseval. From there we took the path right round past Rudh Ghill and by clambering up a gully we eventually came out at the Gap, no mean feat, even by the standards of the old St Kildans. This entirely refuted the assertion made by David Boddington that the soldiers were too lazy or apathetic to go beyond the camp area even on the finest days.

It was during one of these Sunday afternoon rambles that I took a party of soldiers down to the great tunnel under Gob na h-Airde. We managed to walk right through the tunnel from one side to the other at low tide. As we progressed through it a colony of grey seals, about fifty in all, made a hurried and very noisy escape into the boiling current which surged back and forward with a deafening roar. There they trod water, eyeing us quizzically. The stench of the seals' fishy faeces was overpowering so we beat a hasty retreat back over the slippery floor of the cave to the entrance on Glen Bay. Retracing our steps to the top, we skirted the steep, grassy slopes of the bay, across the torrential waters of Allt a' Ghlinne and came to the great caves under the Cambir, the haunt of the great majority of the grey seals.

Although it was only mid-afternoon the light was failing as we tramped back up the steep valley, the boggy ground making for very heavy going, and there were many pauses to get our breath back before we came up to the ridge of Am Blaid again. On our way across the ridge we spotted a most unusual sight, a heron flying low over the valley. Herons are extremely rare on St Kilda, there being no freshwater fish or small amphibians on the island to provide them with food. This one must have been blown off course from the Outer Hebrides in the last big south-easterly earlier in the week.

Only a few minutes later, however, we stumbled across an even rarer phenomenon, a cock grouse which flew off the machair with characteristic whirring wing-beat and raucous cry. In due course I filed a report on both sightings and was astonished to learn subsequently that the grouse was a new record for St Kilda. Indeed, this entry in the official list of the birds of St Kilda is my sole claim to ornithological fame.

This turned out to be quite a day for bird-watching. On my return to the Factor's House I went into my bedroom and found a wren fluttering about. Closing the door and window carefully I settled down to study it at close quarters. It was a wren all right, with the beautiful bar markings on its wings and the distinctive, perky little tail, but almost as big as a sparrow, unlike the tiny reddish-brown wrens of the mainland. With some pieces of bread I eventually coaxed it into the porch where it was confined for the night. In the morning, with whatever light was available, I hoped to take some photographs of St Kilda's most famous bird. I arose early and went into the porch to find it perched on the telephone. What I had not reckoned on, however, was that the poor bird, agitated no doubt at its inability to escape, had crapped itself stupid all night long. I could scarcely believe that such a tiny bird could generate so much shit, but there were splashes of white everywhere, and, most of all, on my service dress hat which was hanging on a peg. Repeated scrubbing failed to budge the most stubborn stains, and for the better part of two years my cap bore the unmistakable evidence of the guano deposited by this lusty specimen of *Troglodytes hirtensis*. Moreover, with my cheap camera, devoid of flash or close-up lens, the photographs I took were pretty poor, though I did get one half-decent shot of the bird silhouetted against the porch window. In the end I gave up, opened the window and let it go. The wren immediately fluttered out, to sit on the street wall opposite, chirping away jubilantly at its new-found freedom.

In the aftermath of the great easterly storm we had another avian visitor. A racing pigeon was discovered in the Minister's Meadow, weak and starving and unable to do more than flutter around ineffectually as it had lost all its tail coverts. It had obviously been blown here, like the heron and the grouse. Duckworth, the medical orderly, built a large wooden cage for it and in no time at all Joey began to perk up, after a good rest and a hearty meal of dried peas, barley and Kellogg's rice crispies. As his new home was actually on the table in the Medical Centre where the post office functioned, some wag wrote PIGEON POST – PLEASE KNOCK on the door of the coop. When we examined the bird we found a ring on his leg inscribed IUUF 49 6188. Eventually I traced this number to the Irish Homing Pigeon Union and early in January a postcard arrived by airdrop from its Secretary, D. Jackson informing me that the pigeon belonged to P. Conlon of 81 Cypress Street, Belfast. When Joey had recovered from his ordeal we liberated him; I hope that he made it back to his loft in the end.

After the complaints about the radio sets in the autumn a fresh supply had been sent to St Kilda, but I am afraid that reception was so poor that it was hardly worth the effort of twiddling the knob and searching the air-waves for something entertaining. BBC reception was so pitiful and obscured by static that we concentrated on the short wave band with quite amusing results. One evening we heard the unmistakable strains of Addinsell's Warsaw Concerto, but the music stopped after a few bars to be followed by an announcement 'This is Radio Warsaw, broadcasting in English to North America, bringing peace and friendship to all nations'. Incongruously, this was followed by a half-hour programme of excerpts from the new American musical 'West Side Story'. Oddly enough, the only other station we received with regular clarity was Radio Moscow. We were at the mercy of Soviet propaganda, without even Radio Luxembourg to bolster our Western ideology. One evening, however, we surpassed ourselves by tuning in to the

Village Bay from Ruaival, LCT on the beach

Signals corporal taking down a message transmitted by WS 19 Mk II, 1959

Voice of America from Tangier (reporting General Eisenhower's tour of NATO countries), first in Greek and then in Turkish; then we got Radio Peking and Radio Budapest (both in English) and finally a Polish transmission from Bush House, London. Later we learned from Radio Warsaw that a terrible frost had hit eastern Europe. The temperature in Warsaw had dropped to minus four but in Berlin it was sixteen below. And here we were on St Kilda, for all our stormy weather, enjoying the comparatively tropical temperature of 47º F, so we counted our blessings.

The following week was exceedingly stormy, with a 30-knot wind blowing straight into the bay, sending great gusts of spray across the top of the jetty and lashing the windows of the camp buildings. Heavy blue-black clouds hung low on Conachair and Oiseval all day and even at noon it was like dusk outside. The wind was too strong to risk taking the trucks beyond the bailey bridge; on the steep hill road they would have been blown over the cliffs by this gale. However, the weather was not allowed to interfere with the unit's mammoth repainting programme, and during this spell the canteen, the Rec Room and dining hall were completely redecorated. It was at this time that the canteen metamorphosed into the Puffin Bar, with some very artistic frescoes and murals to give it a more homely appearance, although very modest by comparison with the splendid Puff Inn of more recent times.

As part of the drive to protect our food supplies from the mice we moved the stores into the old church whose doors and windows had been made secure. In the course of supervising this operation I took the opportunity to study the graffiti on the wooden panelling. The majority of the inscriptions scrawled there dated between 1952 and 1956 and had been made by visiting fishing boats from France, Spain, Denmark, Norway and Sweden, usually a man's name followed by his ship and the date and sometimes a full address. Who was Erik Andreasson of Kladesholm, Sweden who left his mark on 30 May 1953, or Frans Tandberg of MS *Hjerto* who had landed the same year? A French trawlerman in August 1954 even added the pious invocation 'priez pour moi'. One historic entry recorded the visit of the RAF vessel *Bridport* in June 1956, while the most recent inscription was made by Sammy McDowall of 13 Coy Royal Pioneer Corps in 1958. I transcribed all of these graffiti, in their way just as important a record as anything left by the mute remains of the St Kildans and, of course, long gone as a result of the church being completely restored in the 1970s.

During the winter we saw quite a number of trawlers sheltering in the bay. The vast majority of them were Spanish vessels who were content to ride out the storms and made no attempt to come ashore. One Wednesday morning, as I was about to hold the weekly pay parade, the men lined up outside my office were diverted and entertained by the antics of the Spanish trawlermen. The sea was still very choppy and this particular trawler was bucking up and down quite violently. One man, leaning over the steeply angled stern, was washed overboard when the stern dipped into a great trough. Instead of throwing him a lifebelt on a line, his shipmates launched a dinghy, without oars. Somehow he managed to clamber into the boat, soaked to the skin. For half an hour he sat in the dinghy, frantically baling out as the tiny craft wallowed in the turbulent sea. Eventually his dinghy was hauled in on the end of a line and he was unceremoniously pulled over the gunwhale by several willing hands. All the while, a second Spanish trawler had arrived and circled round and round without making any attempt to rescue the poor fellow.

At that time we made no attempt to contact the Spaniards and they, perhaps mindful of the incident with the RAF the previous winter, kept well out of our way. But from the summer of 1960 onwards we gradually established a good rapport with them. We gave them fresh water, carried out minor engine repairs for them and, significantly, provided free medical treatment (including extensive surgery on several notable occasions). In return they plied us liberally with kegs of brandy and vino, gave us unlimited supplies of fresh fish and even posted our letters for us. In the winter of 1960, in fact, we relied quite heavily on the Spanish trawlers from San Sebastian, Pasajez and Irun to take our mail which the skippers often franked with five-peseta stamps. Sometimes, however, they did not add Spanish stamps and the letters were surcharged on their arrival in Britain, although the results were colourful and now much esteemed as philatelic curiosities. To a limited extent we also made use of the crabbers and lobster-boats from Camaret-sur-Mer and Concarneau which also frequented St Kilda from time to time. We even challenged the Spaniards to a football match on several occasions, when the tide was out and the beach provided a reasonable pitch.

Shortly before Christmas a group of Spanish vessels in the bay were joined by two larger trawlers from Lowestoft, the *Captain Fremantle* and the *Captain Hardy*. It was just another day of simply awful weather with a storm hammering the backside of Dùn and sending huge columns of spray over the ridge. One of the Spaniards had a narrow escape near the rocks of Ruaival when she overshot the mooring buoy, but luckily she managed to turn hard to port just when we were convinced that the enormous waves would hurl her, broadside on, against the storm beach. At lunchtime, while trying to pick up the BBC Overseas transmission on short wave, David and I eavesdropped instead on a conversation between the skippers of the Lowestoft trawlers. Unfortunately we could only really hear one of them clearly and he was a monosyllabic individual who merely grunted or occasionally interjected vociferously, 'Bloody hell! No!' while the indistinct voice did all the talking at the other end. It appeared that they were discussing the weather and being stuck in 'this hole Kilda' while their more fortunate colleagues sheltered at Stornoway. Then they began to discuss their plans for Christmas. One said that he planned to take the missus up to London for a day's shopping on Saturday, if he managed back by Thursday or Friday. In unison, David and I had a bad attack of the glums and switched off the set before this conversation depressed us even further.

In the Puffin Bar one evening, over our pints, we fell to discussing the Soay sheep and quite an argument ensued as to the ease or difficulty of catching a ram. Then somebody opined that the meat might be good for eating. As we had been surviving on a monotonous diet of stew made from dried beef, the notion suddenly appealed. The upshot was that Reilly and MacLeay, the two drivers, went out at ten o'clock that night and returned barely an hour later to announce that they had caught and killed a sheep. By way of proof, Bob Reilly produced a bleeding head like a rabbit out of the magician's hat and told me that the carcass itself was hanging up 'to dry' in the garage. Never missing a trick in his capacity as Messing Officer, David declared that we would have roast lamb for Sunday dinner.

Needless to say, all of this was strictly against standing orders and the Ministry of Defence Agreement with the Nature Conservancy Council which stated baldly that 'worrying the sheep' was forbidden. But Reilly pointed out sagely that this particular woollie was not in the least worried – he had merely fallen down dead with fright. Before Sunday came, however, an incident arose to put us right off sampling forbidden flesh. A case of ring-worm had been found among the men, so David ordered a hygiene inspection of all ranks the following morning. Ironically, he told me that every morning when he went up the hill to read the weather instruments he also noted the level of water in the reservoir. That morning he was surprised to find the water level well down, and this he imputed to the fact that the soldiers, in view of the impending inspection, had all taken a bath the night before. We now knew why soldiers are so often referred to as 'old sweats'.

In the course of the inspection David found several cases of athlete's foot which he treated liberally with mycota cream. For good measure, he decided to do all the tetanus inoculations. This was normally given every five years but troops on St Kilda got their shots every year because the tetanus spore was found liberally in the excreta of the fulmars. When I told David that St Kilda babies died of the 'eight-day sickness', the scourge of the island before 1884, and that this was in fact infantile lockjaw caused by the strange custom of putting a drop of fulmar oil mixed with sheep's droppings on the severed umbilical cord of the new born baby, David suddenly hit the roof.

'That's it! There is no way that I could permit the men to eat that sheep. It must be buried immediately!' Despite the protests of the slaughtermen, Reilly and MacLeay, David was adamant, and the corpse was duly interred without military honours. All that was left to remind us of the incident was the head. I put it out in the meadow for the gulls to pick clean, but the birds gave it a wide berth. Perhaps it was not gamey enough for them, or perhaps they were too well fed on the scraps chucked out of the cookhouse each morning. It was still lying there, decomposing disgustingly, when I left the island.

One afternoon David and I were sitting in the Mess when our attention was grabbed by a strange sight in the bay. A huge shoal of fish suddenly rose as one, out of the water, like a vast silver cloud as their scales were caught by the watery sun. We leaped to our feet and gazed through binoculars. The reason for this extraordinary display was obvious, for there was some great creature in the midst of the fish, with a tall dorsal fin. From the distance between the fin and the tail we estimated it to be at least thirty feet in length. At the time we thought it must have been a whale, but the following summer I discussed this phenomenon with Tex Geddes, the Nature Conservancy boatman, and he told me emphatically that it must have been a basking shark. In 1946-8 he had worked with Gavin Maxwell, hunting basking sharks in the Minch and extracting the oil from their livers. Although this project was a financial failure, out of it came Maxwell's first great best-seller, *Harpoon at a Venture*, first published in 1952.

A few days before Christmas Jessup and I paid a routine visit to the Signals Centre. I was intensely annoyed when the duty operator, Signalman Banfield, casually mentioned that last night he had picked up distress signals from two trawlers, one off Northern Ireland and the other near Shetland; but had not informed me as he did not think there was anything we could do about it. I gave him a right ballocking and told him that in future all SOS signals had to be notified to Benbecula immediately, whence they could be relayed to Pitreavie, Kinloss and Ballykelly. When I inspected the barrack-rooms later that day I found that Banfield had not swept out his bed-space and that a pile of cigarette butts had collected under his bed. His summary punishment was to report to the armoury and clean all twelve rifles and the OC's revolver by the following morning.

At mid-day on 23 December I took advantage of the brief watery sunshine to finish the last of a cassette of colour transparencies, taking a few snaps of the camp from above the Street by the Dry Burn. Whenever I look at these slides today I shudder, for more vividly than any words they encapsulate the weird, gloomy half-light of the island on the shortest day of the year. The soggy vegetation is a peculiar dark brown colour and there are pools of water everywhere; but it is that strange yellowish glow that I remember so clearly – and that was St Kilda on a good day.

Christmas Day was a Friday and effectively the start of a three-day holiday. In line with time-honoured tradition two officers and a WOI served four sergeants and twenty-two junior ranks a slap-up Christmas dinner which included turkey and all the trimmings. The festivities had actually begun a few days earlier, with a signal from Brigadier Henderson no less, wishing us all a Merry Christmas. Then, on 21 December, Cyril Sweetman carried out the most successful airdrop up to that time, dropping no fewer than nineteen sacks of Christmas mail. Among the parcels was a case of Johnnie Walker whisky which, unlike my beer-drop, landed without mishap. This airdrop was originally to have been covered by a reporter and photographer from the *Daily Mail* but heavy snow, blocking the Edinburgh-Perth road, prevented them reaching Scone aerodrome. Thus communications with St Kilda were far better than those prevailing on the mainland. The high point of Christmas day was the live link-up with the rest of the British Empire by VHF radio-telephone, part of the hour-long programme which in those good old days immediately preceded the Christmas message from Her Majesty the Queen. I guess this was meant to give our morale a lift, but several of the men were reduced to tears.

After the halcyon days around Christmas, the weather deteriorated sharply once more. Some days the wind strength was so great that it was hardly possible to crawl from the Factor's House to the mess hall, let alone take a landrover up the hill. This nightmarish weather cannot last for ever and, sure enough, it eventually abates. The last pages of my diary of that winter are worth quoting in full.

The Mull *is expected to arrive at St Kilda some time this afternoon or evening. At 5.30am my alarm-clock goes off and I awake to find a calm, moon-lit night. Outside everything is still and quiet and bathed in a silvery, ghostly light which is in sharp contrast to the black silhouette of Dùn rising into the starry sky. It is a moment of pure magic and for a few seconds I feel a pang at leaving this beautiful place…*

Then the peacefulness of the scene is shattered by the steady drone of a large aircraft low over Ruaival. It circles the bay and I make it out easily as a Shackleton, which must be on some night patrol from RAF Ballykelly. I dress and go down to my office and call up the Duty Clerk at Benbecula to find out the latest on the sailing of the Mull*. Corporal Jones [Peter Jones, RAPC] reports that the loading party have already left the domestic site for Loch Carnan where they are to embark at 6am, and in such calm conditions the* Mull *cannot fail to leave South Uist for St Kilda. Later I hear that she has sailed at 6.45am and should be in the Sound of Harris by ten or eleven o'clock.*

I get the night generator attendant, Bracken, to go up to the billets and waken the men, while I rouse the RSM and the sergeants. By 7am the entire garrison is mustered on the jetty, to launch the raft which is moored at the foot of the slipway and serves as a landing for the cutter when it will be plying back and forth from the Mull*. By the light of searchlights and powerful sodium lamps the teams of men haul the heavy hawser down the slipway, anchor it to a bollard and attach the free ends to the raft and the Scammell winch respectively. As the winch is operated, the raft edges slowly forward on to the steep gradient of the roughly paved slipway and all hands are mustered to haul on the guide-lines and prevent the raft from slithering out of control.*

Gradually the raft is trundled down towards the water which is now at high tide. Hodgson directs the movement from his perch on the raft itself, and though the bay is calm the heavy swell which is always present sends the sea-water racing up the slipway, lashing the forward end of the raft and soaking poor Hodgson to the skin. Once she is in the water, however, the raft is easily made fast, fore and aft, to the stanchions on the jetty, with enough slack to allow for the ebbing tide. We estimate that, all being well, the Mull *will be here around three o'clock in the afternoon, by which time the tide will be rising once more, enabling heavy boats like the cutter to come in to the jetty.*

Breakfast at eight o'clock is followed by four frantic hours. I close the accounts, balance the books, check the canteen stock, the ammunition, the rum kegs and a hundred and one other items of lesser importance. The men are sweeping out their billets and tidying up the rubbish dumps; cleaning and polishing goes on all round. Mr Jessup superintends the stacking of crates of stores, empty beer barrels and all the personal kit – suitcases, holdalls, grips and parcels – of the twenty men who are returning to the Outer Hebrides and civilisation on this trip. By lunchtime the jetty is cluttered with all the outgoing bits and pieces.

RASC-V Mull*,*
St. Kilda's winter lifeline

Now we can have our mid-day meal and relax a bit, waiting only for the trawler to put in her appearance. It is a glorious day, not a breath of wind, a lovely blue sky, with the outline of the Western Isles on the horizon. Reilly reports from the top of Mullach Sgar that the Mull *can be seen with binoculars, about twenty miles away.*

At 3.10pm the Mull, *looking dirty and diminutive, steams smokily round the Point of Coll and pays out her anchor chain almost at once – for the* Mull *is notorious for her reluctance to come into the bay. Instead, she lies out near the end of Dùn, about a mile and a half from the jetty.*

We launch the dory and Hodgson and his crew go out to the Mull. *As if there is some jinx on her, the arrival of the* Mull *is the signal for the weather to change – and change it does with dramatic impact. Within half an hour, as darkness falls, the sea is that ghastly, angry steel-grey colour I have learned to fear so much, and great black clouds are rolling up from the south-east. The second trip of the dory is very tempestuous and the chaps come back to the jetty, soaked to the skin and almost swamped. Their cargo of mail from the outside world is saturated with sea-water and David has to lay the individual letters out on the radiators in the Medical Centre to dry before they can be handed over to the recipients, much to the annoyance and frustration of men yearning for the letters of their loved ones.*

The boat's crew change into fresh combat suits, but on their way out to the Mull *again the Seagull outboard engine breaks down and it is all they can do to row to the ship. The* Mull's *cutter is reluctantly launched and the work of ferrying stores ashore commences. Major McGregor, with Will Warner and his successor Desmond Williamson, step awkwardly out of the cutter on to the bucking raft and wobble groggily up the slimy steps of the jetty. We scarcely pause for greetings and introductions all round before continuing the ferrying of stores and personnel from the* Mull. *A chain is organised and kit and baggage is passed from the cutter to the jetty; everyone, officers and men alike, muck in as it is now a race against time. A south-easterly gale is expected at any moment and Village Bay is a danger to shipping when the wind is in that quarter.*

Mac, Will and Desmond have a very quick look round the camp and then head back to the jetty to watch the unloading, now being done in pitch darkness and torrential rain, through which our pitifully small searchlight can scarcely penetrate. An urgent blast from the Mull *tells us that all departing personnel must get aboard at once. All the stores on the jetty to be back-loaded to Benbecula are peremptorily abandoned. Only the precious mailbag, done up in a bright yellow PVC sack, is taken off the island and everything else is left behind.*

The voyage back to South Uist is on record as the roughest yet experienced, the ship spending nineteen hours at sea in a force ten gale. The ACC cook was too ill to prepare meals and the task of heating up tins of steak and kidney pud for the few souls hardy or hungry enough to face it fell to me. I was nothing if not versatile. Later, when the storm was at its worst and I was scared stiff, I put on my life-jacket and took refuge in the bathroom of the ship's officers where I wedged myself into the bath, the only place on the *Mull* where I could be reasonably sure of not being thrown around by the violent motion of the vessel.

11. ALARMS AND EXCURSIONS

Captain Desmond F. Williamson took over as OC of St Kilda on 20 January 1960, and relinquished his command in August 1961, about the same time that I left the Army. He thus served on the island over a period of twenty months, during which time I acted as his second in command (when duties increased with the build-up of military and service personnel in the summer missile-firing season) and then took over when he went off for very well-deserved leave periods.

Will Warner did not leave the Hebrides when his St Kilda tour came to an end, but remained at Benbecula. It is probable that he may have been retained there for the express purpose of alternating with his successor, but he only went back to St Kilda once, in March 1961; but a few days before the annual Admin Inspection he developed pains in his abdomen and left the island precipitately for exploratory surgery at Daliburgh Hospital. At this time his wife Jean and baby son had come up to Benbecula and obtained one of the very first officers' married quarters. Stuck with a further twelve months in the Hebrides, but understandably not relishing a return to St Kilda when Desmond Williamson went on leave, Will devised a novel solution to his problem. If he could make himself indispensable at Benbecula, St Kilda would fade into the background where it rightly belonged. The question of going back to St Kilda was largely academic in any case, so long as there was a crazy junior officer who not only never objected to being sent there but who positively relished the prospect.

Up to that time the permanent staff was headed by Lieutenant-Colonel Cooper as Range Controller and Commandant and Major McGregor as Administrative Officer, but subsequently – probably at the time that Lieutenant-Colonel Geoffrey Brewster took over as Commandant – Major Mac assumed the title of Second in Command (which he was, in reality), while Will Warner took on the role of Adjutant, an important functionary in all proper regiments but one which was curiously lacking in RAGWR. At this remove in time it is hard for me to recall precisely how these subtle changes were wrought, but I suspect that they were, to a large extent, generated from within, rather than created from outside, and that they merely evolved by some natural process without the direct intervention of the War Office or Scottish Command.

I am sure that my own diverse roles in this strange and unconventional unit came about in the same manner. I do not recall, for example, any Part I Orders that specifically appointed me as HQ Troop Commander at Benbecula, far less Relief OC St Kilda. In 1981, when a special postmark was used at St Kilda to celebrate the 25th anniversary of the Army's involvement with the island, the initials of nine regiments or corps were inscribed on it, like the spokes of a wheel, but of the tenth regiment represented there – the RAEC – there was no mention. Perhaps I never existed. Perhaps it was all a dream.

By late January 1960, however, nemesis had caught up with me, in the shape of Colonel A.E.Hargreaves, ERD, the Chief Education Officer at Scottish Command. Apparently he had tried to contact me the previous autumn, only to be told that I was attending a messing course at Aldershot. This would have been rather like sending an ACC officer on a course at the Army School of Education and it was sufficiently irregular to raise the Hargreaves hackles, but when he tried to track me down a few days later I was already safely tucked away for the winter on lone St Kilda. He bided his time, but immediately after my return to Benbecula I was summoned to Edinburgh where he and his GSOI, a lieutenant-colonel whose name I have forgotten, gave me a joint dressing-down. Where were my schemes of work? What visual aids had I created? How many men was I preparing for the Army Certificate of Education Third Class, for example? And so on and so on. Then came the tirade reminding me that I was an education officer and not a regimental officer. I took it all on the chin. What else could I have done? After all, I was only obeying orders... But mindful of Our Lord's precept to render unto Caesar the things that were Caesar's I promised to go off and be a good boy in future.

Back in Benbecula Colonel Cooper's reaction was predictable. How dare Scotco interfere with one of his boys in such a high-handed manner! A quick phone call to Brigadier Goschen, the new BRA, produced the suggestion that I apply for a permanent commission and transfer to the Gunners. I was flattered at their concern, but by this time I was developing a relationship with Mary Jackson (from the first work party of 1959) and she had very definite views on the subject. Her sister was married to a navigator in the RAF, and Mary had no wish to emulate her, with married life in quarters and the constant upheavals of service life. Moreover, I enjoyed life in the Hebrides so much, and St Kilda in particular, that I realised that it would be very hard for me to settle down in a proper regimental setting anywhere else. The annual personal assessment reports I received were fulsome to put it mildly, but I worked hard and rose to every challenge that was thrust in my path.

The gun, ruined Store House, Church, Manse, and Army buildings, 1959

In the end, we compromised. I would continue to take my fair share of regimental duties while Colonel Cooper would ensure that I got an adequate quota of men to be put through the various ACEs. I organised advanced courses for our technicians and introduced evening classes in motor maintenance for the islanders at our REME workshops. I held courses in conversational Gaelic for soldiers seeking appropriate chat-up lines for the island dances, and ran a class in elementary Russian for the more paranoid among us. I even coached Will Warner and Desmond Williamson in Current Affairs and History for their Staff College entrance exams, but the educational work that gave me the greatest satisfaction was with the Pioneers. It will be remembered that a squad of RPC had mysteriously joined us on the inaugural trip to the Hebrides. Thereafter, there was invariably a platoon of Pioneers based at the Range and employed mainly in the loading and unloading of stores from the landing craft. Many of them were National Servicemen with little or no educational attainments and several were completely illiterate. I might add that one of the Gunners was unable to read or write, and yet he was one of the few men who could drive the Scammell tractor up and down the St Kilda road which, near the summit, has the steepest and most vertiginous bend anywhere in the British Isles.

To cut a long story short, over the ensuing eighteen months I held classes in the three Rs for the Pioneers and got a considerable number of them through the ACE III, the first step to better pay and promotion. Unbeknown to me, the fact that somewhere in the Army there was an education officer who was actually giving the Pioneers the time of day had come to the attention of their Corps HQ and thereafter, as soon as one batch had acquired the basic rudiments, they were transferred out and another batch was posted in to the Hebrides. My efforts were rewarded not long before I left the Army when the Colonel Commandant of the Pioneer Corps flew up to Benbecula to thank me personally and present me with a copy of the RPC journal where my educational exploits were chronicled.

Ostensibly it was educational duties which took me out to St Kilda every month in the spring of 1960, and it was during this relatively quiet period that I got to know Desmond Williamson better. Where Will Warner had a rather flexible, pragmatic approach to life and work in general, Desmond was very regimental, a stickler for rules and regulations. When I first joined him he let it be known that he expected me to don my best blues on Wednesday evenings for a formal dinner, and when I queried this he said, 'We mustn't let ourselves get jungly, must we.' So from then on I had to pack my ceremonial uniform for St Kilda, all the more incongruous as it seldom got an airing at Benbecula. We both went through a phase of growing very military moustaches. Indeed, I still have a photograph of myself, on the jetty, in my blues, sporting a large moustache on my stiff upper lip, as Desmond and I prepared to go aboard the *Meteor*, the luxury liner which was then chartered by the National Trust's annual islands' cruise.

In April and May that year I spent several weeks on St Kilda. I went out on the last winter trip of the *Mull* on 27 March and deputised while Desmond got his first furlough after assuming command, and then after he returned on 8 May I stayed on to assist him as the detachment's numbers rose dramatically with the advent of the missile-firing season. At this time our garrison was augmented by a troop of Gunners from 108 Locating Battery under the command of Second Lieutenant Frank Tett, who were under canvas on part of the level ground between the fuel dump and the Signals Centre, where the RAF had camped in the summer of 1957. Unlike the RAF three years previously, the Locating Battery had some of the best weather I ever experienced. For days on end there was not a breath of wind and as the temperature soared the spirits of the soldiers, after a long hard winter, rose considerably. On 29 April LCT 4061 made her first voyage to St Kilda and I took a photograph of her on the beach with soldiers in their swimming trunks, fooling about in the surf. It was an idyllic picture and it is just as well that pictures may excite the eye, but do not reveal what assaults our olfactory senses – for the sea was the only place that spring in which you could escape the awful smell that hung like a miasma over Village Bay, but more of that anon.

The end of Dùn, showing the rugged outline and the great natural arch under the island

On 6 May Her Royal Highness Princess Margaret married Anthony Armstrong-Jones in Westminster Abbey. Almost thirty years earlier, the birth of Princess Margaret Rose at Glamis on 21 August 1930 had been almost driven off the front page of the nation's newspapers by the stories surrounding the imminent evacuation of St Kilda. Now, here we were on this lonely island, actually watching the ceremony as it happened – on television! At that time, there were many parts of Scotland which did not have the benefits of this Scottish invention, the Highlands and Islands being an area where the idiot's lantern was not yet lit. But here on lone St Kilda we had an electronics boffin by the name of Signalman Langdon who had been experimenting with a home-made set up at the Marconi radar station and had succeeded in getting a reasonable signal from the television station in Northern Ireland. The great day of the Royal Wedding was declared a public holiday on St Kilda. We all trooped up the hill and crowded into the Marconi station and there, in the flickering glow, we watched our beautiful young princess marrying her handsome young photographer. Was it my imagination or did our cook sergeant shed a tear? Afterwards it was a free can of beer for all ranks and three cheers for the bridal couple. Life was much simpler and infinitely more idealistic back in those days. Sadly, an attempt to pick up the English FA Cup Final the following afternoon was very disappointing and it was quite a few years later before television was something that could be watched from the relative comfort of the camp.

For two weeks in April we had a party of Paratroop Engineers from the Territorial Army unit in Hill Street, Glasgow under the joint command of Lieutenants Ewan MacLachlan and John Liversedge. Operation Birdwatch had the task of demolishing and removing the boulders blocking the jetty and the LCT ramp. This was a never-ending job every spring, like painting the Forth Bridge. Our puny efforts at clearing the way for the landing craft were set at naught every winter when the storms brought a fresh supply of boulders up from the deep to render navigation hazardous. Ewan was a giant of a man, in civilian life a schoolteacher in Mull. He was also a fluent Gaelic speaker, and soon after my marriage he sent me a very funny postcard in that language, speculating that the married quarters on Hirta might be Tigh Calum Mór. When they were not blasting rocks out of the bay, the Paras entered into the spirit of St Kilda, helped retrieve mailbags from erratic airdrops and went for jaunts round the islands in our dory. One of the youngest members of this team was a certain Sapper Connolly, an apprentice welder in one of the Clyde shipyards and very much the life and soul of the party. I had never met anyone with such a droll line in 'the patter'. Later on, of course, he would make a very handsome living at it.

Harry Russell (Nature Conservancy), Lieutenant Alan Smith, RA, Winwood Reade (BBC Natural History) and Malcolm Smith (resident warden) studying the map, using a dory as their table

LCT 4062 which brought Desmond back from leave also carried a party of naturalists under the command of Dr J. Morton Boyd of the Nature Conservancy Council in Edinburgh. I had briefly met him the previous summer, but now he was accompanied by Graham Gunn of the Hill Farming Research Organisation, Peter Jewell, an archaeological physiologist from Oxford, Bill Dunn (Morton's assistant) and Tex Geddes – 'bearded shark-hunter of Soay' according to the *Daily Express* – who was the coswain of the Nature Conservancy's boat *Fulmar*.

Tex was one of the most colourful characters I met on St Kilda. A native of Peterhead, he had gone with his father to Newfoundland at the age of two. When his father was killed in a logging accident a few years later, Tex was raised by the foreman lumberjack. Tex himself became a lumber monkey whose job was to shin up the tallest trees and lop off the topmost branches. As a teenager he joined the rum-runners who ran the US Coastguard blockade to take cargoes of liquor into Maine and Massachusetts during the Prohibition era. When the repeal of Prohibition in 1932 brought this lucrative career to an end, Tex drifted back to Scotland. In 1939 he enlisted in the Seaforth Highlanders and subsequently became an instructor at the Commando training centre in Arisaig, where he met up with Major Maxwell. Tex's wife Jan had been educated at Cheltenham Ladies College. As previously mentioned, he worked with Gavin Maxwell in the Inner Hebrides shark-hunting venture for several years before settling in the island of Soay – not our Soay, but its almost deserted namesake off the south coast of Skye. Here he wrote his book *Hebridean Sharker* and fell foul of neighbouring author Lilian *(The Hills is Lonely)* Beckwith who once stabbed him in the forearm with a pitchfork and landed in the Sheriff Court at Portree as a result.

The presence of Graham Gunn was explained by a calamity that had befallen the island's sheep. A census of the sheep the previous summer had yielded a total of 1,344, but this spring a horrendous epidemic reduced the flock to 610, including new-born lambs. The decimation of the sheep was due to an ailment which was variously described as grass staggers or pulpy kidney but which, I believe had the technical name of hypermagnesaemia. The epidemic which swept through the sheep began a few days before I landed, but within a week it had created nightmare conditions on Hirta. Scores of rotting carcasses littered the Village area, and it was not uncommon to observe a sheep, appearing to be grazing quite normally one minute, then stagger and fall down dead the next. The corpses that lay in the open were attacked by the birds, but even they could not cope with this unexpected largesse. Furthermore, many of the sheep had crawled into cleits to die; virtually every cleit within the head dyke had at least one corpse, while many had two or three entombed.

As luck would have it, there was a temporary breakdown in the VHF radio-telephone link the day I tried to contact Benbecula for advice, and was reduced to sending a coded signal instead. Back came a two word signal from my new CO, Lieutenant-Colonel Geoffrey Brewster who had succeeded George Cooper. All it said was 'Burn them'. I selected a site for a huge bonfire of broken crates and old rubber tires, and then called for volunteers. Sheep disposal, however, was a fearful task above and beyond the call of duty so I decided to offer a reward. Laughable as it may seem nowadays, I offered the men a shilling (5p) for every corpse they brought to the funeral pyre – and almost bankrupted the detachment's funds as a result. I had completely underestimated the iron constitution of the British soldier. A lucky few were equipped for this revolting business with General Service light respirators but most of the squaddies merely tied a handkerchief over their faces and manfully crawled into the cleits to drag out the bodies, many of which were now in an advanced state of decomposition. One soldier achieved the detachment record by bringing no fewer than 68 sheep to the bonfire, but the awful stench of rotting or burning flesh remained in our nostrils for days. One unexpected side effect of this week-long operation was that most of us became vegetarian for a considerable period.

Somehow the Nature Conservancy Council had got wind of this wretched business, and it was this that had brought Morton Boyd and his colleagues out to the island, hot foot. Morton was positively livid at what we had done. His bald head went several shades of puce as he ranted at me. Why had I burned the sheep instead of burying them? He had wanted to examine them and compile statistics of age, sex and general physical condition. This was an unreasonable and unrealistic stance, as we lacked a mechanical digger for constructing a huge pit, and the handful of picks and shovels in the store would have been totally inadequate. Besides, my men had more to do with their time than bury sheep. Desmond not only backed me up but also delivered a blistering counter-attack. For a horrible moment I thought that the two of them would come to blows. Although they backed off on this occasion, the ugly confrontation undoubtedly got Desmond off to a bad start with Morton Boyd, and the situation deteriorated from then onwards.

We had a new medical officer now, Captain Harry Chester, a jovial Irishman, and it was he who calmed the two belligerents as they squared up to each other. Harry pointed out that all those rotting corpses strewn everywhere were a very serious risk to the health of the Army personnel, and that this consideration was absolutely paramount. He hinted that there was always the danger of some discontented squaddie contacting his MP and creating a stink in Parliament which the tabloids would just love. I think it was the mention of the newspapers which brought Desmond and Morton to their senses. Harry went on to explain that though the pulpy kidney epidemic was not pathogenic to humans, the rotting sheep were a wonderful breeding ground for tetanus, and there was an edge to his voice as he quietly pointed out to the Nature Conservancy officer that as he, Harry, was responsible for the health of the garrison he insisted that the programme of burning the sheep had to continue without any interruption.

Boyd glowered and said no more but turned on his heel and stomped off. This, more than anything else, brought home to me the idiocy of siting a military base slap in the middle of a nature reserve. Inevitably there would be a conflict of interests, and over the ensuing weeks these rose sharply to the surface. Morton Boyd next had a go at us because 108 Locating Battery had pitched their tents outside the area leased by the Ministry of Defence from the Nature Conservancy. This was strictly true, but in all honesty there just was nowhere else to put them. I suspect that the MoD was at fault in not telling the Nature Conservancy that it was proposed to double the size of the garrison that summer.

From Desmond's viewpoint, however, the 'caveman behaviour' (as he put it) of the naturalists was totally unacceptable in what was, after all, the Officers' Mess, and obviously he had never encountered anything like this at Woolwich or Larkhill. The 'hairyologists' turned up at meal-times looking like absolute tramps and lounged around in muddy boots. One lunchtime, as I sat opposite Morton, I was horrified to see some sort of creature crawl slowly out of his beard and traverse his cheek. When I drew his attention to it, he plucked it off his face and calmly told me that it was a sheep tick. Clearly he had been in close contact with one of the survivors, but it was almost enough to turn my stomach.

As relations between the OC and the Nature Warden deteriorated, Desmond got his own back by refusing the Nature Conservancy permission to use the radio-telephone on security grounds – a specious argument considering that the Nature Conservancy Council was a government department. There was a whole host of petty, trivial matters between Desmond and Morton personally. The latter tended to make rather much of the fact that he had been a Staff Officer and Station Adjutant in the RAF and claimed that he had been a squadron-leader (equivalent to a major in the Army and thus one rank above Desmond). This cut no ice with Desmond who coolly pointed out that the War was ancient history and while Morton was on St Kilda he would have to conform to unit regulations at all times. Over the course of the ensuing fortnight there was an atmosphere in the Mess you could cut with a knife. Harry, Frank Tett and I adopted a neutral position, keeping well clear of entanglement in this childish feud.

Secretly I agreed with Desmond, but I felt that he had gone the wrong way about enforcing his authority and, when all was said and done, it was the Nature Conservancy who owned (or rather leased) the island, and the Army was merely their tenant. Harry, Frank and I had our own work to get on with, and in our spare time we went for long walks together. Sometimes we took the canoes out, when the sea calmed down sufficiently, and explored the numerous caves and geos (inlets) around Hirta and Dùn. Here we could escape the clash of personalities that was poisoning the atmosphere almost as much as the decaying sheep had done.

I made some attempt to mend fences between the Army and the naturalists and, in particular, I got on well with Peter Jewell whose double 'ology' intrigued me. I learned that he studied the anatomy of long dead and buried animals and fossils, although whether this fitted him to examine the calcined bones of the recently departed sheep was a moot point.

I also had a good rapport with Tex Geddes and never tired of his racy anecdotes, especially the tales of tangling with Norwegian poachers hunting sharks in the Minch. Tex was thoroughly fed up. He had come to St Kilda to run the *Fulmar*, but after a week he had not had a single opportunity to get it into the water. His book *Hebridean Sharker* was due to be published on 20 May, and I was privileged to have a sight of the page proofs. I was also favoured with the proofs of Morton Boyd's book *St Kilda Summer* which he co-wrote with Kenneth Williamson and which was due to be published that July. I was rather disappointed with it, finding many inaccuracies and omissions, and nothing at all about the RAF or RAGWR apart from passing references to the fact that they were here. Writing home on 15 May 1960 I said 'As a book, it will have an appeal to the naturalist or student of the Hebrides, but I'm afraid that there is startlingly little "human interest" for the general reader'. Desmond was characteristically mordant about it.

'Come on, Jim. How about you and I writing a sequel entitled *St Kilda Winter?*' This was said in a jocular mood but it was an appealing thought and about a year later I actually got around to producing a hundred pages of typescript which, forty years on, has been the basis for the earlier chapters of this book.

One of the objects of the naturalists' expedition was to make a landing on Boreray. Morton had briefly landed there in 1956 and twice in May 1959, and these trips had whetted his appetite for a more extended trip, involving a stay of several days. It was a prospect which intrigued and excited me also, and having read in his proofs about the visits of 1959 in which David Boddington had accompanied him, I did my best to ingratiate myself with him in the hope of being included in this year's expedition. Morton very quickly sized up the situation. We struck a bargain. He would take me to Boreray – that was a promise – but in exchange I would have to deal with the logistics of the expedition. Putting it crudely, it fell to me to scrounge the necessary supplies from the Army stores: emergency bedding, compo rations, cooking equipment and, above all, the vital radio sets which would enable communications to be maintained with Hirta. For several days I busied myself with these arrangements, much to Desmond's disgust and Harry's amusement.

On Sunday the weather began to improve and the barometer rose steadily. At long last, the attempt on Boreray was scheduled for the following day, if all went well. At a 'council of war' that night, however, Morton broke the news to me that, with all the stores they would have to take, it might not be possible to take me along after all. This was a bitter blow, yet, for some unaccountable reason, I had a hunch all along that week that I was being used and that the trip to Boreray was like the carrot to the donkey, dangled sufficiently often to secure my co-operation. I tried to console myself with the thought that I did not much relish having to cross the Chasm, involving a four-foot jump across a sloping ledge with a drop of 150 feet to the sea and the rocks below. 'If I get ashore on Boreray,' I wrote home that night, 'all well and good. But if not, whatever there is of archaeological value can wait for a more propitious moment.'

Inevitably I was left behind. Indeed, the matter was not so much as raised the following afternoon when the five-man team boarded the *Fulmar* and I was mug enough to help them load their gear and even accompanied them, still hoping against hope that I would be taken ashore at the last moment. The fact that I was actually in the boat gave the lie to Morton's excuse that there would be not enough space for me in the boat. Cynically he expected me to help Tex manoeuvre the boat while the four of them jumped ashore. His parting shot was to remind me to contact them by radio at noon and 6pm each day and give them a detailed weather forecast. Desmond could not conceal his jubilation when the *Fulmar* returned that night and in a crestfallen mood I climbed on to the jetty.

'Never mind,' he smirked. 'Now let's start planning what we have to do for our next lot of visitors.'

This was a reference to the National Trust for Scotland's annual cruise by the *Meteor* which was scheduled to arrive on Thursday morning. Desmond was very keen to put on a 'good show' and for forty-eight hours the camp was in a frenzy of spit and polish. It was every bit as bad as the annual Admin Inspection – worse, for there might be peers of the realm, like Lords Polwarth and Wemyss who were the big white chiefs in the Trust, and it would not do one's advancement in the Service any harm to impress them. This bout of frenzied activity only made me even more despondent at not having gone to Boreray, although I admit that, as the *Fulmar* had drawn close to that island it was a truly awesome sight.

In preparation for the liner's visit we had been sent a list of passengers' names and home addresses for security reasons, and as I scanned the list I had a peculiar sensation. Until that time I had never believed in coincidences, but now I got a shock when I recognised one of the names on the list. It so happened that by that time I had switched from stamp-

Puffin perched on the wall at the end of Dùn

collecting to postal history, another name for the collecting of used envelopes and postcards. As a result, I had become a subscriber to an exchange packet circuit operated by M.H. Robertshaw of Sheffield. Every month I would receive a parcel containing a large quantity of such material, individually priced. I would take out what I wanted and send a cheque in payment, then post the parcel to the next person on the list. A parcel had arrived by LCT a few days earlier and I was waiting for the next boat to Benbecula to forward it to the next man on the list. And now, by God knows how many million to one, that very person was on the passenger list! When the *Meteor* anchored off Dùn on Thursday morning and began ferrying the 120 passengers ashore, I put out a message over the PA system asking this gentleman to report to the Commanding Officers' office. A rather sheepish fellow in his late sixties shuffled uncertainly into the office wondering what he could possibly have done wrong.

'Dr Chisholm,' I said. 'Here is your club packet.' As he went out of the office I heard a woman's voice say, 'Oh no! I thought we could get away from stamps for a few days!'

We had a whale of a time that day. We were all on our best behaviour and were on hand at strategic points to show our visitors over the island. I was surprised to find myself treated like a minor celebrity for having found fulmars' eggs earlier than ever before recorded, and I was taped by Elizabeth Adair for a radio programme about the birds of St Kilda – and got paid two guineas for my trouble.

Major McGregor arrived in the course of the day aboard LCT 4062 and in the evening he, Desmond, Harry and I donned our blues and went out to the *Meteor* where we dined with Lord Polwarth and some of the celebrities of the natural world, including Joe Eggeling (Director of the Nature Conservancy), James Fisher (author and broadcaster) and Kenneth Williamson (co-author of *St Kilda Summer*). Ken Williamson intrigued me particularly. As a young serviceman during the Second World War, he had been posted to the Faroe Islands. Now I dare say that that was not everyone's cup of tea, but he made the most of his time there, acquiring a beautiful young wife and gathering the material for his book *Atlantic Islands* which remains a classic of the genre. It was the start of a very distinguished career in which he was successively Director of the Fair Isle Bird Observatory, Migration Research Officer of the British Trust for Ornithology and Editor of *Bird Migration*.

After dinner, the *Meteor* weighed anchor and took us on a cruise round the islands, culminating in the dramatic rescue of Morton and Co from Boreray after they had been marooned there for exactly 72 hours. To give him his due, when he came aboard Morton made a point of coming up to us and singling me out publicly to thank me most effusively for all my efforts before and during the Boreray expedition. All my little niggles about being cheated out of the excursion evaporated in an instant. Whatever his shortcomings, Morton Boyd was, indeed, the Staff Officer par excellence.

Mac and I sailed from St Kilda by landing craft that night, while the *Meteor* sailed on to Fair Isle, her next port of call. We had an uneventful trip and landed at Loch Carnan shortly before noon on Friday, 20 May. I was no sooner back on dry land, however, than I was called into Colonel Brewster's office, to be told that he had a special mission for me. The previous summer the missiles had all misbehaved. Some had travelled a short distance before coming down in relatively shallow seas to the west of the Outer Hebrides, and at least one refractory rocket had gone straight up, then come straight down again, to bury itself in the sand dunes barely a hundred yards from the launch pad. There was the fear that the Soviets might be able to retrieve parts of the rockets, especially the motors and guidance system, so, as a precaution, this summer the *Mull* would be on station off the coast. I was to be the liaison officer between the RAF reconnaissance aircraft, the Rangehead and a team of Royal Navy frogmen on South Uist. When a missile was fired it would be my task to pinpoint any which fell short of the target. We would sail to the point of impact, drop marker buoys and luminscent paint, and radio Benbecula to give the exact location. On Saturday I was given a highly sophisticated radio transmitter and the new NATO cipher and told to make myself conversant with it. What a life! Considering I had joined the Army, I seemed to be spending more time afloat or in the air than I did on the ground.

For several days I was on board the *Mull*, messing with the ship's officers and learning a lot about navigation. There were two cadets on board and I joined them for practical instruction from skipper Donny Ross. By day we stooged around the sea about fifteen or twenty miles out from South Uist, and on one occasion were quite close to St Kilda, but every evening we sailed north to anchor in the lee of the uninhabited island of Taransay (made famous by the *Castaway* documentary series on television in 2000). I would look longingly across at the twinkling lights of Tarbert and fancy a pint in the comfort of the Harris Hotel's lounge bar, but we had strict orders not to go ashore during the missile-firing session as there was a possibility of one or two night firings.

Late on Friday night, 27 May, the *Mull* returned to Loch Carnan and I disembarked. I had signalled our ETA and expected to be met by a Landrover, but instead the staff car was parked on the quayside. Inside was Major McGregor.

'I thought I had better come and meet you,' he said quietly. 'There's a helluva rumpus going on just now and the camp is swarming with newspapermen and photographers. Best if we keep you out of the way. Oh, did I mention it? There are two officers from MI6 who wish to debrief you…'

I was quaking in my boots as we drove through that eerie dusk effect you get in the Hebrides at midnight in midsummer. As we drove, Mac filled me in a bit more on what was going on. It appeared that some lobster fishermen from Grimsay had been out at the Monach Islands two days earlier and had seen this strange vessel. She looked like a trawler, but she was painted grey-blue all over and bristled with radar antennae. Of course it was the *Mull*, but imaginations were working overtime and the lobstermen were convinced that the Russians were spying on the Rocket Range. Back in Grimsay they telephoned the *Daily Express* and within 24 hours the sensational story about the Soviet Spy Armada was all over Fleet Street. While we were calmly sailing past North Uist and Benbecula on our way to Loch Carnan, sundry national newspapers had sent reporters to Benbecula to get to the bottom of the mystery. The camp was quiet and deserted by the time we got there, but there was a light on in the CO's office and here I met the two officers from SIS, both in plain clothes. Their brief was to check the movements of the *Mull* over the past week as we stood before a large-scale map.

'I can tell you exactly where we were and when we were there,' I said, 'for I kept a diary.' And over the next hour or so we plotted the ship's movements, day by day, on the map. The following Monday the story of the 'Russian Rocket Snoopers' was still grabbing the headlines, but by Wednesday, when questions were being asked in Parliament, and the Soviets were roundly condemned for their hypocrisy (they were at that very moment trying Gary Francis Powers, the U2 spy plane pilot), the War Office was becoming remarkably coy about the whole affair. The *Daily Mail's* defence correspondent stated, 'The Government is expected to turn a blind eye to the spying activities last week of radar-equipped Russian trawlers off the secret rocket range at South Uist'. Other papers were frankly baffled at the laid-back attitude of the War Office which would neither confirm nor deny the incident.

I had the last laugh. On 29 May the *Scottish Daily Express* chartered a DH Rapide of Cumberland Airways piloted by Tom Wood and flew a reporter and photographer up to Benbecula where it refuelled before going off to search for the mystery ship. As it happens, I volunteered to go along for the ride and seized the opportunity to drop a bag of mail over St Kilda. The newspapermen got a story of a sort, and a nice picture of St Kilda made the front page of the paper the following day alongside the headline 'Radar trackers pose as fishers'. But the staff reporter never twigged that the guy sitting beside him was the great Soviet spy himself.

Duckworth and Denis Hodgson, BEM on the mysterious drystone rampart at the end of Dùn

Private Duckworth, RAMC with a young puffin

The island of Soay from the bows of the dory; sea dead flat calm – ideal conditions for a landing on Soay

I WAS back on St Kilda for most of August 1960 when Desmond went on leave again. I had fifty men under my command, including a dozen War Department civilian labourers – 'quite a handful' was my comment in a letter home. I do not recall whether this was prophetic, or a laconic allusion to an incident which took place. One morning two soldiers came into the office to complain that one of the civvies had been trying to 'touch them up'. I groaned inwardly. There was nothing in the *Manual of Man Management and Morale* that covered such a situation. Such things were just not discussed. I sent off a signal to Benbecula for advice but all I got back was the laconic comment 'I told the War Office this would happen sooner or later'. Well, that was not much help. Fortunately, a landing craft was expected the following day and I made sure that the offending labourer was packed off the island.

We had a new medical officer, Lieutenant James Gallagher from Glasgow. Unlike Willie Stewart, Jim was game for anything and we took advantage of some very fine weather to make a number of jaunts to the other islands. Looking back on this now I am appalled at my irresponsible attitude, for if anything had happened to the boat on these excursions the results could have been disastrous. But back in 1959 both David Boddington and Will Warner had gone to Levenish, and David had been to Boreray and Stac an Armuinn. Besides, when you are twenty-three and have your own, independent command, you get a bit carried away some times. Denis Hodgson, now a Lance-Corporal, and Private Duckworth the medical orderly were two of the lads who went with us in the dory. Boreray, six miles away was the primary target and having sailed round it with Tex Geddes I was itching to get ashore. For all its fearsome appearance, Boreray was an easy island to land on, for there was a very convenient ledge near the southern tip, at a little cove called Coinneag. Denis Hodgson expertly manoeuvred the little boat at right angles to the ledge and gave us the shout, one by one, as we leapt on the crest of the wave from the bows on to the slippery rocks. Landing was one thing; but climbing up from the water's edge was something else altogether. Not only was the ascent very steep but the flinty rocks were tough on hands and feet. At the top of this cliff was an obstacle which Morton had christened the Bad Step. You had to step over a chasm that dropped sheer to the boiling surf at least 150 feet below; the problem was that the ledge on the other side was tilted at a bad angle. It was probably less than a metre from one side to the other but it was enough to test the nerves of the bravest cragsman.

Once past the Bad Step, however, the rest of the ascent, though a tough slog, presented no particular problems. The climb was well worth it, if only for the completely different perspective it gave us of Hirta; and it seemed strange to be looking down on those terrifying rock stacks, Boreray's satellites, for a change. All the while the sky was blackened by thousands of birds, first the gannets and then the dense clouds of puffins. Near the summit we passed the two bothies which had been used by the St Kildans in bygone times when they spent the summer on Boreray tending their flocks. I was particularly anxious heading for Tigh Stallar, a structure of immense antiquity but of which little now remained, its stones having been plundered to build the bothies. Macaulay's history of St Kilda (1758) related how a party of St Kildans were stranded on Boreray for several months over the winter of 1740-1, while Hirta was ravaged by a smallpox epidemic that left too few able-bodied men to man a rescue boat, and it was not until the factor visited St Kilda the following spring that they were relieved. Just the thought of being stuck on Boreray gave me the shivers.

The previous summer Morton, accompanied by David Boddington and some others, had managed to land on Stac an Armuinn, and on one of those rare days in early August when the sea was like a millpond, although the crags were wreathed in mist, we effected a landing near Am Biran and managed to struggle upwards by wedging ourselves in a diagonal crevice. But the din of seabirds was a terrible distraction, and a shout from Hodgson, concerned at a dark cloud that presaged the imminence of a squall, hastened our return to the water's edge

In his book Morton Boyd made a great thing about his landing on Levenish, where Will Warner had gone with Bob Reilly to erect a radar beacon in May 1959. The following year I accompanied the naturalist Donald Baird (whom I had known at Glasgow University) when he came out to St Kilda to study Leach's fork-tailed petrels as part of his doctoral thesis. Levenish proved to house quite a colony of these elusive little birds and we spent a fascinating day there. Although this little island, little more than a rock really, was often enveloped in spray when there was an easterly gale blowing we landed easily and the climb to the summit was straightforward. My excuse for going there was to check that the radar beacon was intact, but I learned a lot about the birds. Donald found a colony of greater black-backed gulls near the summit, their nesting site littered with the sad remains of puffins which had been slit open and literally pulled inside out so that the gulls could pick off the flesh at their leisure. Black-backs are handsome birds but every time I see that wicked curved beak I shudder at the memory of the poor little puffins. Our boatman on this and other excursions to the lesser islands was Gunner Kenny Macdonald from Lewis.

When it came to the saga of Soay, Morton waxed lyrical, devoting several pages of his book to a blow by blow, hand-hold by foot-hold description of how he clung like Spiderman to the sheer cliff face and gradually inched his way to the top. To be sure, we made several attempts to land on Soay but were beaten back by the swell, the velocity of which seemed to increase sharply in the narrows that separated the island from the Cambir. Even when the surrounding seas resembled a mill pond, that swell seemed ever-present. Then one day when there was not a breath of wind and the time of the month was deemed to be right, we sailed round to Soay once more. At slack water on a spring tide, when the enormous boulders at the foot of the cliff were more exposed than usual, we managed to edge the dory through masses of kelp. We had had calm weather for over a week, and the swell had spent itself. Conditions were absolutely perfect, and several of us succeeded in getting ashore.

Soay Sound from the dory. The virtually inaccessible island of Soay is on the left and the cliffs below the Cambir on Hirta are on the right

The ascent of the cliff was tricky and foolishly we attempted it without the usual paraphernalia of the mountaineer. Come to think of it, we achieved the ascent in our Army issue plimsolls whereas Morton Boyd had landed in his stocking soles, just like the St Kildans of old. Unfortunately, by the time we had succeeded in reaching the summit the wind had freshened up so we had barely a few minutes to look for the wreckage of the aircraft which Morton had thought was a Warwick. Sixteen years of exposure to the 100-knot winds and torrential rain had left little in the way of wreckage, far less human remains. The opinion was that the plane might have been German, although we could find no evidence of wing or tail-fin markings to substantiate that theory.

The descent to the boat was scary, to put it mildly, and several times we slipped and almost fell. Had we done so, we would have been dashed to pieces on those enormous rocks. The tide was on the turn and the swell was ominously more evident by the time we scrambled down the last fifty feet and dropped straight into the water whence we were fished out and clumsily hauled ourselves over the gunwhales.

The euphoria at landing on Soay is difficult to describe. We decided that this feat deserved some permanent memento, so the following day, when the weather conditions seemed just as ideal, we returned. This time we had a bucket of cement and a sheet of metal on which the REME workshop had punched a suitable inscription with the date of our landing. We made an even better landing than on the previous day but ran into a problem as to where to fix the plaque. In the end it was cemented to the top of an outcrop and we scrambled back to the boat with the feeling of a job well done. I have often wondered whether our plaque is still there, but in view of the fact that several landings by helicopter were made in the 1970s to examine the wreck of the Wellington, and no mention has ever been made of the plaque, I suspect that it became a casualty of the dreadful wind and weather of St Kilda.

During this spell on St Kilda I had as my 2IC Second Lieutenant Alan Kennard, RA, a National Service officer. I infected him with my enthusiasm for postal history and for a time he was even a member of the British Postmark Society which we both joined; but I regret to say that he never succeeded in infecting me with his great passion which was bug-hunting. He was, in fact, a confirmed lepidopterist (or 'unmarried moth-er' as one wag put it). He was simply dying to get out to St Kilda to see what the moths and butterflies were like. To this end, he seemed to have rather a lot of kit with him when he disembarked from a landing craft. It turned out that he had a very powerful lamp, complete with his own portable generator, and a contraption that resembled a metal dustbin, all of which he proceeded to erect on the summit of Conachair. This device worked perfectly and I was astonished the following morning when I accompanied him and found the dustbin full of a seething mass of befuddled moths. Every winged insect for miles around must have homed in on the beam from Alan's lamp. He was elated at the results, although I wondered how he was ever going to sort out that horrible mess, far less mount the poor creatures on the boards that cluttered his bedroom in the Factor's House. Clearly I had not reckoned on his single-minded dedication to his hobby.

All went well for several days, until I got a signal from Benbecula. Scottish Command had been on to the Range, and Scottish Command in turn had got it in the neck from an organisation hitherto unknown to me but which rejoiced in the grand title of Commissioners of Northern Lighthouses. It had come to their attention that an unidentified light had suddenly appeared and was confusing trawlers and other fishing vessels coming back from the Rockall Bank into thinking that they were off the Flannan Isles, actually some forty miles north of us. Suspecting that the Army were up to no good, the Commissioners had read the riot act to Scotco and they had delivered a rocket of their own, and now, metaphorically speaking, it had landed on my desk. So Alan was ordered to dismantle his equipment. From then on he concentrated on the butterflies which he could catch on the wing by means of a large net, much to the amusement of the soldiers.

When he left St Kilda and returned to Benbecula a few weeks later he presented me with one of his nets and a killing jar and implored me to continue his good work. I shook my head vigorously. There was no way I would be seen traipsing over the island with the butterfly net. I reminded him that I was the OC and had a position to maintain. He would not take no for an answer but left the net and the jar just in case I changed my mind.

Some time later I was sitting on the toilet minding my own business when suddenly I was aware of an enormous moth with unusual wing markings, resting on the toilet wall. I tore off a strip of toilet roll, carefully scooped up the moth and bore it gingerly across the street, into the house and then popped it into the killing jar. In due course I shipped the moth back to Benbecula. It turned out to be a hitherto unrecorded species and Alan wrote it up at great length in a lepidopterists' periodical, giving me full credit for the discovery – well, not that full, fortunately, for he tactfully omitted to record the peculiar circumstances in which I had trapped it.

12. MY LAST YEAR ON ST KILDA

I took over from Desmond Williamson on 4 August 1960, travelling out to St Kilda on the last landing craft of the season. As if to emphasise this point, the ship was laden down with eight months' supplies of foodstuffs, some frozen but most tinned or dried, which would see us through the winter till the following April. The thought that St Kilda's winter was effectively all the months with an 'r' in them was a depressing one. As usual, we arrived very late at night after an extremely choppy voyage during which many of the passengers had been sick. Standing on the bridge, located aft, I could not take my eyes off the bows which appeared to be turning and twisting this way and that and it occurred to me that the torsion on the ship's sides would eventually cause her to rip apart. Metal fatigue was a relatively new concept, and although it had been detected in aircraft it struck me that something as frail as a landing craft could not withstand such a buffeting by wind and waves indefinitely. We had precious little sleep that night, and all hands were up early the following morning to unload eight months' stores in under five hours. As if to reinforce the fact that we were unloading the winter supplies, the temperature suddenly dropped, exacerbated by a biting wind and a relentless drizzle.

St Kilda had acquired a new landmark since my last visit, a splendid flagpole from which fluttered the Union Jack. The pole, in fact, had been the main-mast of a luxury yacht, the *Avocet*, which had sailed into Village Bay on 3 June with a National Trust work party. Having disembarked the thirteen men and women of the work party, however, the yacht did not immediately depart but remained at anchor in the bay. At 3.20am the following morning the work party were roused from their well-earned slumbers by Bill, the eighteen year-old son of the skipper and owner, John Maitland.

'Hurry!' he screamed. 'The *Avocet* is going on the rocks! My father is alone. Oh, please, hurry!' A gale had risen with sudden ferocity and ripped the yacht from her moorings barely forty yards from the shore. Young Bill had managed to launch the yacht's dinghy but while rowing furiously towards the jetty it had capsized and for a time he was trapped underneath before he managed somehow to struggle free and swim the rest of the way, stumbling ashore more dead than alive, to raise the alarm. Several of the work party threw clothes over their pyjamas and rushed down to the storm beach where they found the dinghy overturned on the boulders but miraculously undamaged. They righted it and tried to row out to the *Avocet* but were defeated by the mountainous seas. By now the wind had veered round to the east-south-east and was blasting straight into the bay. Bryon Harvey and Bill Condie eventually reached the stricken yacht and clambered aboard. For five hours they wrestled with the anchor cables. By now the Army had been alerted and the dory had been launched. Denis Hodgson and his volunteer crew of four made several attempts to reach the yacht and in so doing almost overturned. No sooner had the dory secured the yacht's second anchor than she capsized, and the crew had to swim ashore. If anyone ever deserved a bar to the BEM for gallantry it was Denis Hodgson.

All attempts to tow the yacht away failed. Caught on a lee shore in a force nine gale she inevitably dragged her anchors and

The Medical Centre cum Post Office, Corporal McCarthy and Private Woodburn, RAMC, medical orderlies and postmen, posing with mailbags

ended up on the rocks. When the storm subsided and the tide ebbed she was left high and dry. One of her port-holes burst open with the force of the water which had accumulated in her hull. She lay at a drunken angle, her cabins flooded to the ceiling, A well-meaning attempt by the Army bulldozer to push her off the rocks into deep water merely stove in her bows. Later in the day the *Mull*, despatched from South Uist as soon as the alarm had been raised, entered the bay and attempted to haul the yacht off the rocks at high tide, but by now the damage was so extensive that she was beyond salvage. Maitland was not ready to give up, pleading with the Army technicians to repair the burst port-hole and bows, so that the yacht could be pumped out before the tide came in again, but this was wholly unrealistic. Sure enough, the yacht was pounded to matchwood with the incoming tide and the rising wind. The Army managed to salvage her beautiful brass bell, the masts and some spars but precious little else, and in due course the main-mast was erected in front of the camp. It remained there throughout the rest of my sojourn in the Hebrides but it was subsequently taken down. Strangely enough, it was still lying there, at the top of the storm beach, when I visited St Kilda in July 2001.

Fortunately the only mishap during this trip to St Kilda occurred on the day I left when the mailbag, coming ashore from LCT 4061, fell into the drink and was reduced to a sodden pulp. Two events worthy of note occurred on 19 August. The first was an airdrop by Bill Hamilton. Only forty letters were dropped, as the *Mull* had set off for St Kilda the previous day and, in fact, docked in the bay on the morning of the airdrop, so only the handful of mail which had accumulated overnight was flown. But this was a historic flight, the first under the official contract between the Ministry of Defence and Airworks, and to mark the occasion a three-line rubber stamp, inscribed FIRST OFFICIAL AIRDROP / BENBECULA – ST KILDA / AIRWORKS SERVICES PERTH was applied to the mail alongside the usual oval datestamp. The *Mull*, however, brought with her a Colonel Wellsted, RE who had come to inspect the various installations maintained by our Sappers. In fact he was more interested in getting specimens of the Puffin cachet on his souvenir postcards and impressing on me his earnest wish to have some letters despatched by the next Tin Can Mail. Discovering my interest in postal markings he subsequently introduced me to his brother, the notable postal historian W. Raife Wellsted whose collection of St Kilda mail, much of which emanated from me, is now beautifully preserved in the National Postal Museum, London.

Among the forty letters which arrived by that first official airdrop was one addressed 'For the Mayor or Governing Authority of St Kilda, Hebrides, Scotland'. The writer of the letter enclosed a newspaper cutting from a syndicated column entitled 'Believe it or not' by Ripley. The cutting asserted that, prior to 1930, the people of St Kilda had communicated with the mainland by means of toy boats consigned to the wind and waves. Wayne Harbour of Bedford, Iowa now wrote to enquire whether there was any truth in this allegation. I subsequently discovered that Ripley paid out a handsome reward to anybody who could disprove his statements and clearly Mr Harbour had this cash prize in his sights. His aerogramme ended with a postscript: 'Who do you folks think will be our next President, Nixon or Kennedy?' In my reply, which confirmed the gist of Ripley's claim, I concluded with a postscript of my own: 'Who are Nixon and Kennedy?'

ON my return to Benbecula at the beginning of September 1960 I was immediately thrust into the frenetic business of preparing for our first ever Royal Visit. On 7 September Her Majesty Queen Elizabeth the Queen Mother came to Benbecula and formally inaugurated the North Ford Causeway which linked the island, via Grimsay, to North Uist. In my capacity as Mess Secretary I was involved in the arrangements for the hospitality accorded Her Majesty in the Officers' Mess, the only building on Benbecula which was large enough to accommodate the Inverness-shire county councillors, the Lord Lieutenant and the royal retinue. The officers of the Permanent Staff were banished to the colonel's house for lunch that day, leaving me and Gordon Hume, our ACC officer, to deal with the VIPs.

There was one slight logistical problem; the Officers' Mess did not have a ladies' toilet. Fortunately, the Ministry of Works had the solution, and a few days before the Royal Visit an aircraft arrived from London with a prefabricated building, comprising a toilet cubicle and a little sitting room, which was bolted on to the side of the Mess. A door was cut through the wall, a fitted carpet was laid, and on the eve of the visit I must say that it was a rather splendid addition. All the banging and sawing and assorted upheavals were well worth it, for now we had an extremely useful amenity which meant that, henceforward, our female visitors on guest nights would not have to go across the road to one of the married quarters to powder their noses. The sitting room was equipped with two easy chairs and a table on which was set a silver salver with various glasses and an assortment of bottles of gin and Dubonnet as prescribed by some edict handed down from on high. When the Queen Mum arrived with her lady-in-waiting it was my task to escort the ladies into the Mess and discreetly indicate the facilities. What was most memorable for me was not so much meeting the Queen Mother but her lady-in-waiting, Lady Jean Rankin. During the course of a brief conversation it transpired that she had been to St Kilda in the early 1930s when she and her husband, the naturalist Niall Rankin, had accompanied the Earl of Dumfries, and as a result of this chance encounter I subsequently met Colonel Rankin himself in London and got an interesting first-hand account of the two summers (1934-5) that he spent on the island.

While Gordon Hume supervised the cooks in the kitchen, I donned a mess-waiter's white jacket and superintended our civilian waitresses as they handed out drinks and canapés to the mob of councillors, our Member of Parliament and sundry other dignitaries in the ante-room. There was an ensign in the Household Cavalry, some kind of aide de camp to the Queen Mother, who had rather too much to drink and was throwing his weight around when the waitresses failed to replenish his glass quickly enough. When he saw me he turned his obnoxious attentions on me, until I quietly drew him aside, told him (1) that I was the Mess Secretary and (2) I outranked him, and that if he did not behave I would put him on a charge.

I regret to say that, no sooner had the royal party and assorted hangers-on departed for the actual tape-cutting ceremony at the North Ford, than the Ministry of Works people moved in and dismantled the Queen Mum's loo, which was carted back to London the following day at vast expense.

Such was the hullabaloo surrounding the Royal Visit that the arrival of another personage that very day almost passed unnoticed, but when the VIPs had wined and dined and set off in a cavalcade of specially imported limousines for the Causeway I realised that there was a rather strange individual in the lobby. He was wearing a Norfolk tweed jacket and plus fours and brandished a letter of introduction from 'my old chum, Johnny French' who just happened to be General Sir John French, the Director of Royal Artillery at the War Office. I scrutinised this chit which informed us that the bearer was one Hammond Innes and that we were to accord him every facility. It turned out that he was a novelist and that he had some half-baked notion about writing a thriller about Hebridean crofters and their unceasing battle with the elements to scratch a living from the soil and the sea. In an article which he wrote for *The Scotsman* (1 September 1962) he described how he, 'A Highlander myself, was conscious of the strange fascination of that empty world'.

Well, if he was a Highlander then I was an Eskimo. He was very much a product of London and the Home Counties, and at that time was living in Kersey, Suffolk.

One of my 'dogsbody' duties was to act as guide to visiting Brass and other VIPs and so it was that I got lumbered with Hammond Innes over the ensuing week. Colonel Brewster put a Landrover at his disposal and I drove the novelist all over the Uists. At best he was patronising, at worst supercilious and barely able to conceal his contempt for his 'fellow Highlanders'. But what really annoyed me most of all was the way he put Major Mac down. It will be remembered that Mac loved messing about in boats and his pride and joy was our little cabin cruiser, the *Kirstag*. Mac had the bright idea that Hammond Innes would appreciate a jaunt in our boat. The little islands off the east coast of Benbecula and North Uist were like emeralds set in a deep blue sea and the weather that week had never been better; but the novelist took one look at our little boat and let it be known that he would not be seen dead on such a tub, adding gratuitously that he had sailed the seven seas in his own ocean-going yacht, the *Mary Deare* (named after one of his best-selling novels). Mac was totally crushed by this, and from that moment onwards I loathed Innes and was determined to teach him a lesson.

On 15 September Bill Hamilton flew in from Scone with the intention of flying around the Rangehead as part of the Air Co-operation programme. It was a dreadful day, a total contrast to the splendid weather we had had earlier in the week. Normally we would never have dreamed of attempting an airdrop in such atrocious conditions, but it seemed to me that this was a heaven-sent opportunity to take our bumptious guest down a peg, so I told Bill what I had in mind, knowing that he was always game for such daredevil nonsense. There were only thirty-five letters in the bag but that was sufficient excuse, and soon we took off, myself in the back seat with the mail and Hammond Innes in the co-pilot's seat. The article he wrote two years later under the title of 'Flight to St Kilda' was inaccurate in a number of details, not the least being the date which he gave as 9 September when in fact it was six days later. The 40-knot wind and eight-eighths cloud at a thousand feet were true enough, but his account states that we climbed to 6000 feet to get above the cloud and then let down through the cloud – something that no pilot in the vicinity of St Kilda would ever have done. In fact we flew below the clouds all the way, and as the weather closed in we got closer and closer to the waves, until we were flying at an altitude of twenty feet and were occasionally buffeted by spindrift. Eventually Bill said over the intercom, 'I think we've missed it. I'm turning back,' and gaining height he did a rate-one turn and commenced the flight back to Benbecula. Suddenly the sky darkened ominously. There was a sudden surge of the engines as Bill applied full throttle and climbed so steeply that I was thrust hard back into my seat. I had to struggle to sit up and peer out of the window – to see the jagged pinnacles of Boreray flash past the port wing-tip! We turned hard to starboard and raced across the water, skimming the cliff top and hurtling down the V-shaped gap between Oiseval and Conachair. As we plunged towards Village Bay the eddies and gusts hit the aircraft like a bomber going through flak. Standing on his port wing-tip over the end of the jetty, Bill pulled his ancient, creaking Consul round and roared across the bay, neatly side-stepping Levenish as we headed for home. I had barely a second to chuck the flimsy bag out of the door somewhere over the domestic site as we went.

Back at Benbecula Airport I helped a very ashen-faced Hammond Innes totter out of the plane and across to the terminal building. Bill smirked as he handed me a puke-bag and asked me to dispose of it. Back in the Mess, his hands still shaking from the ordeal, the novelist confessed that that was the worst experience he had ever had.

'Oh, that's fairly typical for an airdrop,' I said as nonchalantly as I could muster. To tell the truth, I was pretty shaken by it myself but took care not to show it Then I added, 'Though I have to admit, when Borerary suddenly loomed out of the mist I thought we were going to be Number Four.'

'What do you mean?'

I then told him about the three wartime aircraft which had crashed on Soay and

Hirta, and with bloodthirsty relish I repeated the hoary old tale about the survivor of the Sunderland who had allegedly fed on the flesh of his comrades. Suddenly Innes perked up and there was a fresh glint in his eye. That evening, after dinner, he borrowed my large-scale map of St Kilda (I never got it back, incidentally) and asked me to indicate on it the sites of the three crashes. He took copious notes while he picked my brains about the Sunderland. Although his *Scotsman* article says that he flew over St Kilda again the following day in perfect weather he never did. Instead he went back to Suffolk and in due course wrote his novel *Atlantic Fury*, the plot of which revolved around the tale of cannibalism on the mythical island of Laerg, but actually Hirta thinly disguised. He eventually visited St Kilda in the spring of 1962, but his book had been written by that time and was published soon afterwards.

He got his revenge on me, though. The characters of the officers at the Rocket Range in the novel were based on real people, and in Ferguson the Adjutant I saw myself. He was described as having 'a raw Glasgow accent', and as I was the only Lowland Scot on the Permanent Staff I took this jibe personally.

On 22 September 1960 I went on leave, journeying south to Birmingham where Mary and I were married in Bournville parish church two days later. Gordon Hume was my best man, but David Boddington came over from Bromyard to attend our wedding. Mary and I spent our honeymoon in Skye. At one extreme we visited the ruined croft in the Braes where my maternal grandfather had been born; at the other extreme we were invited to lunch at Dunvegan Castle by Dame Flora MacLeod of MacLeod, then well into her eighties but remarkably alert. In the public corridor outside her dining room hung a St Kilda mailboat which had been despatched in August 1930 by Alasdair Alpin MacGregor, the last of the mailboats to leave the island before the evacuation. It had been recovered in northern Norway and was now one of the attractions, along with the Fairy Flag and Rory Mór's drinking horn, for visitors to this stately home. Dame Flora's ancestors had been lairds of St Kilda since time immemorial, but soon after the evacuation her father, Sir Reginald, had sold the island group to the Earl of Dumfries, later fifth Marquess of Bute. Sir Reginald was probably glad to get rid of St Kilda and had only hung on to it out of a sentimental attachment to his hardy tenants, but with their departure there was no incentive to retain such a romantic white elephant. Although the sale severed the personal connection of the MacLeods of MacLeod with St Kilda, I was heartened to discover, on a recent visit to Dunvegan, that there is now an extensive display of island relics in the basement gallery, and down in the village the estate souvenir shop rejoices in the name of The St Kilda Connection. Mary and I also made a pilgrimage to the tiny windswept kirkyard of Trumpan at the northern extremity of the Waternish peninsula, and visited the unmarked grave which was the last resting place of Rachel Erskine, Lady Grange, St Kilda's most celebrated resident.

Back in June 1959, when Mary travelled south to return to her home in Birmingham, she had to catch a train at Glasgow's Central Station. Arriving early, she killed time by wandering along Argyle Street and thus stumbled across McLaren's Gaelic bookshop. Going inside, she asked the shop assistant for an introductory guide to the language and for three and sixpence purchased a copy of *Gaelic Without Groans*. The lady behind the counter was intrigued at an English girl wishing to learn Gaelic and by way of explanation Mary said that she had just been on St Kilda.

'Is that a fact?' said Morag Ferguson. 'My husband is a St Kildan!' Her husband John was the younger son of Neil Ferguson, the island's last postmaster. The upshot of this was that Mary obtained their address in East Kilbride and I then got in touch with them. When I went on leave later that summer I visited them and found a right royal ceilidh attended by every other St Kildan then living in the greater Glasgow area. John's brother Donald (shown on a famous picture postcard of 1929 posting a letter in the island's mailbox) was a lighthouse keeper, and on one occasion I cycled along a terrible mountain track to get to a remote lighthouse on the east coast of South Uist to visit him. Neil

Gillies, who had been the coast-watcher for the Earl of Dumfries during the 1930s, lived in Garthamlock and we corresponded for many years and met from time to time.

Of all the St Kildans I met, however, by far the most interesting was John's uncle, the redoubtable Alexander Gillies Ferguson who lived with his second wife in a bungalow, appropriately named 'St Kilda' at Dalnottarhill in Old Kilpatrick. Immediately after my honeymoon I paid him a visit before returning to the Hebrides. He was then aged eighty-seven and terminally ill, but he was as alert mentally as ever. His house was a veritable museum of the island, replete with paintings, framed photographs and even stuffed birds. I have often wondered what happened to these precious mementoes and hope that they have been preserved for posterity. I filled several notebooks with the reminiscences of this fine old Highland gentleman, and some day, perhaps, they will form the basis for another book. He died about two months after my last visit.

I had another stint on St Kilda the following Christmas, sailing out on the Mull on 8 December and returning to Benbecula on 21 January. Unlike the previous winter, the weather was remarkably good, and for once we had something like regular weekly sailings, the *Mull* calling on 14 and 21 December and bringing out our Christmas parcels including boxes of Christmas puddings and cartons of liquor. Two days earlier, however, Bill Hamilton carried out a heroic Christmas airdrop which brought the great bulk of our letters and greetings cards. His colleague Les Bolton made an airdrop on 4 January 1961 which I noted contained no fewer than 520 letters (including a great many late Christmas cards). There was a further airdrop on 10 January, carried out by Cyril Sweetman, so all things considered we did extremely well for mail that winter.

Mercifully for me, the extraordinarily mild weather that winter continued well into the new year with only one cold snap early in January when winds which seemed to be coming straight down from the North Pole brought us a sharp frost followed by a blizzard. It was of brief duration but for about an hour St Kilda was totally transformed. We rushed out to photograph this strange sight before the snow melted. Two years earlier there had been a similar snow-shower of brief duration – just long enough to enable David Boddington to risk life and limb by scrambling up the flank of Oiseval to photograph Village Bay mantled in white. I understand that on one occasion in fairly recent years there was a very heavy snowfall which resulted in drifts up to three feet deep on the summit of Mullach Mór, but that must have been truly exceptional. The generally calm weather, however, broke at the end of January and from then on heavy rain and high winds were the order of the day. Gusts of 78 mph were recorded at Stornoway on 26 January and the following day a gust of 94 mph was recorded. On St Kilda, however, wind speeds in excess of 130 mph were recorded and on several days it was impossible to leave the billets, far less drive up the road. Stephen Gray, who was OC in 1962, later recorded that on one occasion he and his Battery Sergeant Major were lifted bodily into the air and propelled a distance of twenty yards.

During the winter of 1960-1 we saw more and more of the Spanish trawlers. Most of them belonged to the Alvamar company of San Sebastian and rejoiced in names beginning with the same initial letter: *Andino, Arzibal* and so on; but my favourite was the beautiful vessel with a name to match, the *Virgen de la Merced*. We had a new doctor, Captain Noel Roy, and like his predecessors he welcomed the diversion of having some human patients to treat. By and large the soldiers were a disgustingly healthy lot, although I recollect that Sergeant Bennett, our RE Clerk of Works, had to be evacuated by helicopter in July 1960 with a ruptured appendix.

The Sappers seem to have been accident prone for in March 1961 our plumber, William Laity from Camborne in Cornwall, fell and broke his leg. He was airlifted from the island along with a seaman from the San Sebastian trawler *Teresa Lopez*, Castor Lagos, whose foot had been crushed and partially severed when it was caught in the winch while dropping the anchor. Noel amputated the foot in a two-hour operation. On this occasion Desmond acted as anaesthetist and, I think, was also one of the three soldiers who gave a pint of blood for good measure. Both injured men were taken by RAF Whirlwind helicopter flown by Pilot Officer Bill McEachern to the hospital in Oban. Laity's pals erected a concrete plaque in the camp area inscribed TO PLUMB, RE WHO BROKE A LEG WHILE SERVING QUEEN AND COUNTRY. WHAT A SHAME – 40 DAYS TO DO. ROLL ON DEMOB!

I was on the last voyage of the *Mull* that winter when I went out to St Kilda on 6 April. In fact, it was one of the pleasantest voyages, with not a breath of wind and brilliant sunshine all the way through the Sound of Harris, so much so that I got quite badly sunburned. We anchored in the bay at 4.30pm and after the usual frantic loading and unloading of stores and going through the ritual of the handover, the trawler was off again before sunset. The one thing I never got used to on St Kilda was the terrible rush whenever the *Mull* or a landing craft arrived. Their reluctance to remain in the bay a minute longer than could be helped was understandable, but there was always so much to do and so very little time to do it.

This was borne in on me on this particular trip for it was during a two-month period (April and May 1961) that the Directorate of Army Postal Services, based at Post Office Headquarters in St Martins le Grand, decided to bombard us with a daily test letter. Each of these missives was numbered and inside was a questionnaire which had to be completed and returned by the next available post. The trouble was that these wretched questionnaires tended to arrive in bunches, depending on the frequency of ships or airdrops. If a landing craft arrived at 11pm and was off again at 4am, I had to deal with a mass of 'bumf', quite apart from these test letters. I am afraid that when I returned the first batch I enclosed a letter explaining that, quite frankly, we did not have the time to deal with such trivia and that, in any case, what with airdrops in one direction and the adroit use of the Spanish trawlers to augment the infrequent visits of Army vessels – not to mention the occasional St Kilda 'mailboat' – I could not see how we could possibly improve on the service.

The beach in Village Bay at low tide, showing the strip of sand below the storm beach of boulders.

In due course I received a very nice response (in the circumstances) thanking me for my very full and revealing letter. It did not occur to me at the time, but it has struck me now, that this exercise may have had something to do with the decision of the War Office to scrap the outmoded Fleetwood system and award a contract to Airworks, thus making the airdrops official and above board. These test letters, by the way, came in buff envelopes with official 're-use' labels and the certifying cachet of the DAPS, but they were mailed from various parts of London and Kingston-upon-Thames, seemingly at random. Several of them were missent to the Foreign Section or the Home Depot of the Royal Engineers Postal Service at Mill Hill before leaving London, and some were missent to Stornoway or even Lerwick, Shetland before they found their way to St Kilda.

Two or three test letters even arrived by helicopter on 26 May when there was yet another emergency evacuation of an injured Spanish trawlerman. This time, Luis Angel of the *Larra* from San Sebastian was brought ashore after he had been crushed by a hawser. By this time the tenure of Army doctors on St Kilda had been reduced to a single period of about four months and as a consequence we had yet another new medical officer, Captain Donald Bell, RAMC, who had only just been posted to St Kilda from Cowglen. It was clear to him that the Spaniard was suffering severe internal injuries and it was therefore impossible to do anything for him other than try to make him as comfortable as possible. A signal was therefore sent to the Rangehead and Benbecula then alerted RAF Leuchars whence Bill McEachern in his trusty Whirlwind set out again on a mercy mission. From Benbecula the injured man was flown by BEA Heron to Renfrew Airport. Within twelve hours of being put ashore on Hirta he was on the operating table at Cowglen and apparently made a good recovery from his fearful injuries. In due course a letter of thanks in florid Spanish arrived from the head of the Alvamar fishing company in San Sebastian, addressed to 'Sr. Jefe de la Base Militar de la isla SANTA KILDA (Escocia)'.

Actually Donald was only a lieutenant when he arrived on the island, but in the mail which I had to deal with just after my own arrival was a letter from the Directorate of Army Medical Services intimating that he had been granted a short service commission and immediate promotion to the rank of captain. On being apprised of his promotion Donald's jocular rejoinder was 'Well, I suppose that makes me the boss of St Kilda now.' I gently pointed out that this was not the first time I had been in command with a medical captain under me; but it made me wonder how often a lieutenant had commanded a unit with a captain under him. It seemed cockeyed to me at the time, and a third pip would have regularised the position – but then, I was only twenty-three at the time.

The biggest bombshell came the very next day when I received a signal from the Rangehead that Colonel Brewster had decided that it was high time that he inspected this far-flung outpost of his domain before leaving the Hebrides on promotion to brigadier. In fact, I now realise (what seems to have escaped me at the time) that this was the time of the annual Admin Inspection. It poses the interesting question why Desmond Williamson should have been allowed to take some well-deserved leave shortly before. It may be remembered that, on this important occasion, he was relieved by his predecessor Will Warner who, in turn, had left St Kilda a few days earlier to be treated for suspected appendicitis and that was why I had stepped into the breach.

Just my bloody luck to be OC at the time! The colonel was coming out on the first landing craft of the season, scheduled in two days' time. What was more, he would be accompanied by our new quartermaster, Major Arthur Morrall, RA, who would then remain on the island for several days to do a thorough overhaul and inventory of the stores. So for about a week a lieutenant even had a major under his command. I should perhaps explain, for the benefit of readers not familiar with the way the Army worked, that quartermasters were commissioned from the ranks of warrant officers and senior NCOs and although they wore the insignia of their respective grades they did not hold combatant commissions and therefore did not have executive powers. 'Uncle Arthur' was an elderly major who had risen from boy soldier in India to his present position through forty years of soldiering. Not surprisingly, he was one of the best raconteurs I ever met, his droll tales of life in the 'real' (i.e. pre-war) Army being delivered in a strong Yorkshire accent.

At such short notice I could not lay on any bullshit exercise; the men were all extremely busy stacking diesel drums and clearing rocks off the LCT beaching-ramp. Will had pulled a fast one on me, the crafty bugger. By leaving St Kilda a week earlier than originally scheduled, he had avoided having to clear several tons of accumulated boulders which seven months of winter gales had hurled up the beach-head, almost totally covering the ramp. Now that task had fallen to me and I soon found that the edges of the pre-stressed concrete had got more than a little frayed! For two solid days, working round the clock by arc-light, all ranks were press-ganged into clearing the mess so that the ten-ton trailers and assorted vehicles could come off the landing craft at mid-day on Wednesday. The task was made all the harder by the fact that it was accomplished in driving rain and howling winds.

I had barely tumbled into bed on Monday night, utterly exhausted, when I was rudely awakened by Private McBryan, my Pioneer batman, bursting into my bedroom, proclaiming beerily 'There's no fucking justice here!' and more Anglo-Saxon imprecations to the same effect. It seemed that he and the generator attendant had been drinking together when the Camp Orderly Officer, Staff-

Sergeant Hall, noted that the lights were flickering erratically. When he went up to the genny-sheds he found these two, fairly drunk. He immediately put the attendant on a charge, had him replaced by another attendant, and ordered McBryan to bed. With Dutch courage McBryan squared up to the NCO in belligerent fashion and began shouting the odds, and when this failed to elicit an apology from Sergeant Hall the aggrieved Pioneer immediately came up to the Factor's House to get instant redress. The net result of this fracas was that two rather crestfallen and extremely hungover soldiers were on the mat at nine o'clock the following morning.

This situation highlighted the anomaly of my own position. I did not have the full disciplinary powers which captains commanding St Kilda had been granted. I was in two minds whether to remand them for Colonel Brewster the following day, but on the spur of the moment I decided to deal with them myself, within the limits of my powers, by giving them one helluva lambasting with my tongue, putting them on fatigues and extra duties for a fortnight, and banning them from the Puffin Bioscope and Bar for the same period. That settled the matter, and as far as I can gather neither man gave any trouble thereafter.

The night before the LCT was due, several Spanish trawlers sheltered from the gale and recognising one as the *Arzibal* I paid a quick courtesy visit to my old amigo Captain Fernando Hispuria who, on learning that *El Comandante* was coming the following day, presented me with a couple of bottles of his finest vino all the way from the bodegas of Barcelo-Carles of Malaga, which provided a suitably exotic touch to the CO's dinner on Wednesday evening.

Owing to the severity of the weather there was some doubt as to whether LCT 4002 would get to St Kilda. For once in my life I actually prayed for a storm, the longer and more ferocious the better, anything to delay if not prevent the colonel's inspection. To be sure, the weather remained pretty awful, with strong winds gusting up to 85 mph from SSE blowing straight into the bay and low mist everywhere. But with the perversity of the pelagic climate Wednesday dawned sunny and calm and the weather steadily improved as the day wore on. As a result, the landing craft arrived at six in the evening, only twelve hours late. By now I was resigned to my fate, and when the afternoon shipping forecast gave gale warnings for Malin and Hebrides I was actually keeping my fingers crossed that the vessel would manage to nip in, deliver her precious cargo (including the mail) and sod off sharpish, leaving the colonel the absolutely barest minimum for the annual inspection.

In fact, Colonel Brewster conducted his inspection briskly, actually spending most of his time examining the Decca and Marconi radars in some detail and only sparing a cursory glance at the generator sheds and other buildings in the bay area. By eight o'clock we were seated at dinner in the Mess enjoying our Spanish wine. Colonel Brewster was in a mellow, expansive mood, if a trifle patronising when he suggested that I was wasted in the Ed Corps and should reconsider the permanent commission in the Gunners.

'What will you do in Civvy Street, anyway?' he asked. 'I suppose you will become a schoolmaster. Well. It's a shocking waste. The Army needs young fellows like you. With your educational qualifications and Service record you would go right to the top.' I should add that Colonel Brewster wore three medal ribbons only. The first was the Military MBE which he had been awarded for some unspecified duties while serving as Military Attaché in Washington – 'spying on our cousins' was all he would say. The other ribbons were the Defence Medal

Looking south from the summit of Conachair across Village Bay to Dùn

and War Medal which reflected the fact that he had spent the war on home defence duties with Anti-Aircraft batteries. At the end of his year in the Hebrides he was elevated to brigadier and went off to higher things at the War Office.

After dinner, however, the colonel pottered about the camp area, mercifully leaving me to get on with the chores of unloading the technical equipment required to prepare the radar stations for the imminent missile-firing season. Meanwhile Arthur Morrall got down to work on his audit of the stores. The landing craft weighed anchor at three in the morning and having seen the colonel safely aboard I returned to the Factor's House for a well-earned rest and a long lie-in.

With this landing craft came Captain Alan Tatham, RE, in command of a Territorial Army unit which had the task of blowing up those boulders blocking the ramp and the approach to the jetty which were far too large for us to manhandle. Like Robin Ward two years earlier, Alan Tatham occasionally used explosive charges which were far too powerful for the purpose. As luck would have it, demolition was going on one day when I suddenly received a telephone call and found Colonel Hargreaves, the Chief Education Officer at Scottish Command, on the other end. This time he was phoning to congratulate me on the sterling results I had achieved in getting so many soldiers through the various certificates of education. I am not sure whether he realised where I was, as his call may have been patched through from the military exchange at the Rangehead without comment. But as we chatted, quite amicably for once, there was a series of almighty explosions, three in quick succession.

St Kilda at the centre of the world: erecting the signpost indicating Rockall 181 miles west, Nome (Alaska) 7,015 miles, Hirta Post Office 1896 yards east and Moscow 1954 miles

'What the hell was that?' he asked. It was on the tip of my tongue to suggest that the Third World War had just broken out. Going to the office window, which I threw open, I commented as nonchalantly as I could muster, 'Oh, that? Just our Sappers playing silly buggers.' And to underline the point there was another explosion, mightier than the first three, sending an enormous column of water and rubble out of the bay, to rattle down on the corrugated iron roof of the office. The line went dead at that point, but I hope Colonel Hargreaves was suitably impressed by one of his schoolies in the firing line.

One night two Manx shearwaters had got trapped in diesel oil at the generator sheds. One was not too badly soiled and Donald Bell, though not an ornithologist, managed to clean it up sufficiently for it be safely released a day or two later. But the other was choking on the black, viscous fluid and expired soon afterwards. I left the sad corpse outside the Factor's House, meaning to cut off the head later and send it to Mike Knott in Devon, one of my new-found philatelic friends who also had the strange hobby of collecting birds' skulls. I had started with a couple of puffins which had been pulled inside out by the gulls, and from this I had gradually progressed up the scale to gannets whose heads took a considerable amount of boiling to remove all the flesh and brains. Leaving the shearwater out overnight was a big mistake. When I went to collect it the following morning I found nothing but a gruesome pile of bloody bones and scattered feathers; the gulls had beaten me to it.

The severest headache – and biggest let-down – in the communications of this period was the VHF radio-telephone link. Although installed primarily for military reasons it was very quickly thrown open to private use. I do not think there was any attempt to ration outgoing calls, but the rates were so prohibitively expensive and the quality of reception and transmission appallingly bad, that we would probably have been better off without it. In the first place, booking a call through the duty operator was a painfully slow and tedious business. The one public telephone on the island was located in the passageway between the Officers' Mess and the Rec Room and as the walls were paper thin and you had to shout at the top of your voice, you were acutely aware that everybody could hear your side of the conversation. It was no fun either for the wife or sweetheart at the other end. Both parties were constantly reminded that even if the Russians were not lugging in, then the War Office Monitoring Team camping out on Skye were certainly listening to every word – and transcribing it. Every month a bulky registered package would arrive at Benbecula from Portree containing the latest transcripts with pungent comments and strictures added alongside. Foul language was the commonest complaint, but mentioning people by name, or daring to use the K word (Kilda) would earn the detachment a collective reprimand.

Does the Army still use those rather quaint code-names, such as Starlight and Acorn, to designate certain key officers? There may have been conscious humour in choosing the name Seagull for the Adjutant, because, as we used to say, he shits on us from a great height. When I was on St Kilda I was either Sunray or Sunray Minor, depending on whether I was the OC or his deputy, but back at Benbecula I was the Education Officer and the War Office, in its wisdom, had never reckoned on the 'schoolie' being important enough ever to figure in secure transmissions; so we had to invent a code-name and thus I came to rejoice in the name of 'Blackboard'. Obvious, really, when you think of it. In the summertime, when we had an officer of the Catering Corps at Benbecula, naturally he was dubbed Compo...

The lack of proper telephonic communication had never bothered me before, but now I was a married man it assumed paramount importance. The night the colonel was on St Kilda Mary telephoned me while we were sitting in the Mess after dinner. I was terribly embarrassed as everyone could hear me shouting down the line, and to make matters worse Colonel Brewster said, 'Tell her what you're really thinking – the old bugger from the other side is here.'

On this stint as OC I was hampered by not having a Battery Quarter Master Sergeant. This extremely valuable NCO was evacuated a few days previously by HMS *Puma* when a signal intimated that his father was dying. The frigate, which had been stationed off the coast of Iceland when the long-running Cod War came to an end in March, was on her way back to Mallaig when she was diverted to St Kilda to pick him up. Consequently I found myself stuck with Gunner Sturrock who was suddenly and meteorically elevated to BQMS, an extremely difficult and responsible job normally done by a senior sergeant. Sturrock was a GD (General Duties) man who had given me a lot of trouble back at Benbecula, especially when he went absent without leave – not an easy thing to do when you are stuck on an island with precious few means of escape. But now that he had this responsibility thrust on him through sheer necessity, a tremendous change came over him. Overnight he smartened up and I must say he did a surprisingly good job. Perhaps his previous bolshie attitude had been due to his talents going generally unrecognised. 'It is amazing what a little responsibility can do to a man,' I wrote to Mary, but as I re-read these words now it occurs to me that they might equally have applied to myself. So many National Servicemen got stuck in dead-end jobs and regarded their two years in uniform as a sheer waste of time, but I had the time of my life; it was exciting and challenging, with never a dull moment

My arrival that April coincided with the advent of the puffins. Within a couple of days the bay, which had been deserted, was packed with these attractive little birds, skimming the waves or skittering low across them. With Second Lieutenant Alan Smith, my 2IC, I went out in the dory towards Dùn to get a closer look. The sea was beginning to get pretty choppy and it was highly entertaining to watch puffins flying low over the water to escape from us and crashing straight into an oncoming wave. I also noted that the fulmars seemed to be gradually spreading round the bay, as we observed about a dozen pairs nesting on the cliffs by Uamh Cailleach Beag Ruaval (cave of the little old lady of Ruaival) which was quite bare of them in previous years. So much for the Nature Conservancy's fears that the military presence would have an inhibiting effect on the birds. Now, of course, the fulmars are everywhere and, indeed, have successfully colonised the entire coasts of the British Isles.

I returned to Benbecula on 24 April aboard the *Mull*. As usual, the trawler which brought Desmond back from leave arrived at some ungodly hour of the night and it was 4.30am before I went aboard for the journey back to relative civilisation. Immediately I landed I found myself pitched into a strange situation which got even more bizarre as the day progressed. A party of senior French officers from the army, navy and air force arrived by the mid-day plane and I was detailed to meet them at the airport, escort them to the Officers' Mess and be on hand to interpret for Colonel Brewster. It was apparent that, in addition to the Americans, some of our other NATO allies were likely to make use of the Range facilities. We had actually driven down to the Rangehead when we received a signal that a military revolt had erupted in France. In fact, an insurrection had broken out in Algeria over the weekend as the colonists headed for a showdown with President De Gaulle. When the revolt spread to metropolitan France, De Gaulle went on the air to proclaim a state of emergency. The following day, however, the French premier, Michel Debré, announced that drastic measures would be taken against those responsible for the revolt which collapsed a few hours later. Two top generals, Maurice Challe and André Zeller, were subsequently sentenced to fifteen years' imprisonment but the other ring-leaders, Raoul Salan and Edmond Jouhaud, remained at large though stripped of their rank. The reaction of the Frenchmen visiting the Rangehead, on news of the revolt, was predictably mixed and confused. Indeed, for a few anxious hours they were not sure whether they would be allowed to return to France.

Shortly after this Colonel Brewster handed over command to Colonel Ken MacIntyre who, despite his name, was English born and bred, but he was immensely proud of his Scottish roots. Shortly afterwards officers and men from the US 2/82 Artillery under the command of Colonel Elbert R. Curtis flew in from their base in Germany, and my last mission to St Kilda occurred in July when I accompanied a party of them, under Lieutenants Ray Hapeman and Joe Rosenfeld, out to the island so that the Americans could examine our missile tracking systems. We went out by LCT 4074 on 26 July and returned by LCT 4097 five days later. On this trip I think we also had Captain Estlin Waters, RAMC from Cardiff who was taking over as medical officer. Estlin was a dedicated ornithologist and remained on St Kilda for a whole year, during which we corresponded regularly. We were accompanied by William Porter, a journalist from *The Scotsman*, whom I took all over the island. In his subsequent article he referred to Lieutenant James Mackay making 'a last sentimental journey' to St Kilda prior to demob. On my return to Benbecula on 31 July I went on terminal leave. Technically I remained in the Army until 24 August, but I had accumulated so much leave that effectively that was the end of my three years' service.

During those last few days on the island, however, an incident occurred which, though trifling in itself, somehow symbolised the conflict of interests between the Army and the Nature Conservancy. It was a small thing really – a solitary specimen of *Bellis perennis*, the common daisy, which suddenly appeared in the middle of the Minister's Meadow. Now this is a flower commonly found all over the British Isles, and unless you are one of those people who are very pernickety about your immaculate lawn it is not a plant which normally excites any interest. But on St Kilda the daisy had never been seen before. A routine reference to this in a report to the Nature Conservancy, however, had Morton Boyd out like a shot by the next available landing craft. He almost went berserk when he saw the innocent little flower and had it dug up, roots and all, immediately.

'Why all the fuss?' I could not help asking.

'It's an invasive species!' he thundered. 'It should not be here. Do you realise what this means?'

'No, but I'm sure you're going to tell me.'

'It means that there is a shockingly slack attitude here. This plant is only here because some idiot has been witless enough to bring the seed here, either on the sole of his boot or, more probably, adhering to his trouser leg.'

'Ah, I see. But what does it matter?'

He turned a pitying eye on me, as if I were the village idiot. 'Don't you understand anything at all?' he seethed. 'Today it's only a daisy but next year there could be a carpet of them, and that would upset the entire ecology of the island. The Army will have to smarten up its ideas. This is intolerable!'

Really, the way he carried on, you would have thought we had discovered a clump of the dreaded Japanese Knotweed or the awful Giant Hogweed. But clearly his ruthless eradication of this helpless little flower did not do the trick. When I revisited St Kilda forty years later there was quite a carpet of daisies in the meadow.

EPILOGUE

ALTHOUGH I left St Kilda in July 1961 I corresponded with the medical officer, Estlin Waters for a whole year, right up to the time he himself left St Kilda to return to civilian life; for sixteen years he held the Chair of Community Medicine at Southampton University until he retired in 1990. Stephen Gray, whom I had known as a lieutenant, was appointed OC St Kilda in August 1961 with the rank of captain and served on the island until September 1962. He wrote a very interesting account of his time on St Kilda which was published in the *Royal Artillery Journal*, reprinted in Brigadier Spackman's book *Soldiers on St Kilda* (1982).

This book was produced to mark 25 years of the military re-occupation of St Kilda and provides a succinct account of the period up to the time of publication. It recounts such incidents as the time in December 1962 when three soldiers were evacuated by Spanish trawler but when the trawler failed to arrive at Lochmaddy an air and sea search was ordered – only to find the trawler sheltering in Glen Bay during a storm. The soldiers were disembarked at St Kilda and transported to the mainland by more conventional means. The national press had a field day with the story of the soldiers from a top-secret rocket tracking station going missing on a foreign ship.

The officers vacated the Factor's House in 1962 when a purpose built Officers' Mess was erected. Thereafter the Factor's House reverted to the Nature Conservancy and has since been the home of the resident Warden. The domestic site was completely rebuilt in 1969-70, when the installations at sea level were replaced by the huge and ugly buildings we see today. The relatively tiny and unobtrusive sheds that housed the Meadows generators in my day have now given way to a huge power station. When my son Alastair visited St Kilda in 1997 this building bore a huge sign inscribed KGB to denote the Kilda Generating Board. Other manifestations of unconventional humour included the pillar box at the roadside (where you could post your Christmas cards well in advance, for it was only emptied once a year) and the pedestrian crossing near the radar stations. There was also a bus stop at the top of the ridge, but no red London double-decker ever came along.

On 12 August 1971 HM Royal Yacht *Britannia* brought Her Majesty the Queen, Prince Philip and their four children to St Kilda, the first Royal Visit in the island's long history. The Royal Family even landed on Dùn by Gemini rubber boat. It is recorded that the weather during the Royal Visit was unusually benign; but characteristically it turned really nasty as soon as the Royal Yacht and its attendant frigate had left, and St Kilda endured the worst and most sustained period of stormy weather ever recorded, continuing with no let up until the following February.

In June 1981 Brigadier Tony Spackman, by that time Range Controller and Commandant, wrote to all the officers and ex-officers who had commanded St Kilda over the intervening quarter of a century, inviting them to a reunion the following year. Unfortunately I was in Australia at that time and unable to attend, but it was interesting to study the names on the distribution list and see what had become of everyone that I remembered from my time on the island.

Lieutenant James Mackay, RAEC (Relief OC St. Kilda) and Major A. D. McGregor, MC, TD, RA (21C Benbecula), dressed up to go aboard the cruise liner Meteor, *June 1960*

Tony Riach had retired with the rank of major, but had been awarded the MBE. George Langford, the reluctant captain of 1958, had attained the rank of major before retiring to Kingussie. Will Warner was now a full colonel, the Deputy Commandant of 6 Field Force at Aldershot, but his immediate successor, Desmond Williamson had only progressed to the rank of major and was then attached to Liverpool University OTC. Stephen Gray, Desmond's successor, was now a lieutenant colonel, with the MBE and a staff job at the Ministry of Defence, while his successor, whom I remembered as a lieutenant with one of the guided weapons regiments, Alan Walpole, was now the training major at the Honourable Artillery Company. Of the other names on the list I knew nothing, but I was intrigued to note that two of them were already lieutenant colonels, General Staff Officers grade I at the Royal Military College of Science, Shrivenham – so clearly a spell on lone St Kilda had not hindered their subsequent careers. And now, twenty years on, it is a sobering thought that some of them may be dead, and most will have retired long ago.

Dougal Andrew, who used to take charter parties to St Kilda, told me recently that in 1995 he happened to visit the island when there was a handover from one OC to another, and the incoming commander was a woman! I thought I was unique – but clearly I was not as unique as all that. And now the Army has departed, its radar stations and domestic site since 1999 in the capable hands of a care and maintenance unit. Initially this was operated by Serco, a division of the Ministry of Defence, but in 2001 it was privatised under the name of QinetiQ. The story of the 'privatisation' of the former military base has already been recounted and, in particular, the fact that the Puff Inn now requires a license like any other pub. But what are the long term prospects for the island now that the army has gone, and will probably never return. The Rocket Range itself has become a casualty of the Peace Dividend, and it remains to be seen how long the cost of running the base, even on a care and maintenance basis, can be kept up. Perhaps, eventually, the military base of 1957-99 will be abandoned altogether and allowed to take its place amid the other relics of civilisation in this remote place.

INDEX